Demystifying Bigotry

Demystifying Bigotry

THE BEST OF THE
AMERICA'S RACE PROBLEM BLOG

Paul R. Lehman

Library of Congress Control Number: 2017913819
ISBN: Hardcover   978-1-5434-4971-6
                 Softcover   978-1-5434-4972-3
                 eBook   978-1-5434-4973-0

KJV
Scripture quotations marked KJV are from the Holy Bible, King James Version (Authorized Version). First published in 1611. Quoted from the KJV Classic Reference Bible, Copyright © 1983 by The Zondervan Corporation.

NIV
Scripture quotations marked NIV are taken from the Holy Bible, New International Version®. NIV®. Copyright © 1973, 1978, 1984 by International Bible Society. Used by permission of Zondervan. All rights reserved. [Biblica]

Print information available on the last page.

Rev. date: 09/14/2017

To order additional copies of this book, contact:
Xlibris
1-888-795-4274
www.Xlibris.com
Orders@Xlibris.com
767387

Contents

POLITICS

POPULAR CULTURE

This book is dedicated to my family and friends who encourage me to always seek after wisdom and truth. Blessings.

Introduction

In the popular blog, *America's Race Problem*, Dr. Paul R. Lehman never shy's away from unveiling the hurtful and far-reaching effects of bigotry in America. Impassioned by a desire to see his country liberated from the limitations and social erosion caused by cultural bigotry, Dr. Lehman's blog reflect his heart's deepest desire - to heal and educate his readers about the harm of sectarianism.

In *Demystifying Bigotry*, Dr. Lehman presents a collection of his most provocative and thought-provoking blogs, allowing current and future fans to revisit these popular blogs and experience his compelling point-of-view.

America's Race Problem presents the voice of courage in a day when the social climate has grown more and more polarizing due to social inequality. Tackling every topic imaginable, *America's Race Problem* has evolved over the past seven years to capture the attention of a loyal fan-base and has gone on to reach millions of readers, through its republishing in blogs, newspapers, and online publications across this nation.

Hoping to present a simple answer for the complex problems of bigotry in this country, *Demystifying Bigotry* continues the dialog that Dr. Lehman began over 20 years ago, and challenges readers to disempower provincialism by choosing to see each, unique person in this world as a part of the same God-given fraternity – the human race.

Dr. Lehman's books and blog has helped to transform the way that I, too, see the world. No longer willing to comply with the deception and limitations of the concept of race, I have found that my choice to evolve in this area of my life has brought with it an unexpected liberty and joy that I didn't know was possible.

I think that every person deserves to educate to elevate and *Demystifying Bigotry* is a great vehicle for transcendence for anybody looking to embrace the best, highest version of themselves.

~ **Saraa Kami**

ROOT CAUSES

*"I freed a thousand slaves.
I could have freed a thousand more
if only they knew they were slaves."*

HARRIOT TUBMAN

Race, Myth and Illusion

December 26, 2009

Race is a subject many Americans do not like to discuss simply because they feel inadequate or ill equipped to talk about it. America has endorsed, supported, and promoted racism since Africans were added to the list of American slaves. Prior to American slavery, the need for color as a symbol of personal worth or value was not needed or used, except by Europeans who referred to themselves as "white."

The primary driving force in the use of color as a marker for race is based on value, personal worth. The wealthy decided the value of everything in society. As a matter of fact, they still do. But that's another subject. The time has come for America to grow up.

As children, many Americans believed in Santa Claus, however, once they reached an age where some discernment arrived, they realized that Santa was a myth, an illusion. In other words, they started to grow up and view life from a new and different perspective. America has to do the same with respect to race.

The fact that all human beings are of one race has not yet taken hold in the American psyche; and that is part of the problem.

Understanding Race, Ethnicity, and Culture

January 2, 2011

From the comments received at this blog, the primary problem for readers seems to be discerning the difference among the terms race, ethnicity or ethnic group, and cultural group or cultural identity. So, in an effort to make clear the distinctions among these terms the tomato will be used as a paradigm to underscore the relationships and differences. This example is based simply on common sense and should not be construed as a scientific study, although it could stand up to close scrutiny.

Like the term race, the tomato is more often than not misunderstood in that most people think of it as a vegetable; it is a fruit. The website Tomato.org provides the following information regarding this fruit:

> "TOMATO, whether pronounced Tuh-MAY-toh or Tuh-MAH-to, is a delicious, nutritious fruit, more widely known as a vegetable. Botanically, a tomato (*Solanum lycopersicum*) is the ovary of a flowering plant, therefore it is a fruit, or, more specifically, a berry."

Regardless of what science says, most people when asked to label the tomato will call it a vegetable. The term race is similar in being misunderstood.

The term tomato is the family name or reference to a family of fruit, and regardless of what they look like, they still are tomatoes. Human beings also belong to family called *Homo sapiens*. The word family can be interchanged with the word race because regardless of how a human being looks, he or she belongs to the family of *Homo sapiens*. Multiple families of tomatoes do not exist; just as multiple races of people do not exist. The problem with understanding the single human family concept comes from years of false information without any concerted effort to correct it—like the tomato being a vegetable.

Today some people use the word ethnic or ethnicity as being equal to or the equivalent of race. As we observed earlier, the word race can be interchanged with family, but not ethnic or ethnicity.

The reason for this is simply that, like human beings, "There are many different varieties of tomato plants and most produce red fruit, but there are also tomato plants that produce yellow, orange, pink, purple, green and white fruit. Tomato plants vary in size from small cherry tomatoes to elongated plum tomatoes." The variety of tomatoes then can represent the variety of ethnic groups in the world.

Some people mistake the variety of human beings as representative of many races. For example, some people might see the Pygmy of Africa as a separate race from the Aborigines of Australia when, in fact, they belong to the same race or family. Just because they look different does not mean they do not belong to the same family. So, the words ethnic, ethnicity, or ethnic group pertains to the variety of human beings within the family of Homo sapiens.

The words culture, cultural group, and cultural identity are often misunderstood and associated with the words ethnic, ethnic group, and ethnicity. The primary difference among these words rest in the fact that cultures can be changed whereas ethnicities cannot be changed. For example, cherry tomatoes represent a specific variety of the tomato family and cannot change their identity or ethnicity. However, the use to which the cherry tomatoes can be employed can vary with the cook. The cherry tomatoes could be used in a variety of ways such as in marmalade, ketchup, salsa, paste, sauce, etc. The way they are used determines their identity.

For human beings, the cultural setting in which they reside or choose to reside represents their culture. For example, a person of Asian ethnicity might choose to live in America and become a citizen of that country. He has, in essence, changed his cultural identity from say Chinese, to Asian American. Human beings can change their culture but not their race or ethnicity.

One of the problems involved in a person giving up his or her belief in the fantasy of race depends on how they identify themselves. If his or her identity depends on an association with a so-called race, then all the privileges and benefits will be forfeited.

However, a new self-image will replace the vague and nebulous old one. In other words, if someone refers to himself as a black, that term makes only symbolic reference to identities throughout the world. No country or culture is referenced in the word black. So, if that word is dropped for the words African American, then not only is a country identified but also a wonderful culture with a history unmatched by any other ethnic minority in the world.

Similarly, those who identify themselves as white instead of European American are simply holding on to a fantasy about race. For too long America has allowed its citizens to accept the falsehood of race until hate groups who base their identity on being white have decided to protect and defend their false belief. If society was to take away the concept of a white race, an Aryan race, and a Caucasian race, where would that leave all the groups that have built their existence on this concept?

If the leaders of these ethnic hate groups did a little investigating, they would have discovered that the word Caucasian or Caucasian race did not exist prior to 1795. The word actually referred to the residents or native people of or near the Caucasus Mountains. A German scientist, Johann Blumenbach, is responsible for introducing this word to describe the people of Iranian and Turkish descent. However, Caucasian has been misused to represent the white race, just like the tomato has been misidentified as a vegetable.

Also, the word Aryan is simply another way of spelling Iran, so those people who profess membership in an Aryan race definitely do not belong to a so-called white race; their ethnicity would be Iranian and/or Persian.

Understanding the words race, ethnicity, and culture in their appropriate context is an empowering experience. Once one understands the context and application of these words, he or she can better understand us, our society, and other societies around the world that are still trapped in the race box.

Bigotry is Still a Problem in America

December 27, 2010

America today seems to be in the midst of arguments that were supposedly laid to rest over two hundred years ago. A number of popular politicians and statesmen have been talking about things like secession, state's rights, and—indirectly—the value of slavery. The mere fact that these topics are being discussed points to our lack of knowledge concerning history, the Civil War, secession, and slavery. Could ethnic bias be the motive behind these topics?

The references to states' rights seem to suggest that the states should supersede the federal government by making their own laws when they want to and covering whatever they want to cover. Lest we forget, the 13th, 14th, and 15th Amendments as well as the Civil Rights Acts of the 1960s were all created and passed because the states failed to do right by some of its citizens in administering justice. In essence, the states could not be trusted to protect the rights of all their citizens. In fact, some of the states were complicit in preventing some of their citizens from enjoying their rights.

The appeal to people wanting states' rights is really an effort to resurrect old biases that allowed states to discriminate against ethnic minorities, women, and children. For example, as recently as 1969 in Oklahoma, by law, an African American could not marry anyone but an African American, or women and children could not establish a legal residential address independent of a husband, brother, or some other male. Other state laws supported discrimination and ethnic separation in schools as well as housing and public places.

The federal government had to step in and protect the rights of these citizens. The proponents of states' rights now want to try and gain back some of the control they believe they lost to the federal government. They want to impose their will on some citizens they feel are a threat to them economically and/or politically.

What many of the proponents of states' rights will not discuss are the strengths and privileges derived by the states from being part of a union of states. Prior to becoming a unified body, each of the thirteen colonies were separate governments and realized the problems and challenges that were created from their being separate. Once the states realized that many of these challenges and problems could be easily addressed by joining forces, they were ready to compromise. Finally, when the federal constitution was ratified the states knew the significance of *E PLURIBUS UNUM.* Of course, many of the powerful state citizens were not pleased with some of the rights and privileges the states had to give up.

Still today, many Southerners are not happy with some of the power the states gave up or lost after the Civil War. Just recently a secession celebration was held in South Carolina revisiting the act committed 150 years ago of seceding from the Union. Why? What did they celebrate? What was gained by bringing up the reason for the secession in the first place—slavery.

The most powerful and significant element given up by the Southern states was the power to own slaves. The irony of this entire episode is that one usually hears southerners complaining about African Americans for speaking about slavery and its legacy, and exclaiming to them to "get over it." Well, look who brings it up now. Governor Haley Barbour thought the celebration was in keeping with honoring the courageous Southerners who signed the papers to secede. To him, one might suppose, they are heroes.

This business of states seceding from the Union is nothing but biased ethnic baiting. First of all, seceding is unconstitutional and unpatriotic. However, even if it was permissible, the state or states doing so would be in peril because they would have to divest themselves of everything owned by or controlled by the federal government. Just imagine what life would be like if all federal roads ended at the state border, or all federal instillations— military bases, VA hospitals, FDIC for banks, no Social Security and Medicare, money for schools was no longer present. In addition, trade across state lines would be discontinued because all trade outside the seceded states must be approved by the federal government.

These are just a few examples of some of the problems these states would have to contend with by virtue of not being part of the Union. So, when some politician starts to talk about secession, please know they are trying to stir up some bias that would invite unsuspecting citizens to join forces with him in some other cause, but not secession. That is, unless the politician is niece or foolish.

One politician who campaigned on states' rights and secession was Texas Governor, Rick Perry. Why would a supposedly intelligent statesman deliberately create such illusions for his supporters? He knows full well that secession is not even a remote possibility for Texas or any other state, for that matter. Chances are he wants to appeal to a certain segment of the population that yearns for "the good old days" when "the good old boys" were in control of everything in the state.

What is happening today? The Civil War has been over since the late 1860s, yet many Southern Americans seem to think that the war is still going on. Evidently they were under the belief that slavery was good and their state had the right to keep it. Their attitude is something akin to them believing that God gave them slavery and it was wrong for the Union to take it away from them.

Governors Rick Perry and Haley Barber seem to want to go back to "the good old days" of slavery and states' rights. Rand Paul, Jim DeMint and other politicians want to revisit the 14th Amendment which identifies and protects civil rights. They say it is because they want to protect America from illegal immigrants. If that is the issue, why not deal with the issue of illegal immigrants rather than trying to change the 14th Amendment?

Since the election of Barack Obama as president, the country has been bombarded with negative assertions and accusations about the direction in which Obama is taking the country. Why all the negativity? Prejudice against Obama because of his ethnicity seems to be one of the reasons. But where did this prejudice come from? If we take a moment to look around and see who is spreading this hate and venom, the answer becomes apparent. Would good Christian people never have a positive word of encouragement to say about the president or his handling of the country? Or wish him God's blessings as he goes about his business of leading the country?

Some people need to know that the South did indeed lose the war, and that the questions of secession and state's rights were settled regarding slavery. If some people want to continue believing that slavery was right and God's gift to the South, that is their personal privilege, but they also need to know that since it is contrary to the law of the land, it must remain personal. Negotiations over the Civil War and Reconstruction are over.

Race Terms No Longer Effective

January 7, 2010

A recent article, "Rate of Survival Rises for White with Melanoma" by Landon Hall, points out the problem we have in America where the terms race, black, and white are no longer useful, accurate, and acceptable.

The article makes the statement, "Whites are surviving melanoma at much higher rates than decades ago, thanks to public awareness and early treatment." Hall continues by stating, "The trend hasn't extended to blacks and Hispanics, however; those groups develop skin cancer much less frequently but tend to have more advanced progression at diagnosis, according to the study."

While the intent of the article is to provide good information regarding the treatment of cancer and those who can benefit from it, much is lost in the language relative to race. First, the term race is no longer a valid term since science has determined that all humans are 99.95 percent alike. We are one race. Why do we keep using the term and applying it to other human beings? We should use the term ethnic or ethnicity when we are referring to someone's cultural or ancestral identity. Let's look at a few examples of the problem with the three terms.

First, we should all know that color does not define or identify a person's biological identity or race; it does not matter what color. So, when the article in discussion uses the term 'white,' what does that mean? Does it mean all fair-skinned people or people regardless of your skin complexion who refer to themselves as 'white'? The term 'white' is reserved for European Americans, but other fair-skinned Americans refer to themselves as white. So, just who is the study directed toward—people who call themselves white or those with fair-skinned complexions?

Also in the article, we find the use of the term 'black.' Does this term refer to all people with dark-skinned complexions or people— usually African Americans—who often refer to themselves as black? Many Americans of varying ethnic identities have dark complexions. Should they be included in this group? Because the terms are too vague and not ethnically specific, the information lacks benefit to those not included or identified.

The term Hispanic is the only one used in the article that accurately identifies a cultural/ancestral group. The term Hispanic, however, covers a wide range of people with different cultural identities from all Spanish-speaking cultures. So, who is to take heed of the information?

Should very fair-skinned and very dark-skinned Asians, American Indians, and other ethnicities ignore the warning that singles out blacks, whites, and Hispanics? The reader is at a loss to know because the terms are too general, confusing, and stereotypical. We need more clarity and accuracy in describing people. As one race of people, we can easily refer to a person's ethnic or cultural identity rather than lump them together on the basis of color or so-called race. No one's identity is ever based on a color because color has symbolic value only. One is usually identified through geography or cultural or both.

In America we have reached the point where we need to re-educate ourselves regarding the idea of race. We should no longer use the term race when referring to a person unless it is to underscore their humanity. The term race carries with it some connotations that unites and separates people into groups of humans, some thought superior to others. This assumption is false.

The appropriate term for people who refer to themselves as black is African American. The term black is the same as negro and both have little positive value except in the so-called black community and the history of American slavery. If some people choose not to identify themselves as African Americans, they are free to identify themselves as 'other.'

According to the Supreme Court, the correct term for people who identify themselves as white is European American. The term Caucasian race is a misnomer because all so-called white people are not descended from the Caucasus Mountain area and humans constitute only one race. Once, again, people who identify themselves according to a color do not really identify themselves; they simply refer to a symbolic social group that no longer exist.

In due respect to the article, the study was meant to provide some worthwhile and useful information, and that should be encouraged, but when we look at the language relative to ethnicity and culture, we must wonder: who will it benefit?

Americans Passing and Crossing for European American (White)

November 21, 2010

When the European Americans created a privileged group of people called the white race, meaning themselves, they also created the phenomenon known as "Passing." The concept of Passing is embodied in the term, a term used to identify non-European Americans who possess physical features of European Americans, and use them to assume a European American identity.

During the late 1800s and early 1900s, many Americans of varying ethnic groups engaged in this practice to gain as many advantages that being "white" offered. Today, thousands of Americans participate in this practice knowingly or unknowingly. Some of the ethnic groups singled out early on for exclusion from the white race included—but was not limited to—the Irish, Greeks, Italians, Jews, and of course, Americans Indians, Hispanic Americans, and African Americans.

History records the experiences each of the above ethnic groups encountered at the hands of an American society that wanted to preserve its specialness and privilege reserved for its group alone. Since the white race was the only normal race in America, it set the standards for everything, but especially, for physical appearance. Being white, in many instances, meant living or dying, eating or starving, working or not working, having housing or no housing, and a plethora of other vital necessities. With so much importance attached to being white, little wonder that anyone who could pass safely, surely entertained the idea. American literature is replete with stories in a variety of genres that capture the experiences of non-European Americans facing the challenges and dangers of passing.

Some of the more famous works that contain an aspect of Passing include Harriet Beecher Stowe's "Uncle Tom's Cabin," James Weldon Johnson's "Autobiography of an Ex-Colored Man," Harriet Jacobs' "Incidents in the Life of a Slave Girl," and even Walter Mosley's "Little Scarlet" —to mention a very few. Movies such as "Pinky," and "Imitation of Life," to name a couple also treated Passing or has some refer to Crossing—the color line. Regardless of the medium, Passing and Crossing have been facts of American life since emphasis was placed on race. The limits to which people get to experience the privileges given to European Americans are too numerous to mention here, but suffice it to say they are serious and drastic in many cases.

Many of the ethnic groups mentioned earlier gained partial admittance, over a number of years, into the 'white race.' The word partial is important because in some sections of the country, certain ethnic Americans regardless of their looks are still viewed as less-than-white.

In Louisiana, for example, some Creole people who could pass for white in New York, would not be accepted as such in Louisiana. Or in Oklahoma, some European Americans with American Indian heritage would not be accepted as white in Oklahoma, but would easily pass in other states. In Oklahoma, some European Americans who try to pass for American Indian must prove their heritage before they can use that heritage for commercial purposes.

Although most experiences of Passing/Crossing involve non-European Americans trying to pass as European Americans, a number of experiences show just the opposite. Seemingly, when the possibility of financial gain is present, people will go to great lengths to qualify as whatever is needed to get their hands on money—even if it means going from European American to African American. A number of books on the subject are available, such as "Crossing the Line," by Gayle Wald.

The quest to become European American (white) took a major turn in 1964 and after, because the privileges and special treatment enjoyed by European Americans became available—to a point—to all Americans. The 1964, 1965 and 1968 Civil Rights Acts passed making all public accommodations, housing, and jobs available to all American citizens. For certain the problems of bigotry, prejudice, and discrimination were still present and visible; the opportunities that were reserved for European Americans in the past were now becoming available to other ethnic Americans. No

longer would non-European Americans have to worry about their
naturally curly hair, or almost too brown complexion. With the
door of opportunity open to all, there was no need to hide behind
the mask of race.

Education has brought us to the knowledge of our human
family and the fact that no superior race of human beings exists
on planet Earth. A great American civil rights activist once
commented to the effect that we human beings can learn to live
together as friends or perish separately as fools.

Unfortunately, many of our national leaders have not yet
accepted that concept; they still try to play the idea of race as a
factor in gaining support for their objectives. Once people realize
that race was and is used as a ploy to play on human weaknesses
of bigotry, fear, and anger by people who know the art of political
manipulation, they can begin the growing process toward peace
and joy.

The actions of Passing and Crossing are as false and confining
as believing in a white race and it biological superiority. Both stifle
growth.

Race Irrelevant and Confusing to America

February 18, 2011

For some time now this blog has been advocating for the removal of the word race used to classify and characterize humans of varying ethnicities. The claim has been made as well as substantiated that the word race is inaccurate, inappropriate, and ineffective in the task it has been forced to perform.

Again, for the record, race is the term that includes all human beings—as in the human race. The use of race in regards to color or geography is useless because it simply adds to confusion rather than making clear the relationships of all humans. People with black skin complexions and those with white, brown, tan, pink, and other complexions are all part of the same race; their ethnicity and culture, however, will vary.

In an effort to underscore the problems caused by our use of the term race, we will call attention to a recent article written by Jeff Jacoby from the *Boston Globe*. In his article titled "Irrelevant Racial Criteria," Jacoby makes the following statement: "Spend a while with the census search engine, and you could be forgiven for thinking that the nation's racial composition has never been defined with such pinpoint accuracy." To this statement he adds,

> "In fact, the nation's racial composition has probably never been defined with less accuracy, and the margin of error is widening. Why? Because of the growing number of Americans like Michelle Lôpez-Mullins, who render the government's racial categories meaningless or obsolete?"

What Jacoby means by the last statement is that Michelle, because of her multiethnic ancestry, has no category available to her on an identity space with the exception of "other." She is identified as a University of Maryland student who is 'Hispanic,' but "the government agency that tracks data on births and deaths, would pronounce her 'Asian' and 'Hispanic.'" Her birth certificate from the state of Maryland omits race altogether. So, we can readily see the problems using the term causes.

Jacoby makes the statement, "Though most Americans may still think of themselves as belonging to a single race, the multiracial population is surging. Racial boundaries are more permeable and easier to ignore than ever before." One might be willing to agree with Jacoby, except for the simple reason that he makes the same mistake as does the government—accepting the word race as legitimate and accurate. If we as a society accept the fact that all humans are of one race, then we do not need to continue using race in identifying people of differing ethnicities and cultures as belonging to a separate race.

Jacoby takes notice of the changing complexion of society with respect to what he calls interracial marriages or new marriages that have increased greatly from the 1960s to 2008. He states, "When Barack Obama was born in 1961, less than one new marriage in 1,000 was, like his parents', that of a black person and a white person. 'By 1980, that share had risen to about one in 150 new marriages,' Pew notes. By 2008, it had risen to one in 60." Unfortunately, the words black and white do not identify other ethnic influences that might have been reflected in these individuals.

Underscoring the problem that not only the word race creates but also words used to identify these so-called races, Jacoby cites the fact that President Obama identified himself in last year's census as 'black.' However, it was pointed out that many young African Americans prefer this latter term to represent their identity.

The problem of using the word race is clearly shown in Jacoby's comment that "The Census Bureau currently recognizes 63 possible racial labels, but that taxonomy is as limited and artificial as the one in an earlier age that subdivided Americans into the categories of "White," "Japanese," "Chinese," "Negroes," "Mulattoes," "Quadroons," "Octoroons," and "Civilized Indians." By what logic, for example, did the 2010 questionnaire classify Korean, Chinese, and Vietnamese as separate races, yet, lump Scandinavians, Arabs, and Slavs together as "white"?

As has been stated many times here, as well as in my last two books, the word race was forced to perform a service for which it was not suited. To make matters worse, accompanying the use of the word race is the assumption that a separate biological uniqueness is accorded.

For example, if someone is identified as being of the Korean race, then that race would be interpreted as not belonging to the family of human beings who identified themselves as white. What the Census Bureau and the government have done is compound the confusion by retaining the word race instead of using the words ethnic or ethnic group. American has fallen in love with ethnic colors and all their stereotypes, which keeps society from making needed social progress.

Our refusal to deal honestly with our race problem will cause the confusion to not only continue, but also to multiply.

So, how should our society address this growing problem? We can start by eliminating the word race as part of an individual's identity since all people belong to the same race. What will this simple action produce?

First, it would eliminate the stereotypes associated with the reference to a person's race. The concepts of racism and racist would be eliminated because there can be no superior race if only one race exists. The idea of a racist would no longer be applicable because more than one race has to exist in order to compare or contrast them. Also, the concept of races as a biological certainty would be dismissed and those social groups who have built their identity on the idea of multi-biologically separate races would be null and void. What would not disappear from avoiding the use of race are prejudice, bigotry, discrimination, anger, and hatred. Each of those concerns is unique to individuals, not groups.

So, Mr. Jeff Jacoby should be applauded for his comments and findings regarding not just the Census Bureau's confusion regarding race. He does, however, miss the part that the word race plays in this story. American societies seem to lack concern for the race problem. The more we procrastinate, the more confusion we heap on ourselves and especially our children. Children need to understand and know that they are more than colors; they are members of a human family.

Race, Biracial and Multi-Racial
Fallacy and Fantasy

November 28, 2010

Race, biracial, and multiracial are concepts based in fallacies and fantasies. The fact that many Americans embrace them, they create serious problems for all concerned. Many Americans grow up thinking that just because one of their parents belongs to a different ethnic group than the other it means that they are biracial. In order to understand the challenges these terms represent in America, we need to examine the problem, the effects, and the solution.

The primary problem comes from the fact that the false concept of many biological races exist. If one would apply common sense to the knowledge available to them they would realize that no pure race of man exists other than the human race—*Homo sapiens*. A brief look at world history shows the influences that went into changing the blood lines of people the world over. All one has to do is look at the experiences of people like Genghis Khan, Alexander the Great, Hannibal, Julius Caesar, Chaka Zulu, or the impact of the Crusades, the Norman Conquest, and the American Revolutionary War to understand the mixture of ethnicities and cultures in the world. Yet, the fantasy of race persists.

The problem with the various aspects of race stems from the economic influence of slavery. When the Europeans first started to explore the world, the one thing that stood out to them when in the company of other people was their color—white; eighty percent of the world population is of color. The Europeans began to refer to themselves as whites, and the white race. When they came to America and met the American Indians, they called them red men. Later, when the Africans came and were brought to America, they were called black men.

However, in the system of slavery, white was of premium value since the most important people in society were white. That value, however, was only in economic terms. A mixed bred Indian or African brought more money at the slave market if part of their ethnic identity included Europeans and was obvious in their appearance. Some of the names given to these mixed breeds were mulatto, quadroon, etc. for African Americans and half-breed for American Indians. Certainly, some of the offspring of the master, overseer and other European American men received special treatment. Some of the females were forced into prostitution, housework, nursemaid, and other jobs making profit for the master; some of the males were called "house slaves" and did work that kept them out of the fields.

The treatment received by these slaves of mixed ethnicity made many of them believe that they were special because they had some of the European blood in them. Because many believed and behaved like they were more valuable than the other slaves, this attitude made them not readily accepted within the slave community or tribal community. Their specialness was only available on the plantation; in regular society, they were still seen as ordinary slaves. For the so-called biracial, buying into the fantasy of a superior white race was at the base of their problems.

After the Civil War, no special provisions were made for the freedmen who saw themselves as biracial. However, since many of them thought themselves better than other African Americans, they formed groups of like people and created small communities and clubs that catered only to the so-called biracial people. All their efforts made a difference only within the African American community. European Americans could care less about the games they played trying to imitate them. The effects of their actions were, in part, to separate them from the European American as well as the African American communities.

Many saw themselves as a special race of people—a mixture of the white and the black race. In reality, no one cared about their so-called special racial status but them. The primary factor in this fantasy is the value placed on the European American (white) that would transfer to them in part because of their biological connection.

Today, after the Civil Rights movement, the Cultural Revolution, and the Gnome Project, for someone to identify himself or herself as biracial would underscore the ignorance that speaks to the fallacy and fantasy of race. The world now has the knowledge confirmed that people are more alike than penguins, and more human differences occur within a family with the same biological parents than with other people in the world. So, where is the value in identifying oneself as biracial?

As long as people hold on to the false concept of many races of human beings, the chance of creating a superior or inferior race is possible. The best way to deal with the problem of biracial is to clarify it. What has been thought of as race is simply ethnic and/or cultural differences. When we eliminate the word race and insert ethnic group or cultural group we change the human value so one group cannot be humanly superior or inferior to another since they are all human. All people are multi-ethnic, and many are multi-cultural—just ask someone who has had a DNA study of himself or herself performed.

Cultural and ethnic differences have been a fact of life almost since life itself. When one looks at the Bible, cultural and ethnic differences readily appear. Select practically any book and chances are aspects of culture and ethnicity will play a part in it. The fact that the idea or concept of race never comes up should underscore its lack of importance in the lives of biblical people in general. Evidently, looking at world history and biblical history and finding that people the world over are more a conglomerate than a single source, provides a lesson worth considering.

As stated in my book, America's Race Problem, the primary problem for all Americans regarding race, biracial, and multi-racial is the fallacy of accepting "race" as a legitimate term. The problem compounds when we began believing and acting like the term is real when we know it is fantasy. The idea of a person being part of two biological races is a joke. One part for certain would be *Homo sapiens*, but what would the other part be?

History and Bigotry Give an Insight into Today's Challenges

July 8, 2012

Many Americans are led to believe that all African Americans are the descendants of African slaves and that the freedmen were only abused, beaten, and murdered after the Civil War, during the Reconstruction period. American history does a poor job of telling the story of the African Americans who were not slaves, and called free persons of color.

That freedom enjoyed by these persons of color was so restricted in certain states that little difference of treatment existed between them and their slave brothers. Prior to the creation of the hate groups, such as the Ku Klux Klan and the Night Riders, whose jobs were to keep the persons of color in their place, each state made laws to restrict the movement and manage the activity of the free persons of color. In many instances the laws also gave specific instructions regarding the actions of free European Americans (whites) and their relationship to African Americans, slave and free.

Many people are puzzled at the attitude and behavior of some European Americans relative to the treatment of African Americans today, especially since the election of Barack Obama as president. A quick look at one of the state laws prior to the Civil War might shed some light on this subject. A bill went into effect in South Carolina in April 1835. The bill was No. 2639 An Act to Amend the Law Relating to Slaves and Free Person of Color:

> Be it enacted by the honorable, the Senate and House of Representatives, now met and sitting in General Assembly, and by the authority of the same: If any person shall hereafter teach any slave to read or write, or cause, or procure any slave to read or write, such person, if a free white person [some European Americans were still slaves at this time] upon conviction thereof shall for each and every offense against this Act be fined not exceeding one hundred dollars and imprisoned not more than six months; or, if a

free person of color, shall be whipped not exceeding fifty
lashes and fined not exceeding fifty dollars, at the discretion
of the court of magistrates and freeholders before which
such person of color is tried; and if a slave, to be whipped
at the discretion of the court, not exceeding fifty lashes:
the informer to be entitled to one-half of the fine, and to
be a competent witness. And if any free person of color or
slave shall keep any school or other place of instruction for
teaching any slave or free person of color to read or write,
such free person of color or slave shall be liable to the same
fine, imprisonment, and corporal punishment as are by this
Act imposed and inflicted upon free persons of color and
slaves for teaching slaves to read or write.

The careful reader will recognize the unequal and contrasting
treatment regarding a free European American (white) and that of
a free person of color. The European American was to receive no
whipping, just fines and imprisonment as the magistrates saw fit.
So, the concept of privilege for European Americans was written
into the laws very early on in society. The objective in all cases
was to prevent the African American, slave or free from learning
to read and/or write, thereby keeping them in a system of perpetual
slavery.

Prior to this law, a number of citizens, European Americans
and African Americans kept school of instruction that included
both European Americans and African Americans as students. The
law was meant to put an end to any kind of instruction to not only
African American slaves, but to free persons of color as well. As a
matter of fact, the way the law was written, it would be a crime for
an African American parent to teach his or her children to read and
write. Remember, the law reads: "…for teaching any slave or free
person of color to read or write…" So, being a free person of color
had its limitations and dangers in that if he or she was known to be
able to read and write, he or she would be in constant fear of being
accused and convicted of a crime.

Most states had laws restricting the lives and actions of both
slave and free African Americans while at the same time showing
privilege to the European Americans. After the Civil war, the

emphasis centered directly on the African American in the form of the Black Codes and later Jim Crow laws and practices. So, the lack of education of the African American has never been a concern for certain segments of society. The more they can remain illiterate, the easier they are to manage, manipulate and exploit. The idea behind this concept is simple—the more education the African American acquires, the more they contend for fair treatment in society, and the more they become a threat to the privileges enjoyed by the European Americans.

Today, many European Americans recognize that the clock is ticking away the time they can continue to enjoy the privilege of being "white." With President Obama as the leader of the country, their sense of superiority is under threat, so they must try and forestall any additional encroachment on their value.

One of the things that President Obama brings to the mix is something the bigots have little or no defense for, and that is an absence of a direct American slavery legacy via his parents. This fact of ancestry makes it difficult for those biased against him to try and find some line of attack based on the general stereotypes associated with African Americans.

Fortunately, no law is available to help them remedy their problem.

The Concept of a Post-Racial Society Conceals the Misdeeds of America's Past and Present

April 14, 2013

An article that appeared in the *Grio* posed the questions, "has the nation lived down its history of racism and should the law become colorblind?" (4/1/13) These questions were asked in conjunction with the two cases before the Supreme Court, one case deals with affirmative action, the other focuses on voting rights. Although both questions involve some aspect of the same topic—race —they need to be addressed separately, and in a different context from the general public concept. Let us look first at the question about racial preference and racism.

The first thing we need to address is the fact that America and the government created race based on color. Two races were created, one black and the other white. These races were not created on anything other than the color of a person's skin. Later many scientists, scholars, ministers, and a host of other players tried to justify race from a biological perspective, to no avail because any person who looked white could be white. So, while the definition protected people with fair complexions, it was no guarantee that the race of these people was correct or valid.

So, society added ancestry to the definition of race via color, but only African ancestry. In other words, if a person had any African ancestry, that person was considered black regardless of how they looked. The problem with race defined by color was finally addressed by U.S. law in Plessy v. Ferguson (1896) but proved to be something of a joke—Homer Plessy's complexion was so light, that his arrest for sitting in a seat reserved for white-only had to be staged. None the less, the law was kept in place.

America made these two races distinct in that they represented opposite values. The so-called white race was given power, privilege, and prestige. If one was upper-classed white, wealthy or educated, then he or she was considered normal. Otherwise, being white just placed one above all other non-whites. For the so-called black race or negroes, as they were also called, they represented negative stereotypes that included ignorance, laziness, worthlessness, untrustworthiness, and repulsiveness along with a host of other despicable characteristics. All these elements were promoted by the so-called white race to be biological features of the so-called black race. Society created, promoted and enforced laws and practices that discriminated against and segregated people of the so-called black race.

Before and during the time of the Civil War, many people, European Americans as well as African Americans, worked towards eliminating slavery and discrimination of African Americans. Once the 13th and 14th Amendments were passed by Congress with pressure from President Lincoln and others, African Americans were recognized as citizens of the United States of America. That meant that only whites and blacks were citizens since no other race was recognized.

For African Americans, being citizens of the United States did not end discrimination, hatred, and bigotry. As a matter of fact, negative feelings against African Americans began to manifest in acts of violence by so-called white vigilante gangs that included acts of lynching.

Although America has always been a diverse society, it acted like a monolith of European Americans. They still held on to the philosophy of Manifest Destiny—this country belongs to them because God gave it to them to take and possess. Although many diverse societies existed in America, the country projected two so-called races—black and white, under the rubric of one country, America. The so-called black race was never treated fairly nor equally by society until the laws of the country was challenged in courts, and especially, the Supreme Court.

The 1954 Supreme Court decision of Brown v. Topeka began the change in the social structure of America. According to the law, African Americans could no longer be treated as unequal in public facilities. Unfortunately, the change in the law did not affect the minds of many Americans who saw the law as a form of discrimination against their rights. Therefore, they continued to maintain and enforce an atmosphere of segregation and discrimination against African Americans until the Civil Rights Acts of 1964, 1965, and 1968.

During the time from the beginning of America creating to two races until the Civil Rights Acts, the race America called white enjoyed the liberties of freedom, life, and the pursuit of happiness without reservation. Now that America has decided to live up to its promise of fair and just treatment for all its citizens, the so-called white race wants to cry discrimination because it cannot continue to discriminate on the basis of its so-called race.

The court case involving university admissions at the University of Texas is said to be based on racial preference for African American students. Actually, if the University of Texas did not show some preference to African American students, it would still be discriminating against them based on past social history and practice. They were formerly denied admission based on their so-called race, so not to consider their so-called race for admission would be seen as unjust or unfair.

Another problem exists regarding this case, that is, how will race be defined since color is not a reliable indicator of race and DNA will show that all people have some African ancestry?

The fact that America created two so-called races based on color has come back to haunt and trouble us since the European Americans no longer control the definition of race in America. Race should have been replaced by ethnic group and ethnicity since the 1940s, but to do that would have meant a loss of power, privilege, and prestige for the European Americans. What society could not bring it to do, Mother Nature is doing for it. In a few more years, the ethnic minority in America will become the majority and the concept of a black race and white race will become so complex and confusing that it will have to become a thing of the past.

So, if the court wants to avoid the problem of having to deal with race, it should simply look at the people who have been denied social and economic justice in our society and do the fair and just thing by them without regard to a so-called race. The idea of a post-racial society is just a way of trying to avoid the realities of discrimination and bigotry that have been a part of America's history.

America created the problem; it can resolve it.

Understanding the Emancipation Proclamation and the 13th Amendment

December 24, 2012

When some people hear the words Emancipation Proclamation (EP), they generally think about it as the document President Lincoln issued to free the slaves. Unfortunately, they would be incorrect; the EP did not free a single slave. So, why is it that people believe it did free the slaves?

The reason for that belief probably has something to do with their schooling. Our society, in certain parts of the country, treats the EP as a special document relative to the freeing of the slaves. The document that should be celebrated more is the 13th Amendment.

When the EP was issued by President Lincoln in 1863, its primary purpose was not directed at freeing the slaves. Initially, Lincoln used the EP as a war measure in hopes of bringing the war to a close. He did not get the reactions from the EP that he expected, so he had to push for something more dramatic, the 13th Amendment. One of the problems associated with the EP was that it freed the slaves in only the states in rebellion. Since the states in rebellion had no reason to acknowledge or accept any proclamation from a president they did not recognize, it fell on deft ears. The only two entities that had cause to react to the proclamation were the government and the armed forces.

For the slaves in the rebellious states, the proclamation was cause for more concern than the problems visited by the war. Just what did this freedom mean? The slaves, when freed, had no home, no money, no security, no job, and no place to go. If they decided to leave their present residence and go to a state not in rebellion, the chances are the state they chose was a slave state. Hence, they would be subjected to slavery again. The proclamation did not provide any safeguards for the slaves that any state would accept or respect as valid. No procedures for making the transition from slave to free was created or provided for the slaves. So, what good was the EP to the slave?

Fortunately, President Lincoln realized that his proclamation had some problems that had to be addressed. For example, since the EP was a war measure, that meant it was temporary; it would expire when the war ended. The Confederate States would resume their form of slavery. That being the case, what would happen to the slaves that fled the South and joined the Union Army? What would happen to the slaves in the non-rebelling slave states? The answer he finally decided on was the 13th Amendment, which abolished slavery in the United States and provided "neither slavery nor involuntary servitude, except as a punishment for crime whereof the party shall have been duly convicted, shall exist within the United States, or any place subject to their jurisdiction."

Had President Lincoln and other like-minded Congressmen not pushed through the passing on January 31, 1865 and subsequent ratifying of the 13th Amendment on December 6, 1865, we can only wonder at the chaos that would have ensued at the war's end. What, in effect, started out as a war measure actually triggered a human measure and helped to save the country. This amendment underscored the rights of African Americans to pursue the liberties that European Americans had been enjoying for years. In addition, because the 13th Amendment is federal legislation, any effort by states to deny citizens their rights could and would be challenged.

The 13th Amendment, more than the EP, established the case for the African American's humanity. Under the First Article of the U.S. Constitution, a slave was defined as three-fifths a man or human, the rights granted via the 13th Amendment elevated him to a full-fledged human being. Without the federal authority of the 13th Amendment, the South could have continued its ways of life without further interruption.

Since we are a society of laws, we should not neglect the EP, but give more attention to the 13th Amendment since it is a very important law.

For many Americans, the idea of the Civil War being fought over slavery is incorrect; they see it as a war over different lifestyles and cultures, economics, and politics. Be that as it may, however, regardless of any or all of these reasons for the war, none can be divorced from the influence of slavery. As suggested earlier, President Lincoln had no thoughts of abolishing slavery. As a matter of fact, early in his presidency, he actually protected it with legislation. Fortunately, for African Americans, Lincoln's concern for the casualties of the war brought about a change in his method for achieving his objective; and we were blessed to receive the EP and the 13th Amendment.

Civil Rights for All Americans is a Constant Battle

December 2, 2012

Most Americans do not dwell on the fact that America was created as a biased society and that the government was one of the prime movers in creating, maintaining, and promoting segregation and discrimination.

After all, the government is not some strange, mysterious organization that influences the lives of the people. No, the government is not strange and mysterious; the government is the people and the mind-set and perceptions of the people in control of the government does affect and influence the lives of the people. Since American society had distinct biases against African Americans that were spelled out in the laws, those laws had to be challenged in order to effect change. Many of the laws were neither just nor fair, but they were legal. Many of the laws created problems for society because they were contrary to the ideals and values that America promoted to the world. For example, the government sanctioned laws of segregation that discriminated against African Americans.

The rights of the people are protected by the 14th Amendment to the United States Constitution, so any challenge to an existing law must eventually go through the Supreme Court. For example, the concept of separate but equal laws that supported segregation in society had to be challenged and brought before the Supreme Court. In 1954, the case Brown v. Board of Education which involved a young African American student, Linda Brown, who was prevented from attending a white neighborhood school, was successfully argued before the Supreme Court. As a result, the law was changed and schools were ordered to desegregate.

To some Americans, this ruling was wrong because it took away their rights to segregate in spite of the fact that to do so was considered un-American. The anger came from the fact that the government had been aiding and abetting the concepts of segregation and discrimination against African Americans, women, and other ethnic Americans since after the Civil War. Many citizens believed that America belonged to European Americans only and that they had the right to live any way they pleased. The concept that living in a society had responsibilities as well as benefits for all individuals was lost on many European Americans.

So, when groups like the NAACP began challenging some of the laws that had prevented African Americans from enjoying the pursuit of life, liberty, and happiness, they were vigorously opposed. The belief was that when a law was changed to correct a long-standing abuse, that change in the law gave the plaintiffs an unfair advantage.

The resentment of some Americans regarding the rights given to African Americans in particular, resulted in a number of cases challenging, for example, Affirmative Action that allowed race to be considered in college and university applications for admission. Several cases have become part of our common knowledge including a recent case involving Abigail Fisher, a young European American female, who claimed she was discriminated against because she was white. In essence, she claims that she was denied admission to the University of Texas in favor of an African American with lesser academic qualifications. What most Americans do not know is that Miss Fisher's case was used as a test case to challenge the use of race in college and university admissions.

In a November 15, 2012 article in the *Washington Spectator*, Lou Dubose, the writer, introduces us to the crusader who wants to undo many of the civil rights laws: "Edward Blum's campaign to dismantle statues and case law that provide advantages to minority groups began in 1992. After Blum, who is white and ran as a Republican, failed to unseat a black Democratic congressman, he filed his first lawsuit." Blum is the behind-the-scene backer of the Fisher case.

Although what Blum does is legal, one wonders why he believes hundreds of years of preferential treatment favoring European American is acceptable and need not be changed when we witness the results of years of injustice in education every day. Dubose notes, "Blum confirmed that his litigation is funded by

Donors Trust and that the names of contributors to the fundraising collective are not available to the public." Dubose does mention that there might be some connection with the Koch brothers via the Donors Trust.

So, while many Americans view the language in our national documents that describe life, liberty, and the pursuit of happiness for all its citizens, some Americans have yet to accept the concept of democracy and the diversity that makes this country strong. Many of the people Blum represents in his lawsuits have a mind-set that speaks to the idea of "just us" as opposed to "justice." He identifies these people and says, "The Reagan-era cabal of Federalist Society lawyers and think-tankers co-opted the 'equal rights' language of the civil rights movement and managed to turn the Equal Protection Clause of the 14th Amendment against the people it was intended to protect."

What this writer finds difficult to understand is how the courts can omit or discount the conditions that resulted from the laws and not consider them in the reasons for wanting to over-turn the laws. If Affirmative Action was created to address some social ills based on race, how can race be removed when trying to correct the problem? If race is removed, what is left to combat the problems of segregation and discrimination that existed before Affirmative Action?

None-the-less, Dubose notes, "Meanwhile, the consensus of legal scholars has the Court wiping out some, if not all, of the race-based college admissions practices that Fisher and Blum are challenging in Texas."

What seems to be the primary reason for some Americans wanting to proscribe the rights and privileges of ethnic and minority Americans is bigotry. In spite of our history of injustice, discrimination, segregation, prejudice, and bigotry, some people would like society to not address these detrimental features in an effort to create a better, more democratic and just America. They, in fact, want to destroy the progress we as a society have made. So, now we know that the fight for civil rights for all Americans is a continuous battle.

Racism is Kept Alive and Protected Through America's Ignorance

November 22, 2016

The subject of racism has been at the top of the list of topics in America before the recent presidential election. A good assumption regarding racism is that the majority of Americans think that they have a good grasp of what racism is. From observations of and listening to many Americans, what they think they know about racism is incorrect.

The Encarta Dictionary offered the following definition of racism: "the belief that people of different races have different qualities and abilities, and that some races are inherently superior or inferior." Another definition is also offered: "prejudice or animosity against people who belong to other races."

While the first definition mentions nothing about hatred, the second definition juxtaposes prejudice and animosity as if they were the same; they are not. Hatred does not have to be an element of racism unless it is focused on something specific regarding the biased race in question. Otherwise, bias against someone simply because he or she looks or acts differently from one's self is irrational; as is racism itself. Nonetheless, we are told that racism exists in America and we are shown evidence of it via media. What we do not see concerning racism, however, is the lack of understanding in what we see, and what we think we know.

In America, the concept of races is generally accepted by many who ignore history, science, and reality in favor of the illusion given to them by society. The concept of a black race and a white race is bogus, untrue, false, has no basis except as an illusion. The social conditioning of Americans by society to accept the concept of races has never lessened or suffered a weakness from the truth.

The system of European American (white) supremacy and African American (black) inferiority was built on the concept of races with the objective of controlling the poor European Americans and African Americans. Today the system is still alive and doing well. Unfortunately, many European Americans do not see themselves as part of the system because they were conditioned to see bigotry on their outside, not their inside. Many European Americans associate racism with something that an individual projects, such as hatred and fear for a person of an ethnic group different from theirs. Therefore, if they, individually, do not hate or fear another person because of that person's ethnicity, then for them, racism does not enter into the mix.

When the statement is made concerning racism being a part of the American social fabric, the reference is directed at the entire society—no exceptions. All of America's institutions are tainted with the element of racism as are all Americans, whether or not it is understood by them. Unfortunately, too many Americans do not know that the concept of racism as well as "race" itself is false. If the reality regarding race is that it is a bogus concept, then so is the concept of racism. Since the term racism is inaccurate, the correct term to use is bigotry.

Bigotry against people of other ethnic groups—not races—is ethnic bigotry.

American society has been persuaded and encouraged to accept things that are irrational, misleading, and illogical for so long because they hide the truth of bigotry from us and keep the system of bigotry protected. For example, when we hear terms like equal justice, equal rights, equal privileges or even equal opportunity, we tend not to question them believing that they are positive and all-inclusive. The fact is these words serve to protect the system of bigotry in that the term "equal" relates primarily to mathematics, not social or human endeavors. If no two people are equal, how then can there be an equal opportunity?

In order to make two people equal, one person has to stop developing in order for the other person to catch up, so even if the other person catches up they would still not be equal. The problem comes from trying to define the term which is relative– even identical twins are not equal. So, using the term equal instead of "fair" or "fairness" conceals the fact that equal can mean anything the user chooses.

Society even accepts the oxymoron phrase "reverse discrimination" as legitimate when common sense tells us that

discrimination exists or it does not exist, like pregnancy either is or
is not. The fact is discrimination cannot be reversed. Little wonder
how our Supreme Court failed to see the defect in their finding
in the Alan Bakke case. The problem is in the language that is
used by law and society that keeps the system of bigotry in place
because no useful definitions are ever offered to make clear the
meaning or intent of what is being said. In many cases, some things
that are meant to be condemned are in fact legitimized in the very
language used to condemn it.

For example, when the Fair Housing Act of 1968 was passed,
instead of saying that discrimination will not be permitted, the
law included qualifiers such as race or color. The fact that the
terms race and color are not defined, but are mentioned in the law
indicates that they are in existence and accepted by society, but
just not to be considered in acquiring housing. We too often make
the mistake of interchanging fairness with equal; they are not the
same. African Americans, as well as all people, want to be treated
fairly because they know that "equal" is relative and elusive.

With the demographic changes taking place in America, the
need to use words and phrases that support the concept of ethnic
supremacy is rapidly diminishing. Terms like racism are used
so often until they have little impact even though they are often
misunderstood by the users. To be clear, racism is not about hating
others; it is about controlling and feeling superior to them. The
element of fear plays an important role in the control aspect of
the system, in that it is used to control the European Americans,
not the African Americans. Fear of African Americans is part of
the social conditioning received by European Americans. Fear,
however, should not be confused with hate. The opposite of hate is
not "love," but ignorance.

America has not been able to solve the problem of racism
because of its ignorance in not realizing that we keep the system of
ethnic bigotry alive and protected without knowing it.

Racist in Heaven?

March 22, 2010

A newspaper article, "Can a Racist go to Heaven?" written by Alan Day, senior pastor of the First Baptist Church of Edmond, recently appeared in the local paper. The article was eye-catching for its honesty and straight-forwardness in discussing the complicity of the church in general and the Southern Baptist in particular in supporting, maintaining, and promoting injustices towards African Americans. Pastor Day took a trip down memory lane in recounting elements of American social and church history that underscored his point that the church did not value African Americans.

In a number of places in the article, Day mentioned significant points such as a reference to the Ku Klux Klan in the early 20th Century having "approximately forty thousand ministers" whose Grand Dragons were Protestants from the states of Pennsylvania, Texas, North Dakota, and Colorado. He also underscored the frequently made fact "that the most segregated hour of the week was 11:00 a.m. on Sunday. Bringing in a personal experience from his youthful days, the Pastor related an incident when good Christian members of his home church armed themselves with guns in an effort to prevent African Americans from worshiping with them.

In addition, Day touches on some questions of Christianity, race, and science and their influence in promoting and maintaining injustices against African Americans. With a reference to Christianity he states, "True Christianity teaches that there is only one world created by the one true God." He continues regarding race that, "It [The Bible] teaches that there is only one race—the human race (Acts 17:26)." Concerning science, he mentioned Charles Darwin and how some pseudo-science helped to encourage racism in America.

Day showed great courage and sincerity in making the statement, "Racism blights humanity. It is a scandal in the church. It dehumanizes people and dishonors Jesus Christ." He then posed the question which is also the article's title, "Can a racist go to heaven?"

He admitted that only God can answer that question. He then changed the question to, "Can a person believe in Jesus and still embrace racial prejudice?" Again, he left the answer to the reader, but added, "If I were God, I might let persons with prejudice in their hearts go to heaven. I suppose they could ride the Glory-bound Transportation System to Beulah Land. But they would have to sit in the back of the bus!"

Pastor Day should be applauded for his efforts in bringing forth the issue of injustice by the Southern Baptist Church towards African Americans. In 1989, the Southern Baptist Convention apologized to America for not having supported a single piece of Civil Rights legislation since its separation from the Baptist Church in 1850. Since that time, the good Christians must have felt comfortable with their un-Christian attitude towards ethnic Americans of color.

Evidently, the apology was not enough to correct the decades of bigotry in the church, because some of that attitude still exists in the last three sentences of Pastor Day's article where he, probably unintentionally, employs dark humor to end his comments.

What Pastor Day did not touch on concerns me more than anything he said. For example, he mentions that all people belong to one race, the human race. If that is the case, then racism should not exist. The people who practice this so-called racism should be identified in truth as bigots. If they are, in fact, bigots, then they cannot be racist because racism is a fallacy. The question should be changed to: "Can bigots go to heaven?"

As a layman, I do not purport to speak on the existence or non-existence of heaven. What I can say is that my learning and experiences regarding Christianity offered me three religious challenges if I was to identify myself as Christian. Those three challenges are to not judge anyone if I do not want to be judged, to treat others as I want to be treated, and to love my fellow man. No restrictions, qualifications, or conditions were placed on whom I should direct these challenges—my fellow man is inclusive of all human beings.

For a bigot to meet and accomplish these challenges would be unlikely. So, common sense dictates the answer. Bigotry and common sense cannot share the same house. Understandably, Pastor Day elected not to deal with that part of the question in that it involves some elements with which he may not be familiar.

For example, using the word race and its derivatives, only serves to underscore the myth of the legitimacy of those words. So, by referring to someone as racist, that person is being rewarded for his false belief in races. Scientists back in 1941 agreed that the words ethnic and ethnicity should replace the word race because they did not carry a supposed undertone of superiority and inferiority; race was a scientific term, not a social one.

Pastor Day should be encouraged for his efforts as far as they went. However, before the article ends, no mention is made of any ways the status quo can be changed; that is, what Day and others in the Baptist and other churches, for that matter, are doing to change the negative attitude of some so-called Christians regarding African Americans and other ethnic Americans. Day does make reference to the hypocritical practice of some churches supporting missions in other countries, but not inviting or caring for ethnic Americans across town or even down the street.

However, talk without action has no value. Carrying a Bible and going to church does not make one a Christian any more than carrying a guitar and going to concerts makes one a musician.

What can be done? If Pastor Day is serious is doing something about the issue in addition to speaking about it, a number of practical things can be initiated. For example, members of the clergy can meet together and invite some knowledgeable person to help them better understand this phenomenon of race in America. Too many people think they already know about race in America, but only know it from a particular perspective. In order to teach and preach truth, a person must be armed with current and appropriate information.

A clergy with an understanding of race and ethnicity in America can have a tremendous positive impact on their congregations by offering sermons that speak to the humanity of all people, by organizing adult and children study groups. These groups should be led by informed leaders who examine the facts of ethnicity and Christianity in an effort to make the group members both better citizens and Christians. The clergy can even meet with ethnically diverse colleagues with the intent of exchanging visits of pastors as well as members.

Many positive things are possible when a challenge is met with an open mind.

These comments were not written to in any way discredit or create a negative attitude toward Pastor Day. They were offered to help in a constructive way to try and clear a path for positive actions by the clergy and the church. Finally, the answer to question asked by Pastor Day should not be left in the air. What can the church do to reduce the number of bigots?

If any doubt exists that bigotry is a sin, then it is part of the church's responsibility to try and help change the bigots and their chances of getting to heaven.

Innocence, Ignorance, and the Confederate Flag

December 12, 2011

The phrase "a little learning is a dangerous thing" is attributed to Alexander Pope (1688 – 1744), in *An Essay on Criticism*, 1709. For most people, the point is well taken. However, for others, it falls on deaf ears.

A case in point was reported by the Associated Press (12/2/11) when it published "A black college student who drew complaints for displaying a Confederate flag in his window said he sees the banner as a symbol of Southern pride and not racism." Byron Thomas, a 19-year-old student at a South Carolina University, evidently did not read far enough in American history to discover or gain an understanding of the historical symbolism of the flag, the impact of the flag on many African Americans, and the nature of bigotry.

If Thomas had progressed far enough in his study of history, he would understand that victorious countries do not fly the flags in honor of the countries they defeated, for what should be the obvious reason—they lost the war. In addition, the flag conjures up many negative and painful emotions that could lead to resentment, hatred, and anger.

He must acquaint himself with the history before he jumps to the conclusion that no hard will is created by flying the Confederate flag. He needs to read about the Reconstruction period from a number of perspectives—at least from one that tells about the Black Codes and how they were implemented relative to African Americans. He also might want to visit with some mature African Americans for their opinions relative to flying the Confederate flag today.

Thomas needs to know that the Confederate flag is a symbol of the inhumane treatment of African Americans by the South. The South resented the fact that the North would not accept slavery as a feature of American democracy. Having slaves made America appear hypocritical to the world. African Americans were viewed as the primary cause of the war, so the South sought to make them pay by intimidation, discrimination, physical abuse, and murder. The Constitution had already defined the slave as less than human—three-fifths a man. The reference to slaves in the Constitution was translated as negroes, blacks, coloreds or any slave of African ancestry. These are a few of the things Thomas needs to know in order for him to gain a better understanding of the symbolism of the Confederate flag.

For many African Americans, seeing the Confederate flag displayed serves as a reminder of the lack of respect that the South had for them as human beings. To display it today would mean that one is not aware of the symbolism it carries or else he or she knows, but still wants to communicate that same negative message.

The history associated with the Confederate flag cannot be erased any more than the history associated with the Nazi swastika. To understand and appreciate history, one must first learn it, something Thomas has yet to experience. Had he studied American history and the specific parts played in it by African Americans, he would realize the debt he owes to all the people who sacrificed so that today he can attend a predominantly European American university in the South. He owes it to them and himself to get the best education available to him, but one that includes his story and not just history.

From some of the comments he made concerning the incident, we can surmise his youth and innocence. For example, he said that "he's unhappy about such things as labels, and he doesn't like the term 'African-American,' which makes him feel like 'a half-citizen,' since he wasn't born in Africa." If he would take a moment and think about his self-image, he would realize that being labeled as black says absolutely nothing about who he is. The label black, along with negro, colored, and slave were all given to Africans as well as African Americans by the majority. These labels were given to them to deprive them of the knowledge of who they really were—not labels, but human beings with personal identities that disclosed their ethnicity, culture, and history. One does not have to be born in Germany or England to have ancestry from those countries. The same applies to the continent of Africa.

Thomas mentioned that his parents didn't like his actions with the flag, which should have given him a clue about the appropriateness of his displaying it in his dorm window. In addition, the school missed a teachable moment when it failed to do its job; first, by telling him to take down the flag, then, by telling him it was OK to put it back in the window. No reason for each action was given.

As a result of his ignorance and arrogance, Thomas was made to look like an uninformed young fool. We can only hope that he learns from this experience about acting on too little information.

What Thomas needs to recognize about his actions is that he participates in denigrating himself without knowing it. By displaying the flag in his dorm room he is saying, in essence, that he agrees with all the negative stereotypes of African Americans created by a bigoted South and symbolized by the Confederate flag. He supports all the flag symbolizes. In so doing, he is exposing himself to things which he knows nothing about.

Again, the reference to a little learning being a dangerous thing is underscored in the words and action of Thomas. Someone needs to send him an *Ebony* or a *Jet* magazine.

Kilpatrick's Old South's Ignorance and Prejudice

September 26, 2010

In a recent article published in the *Oklahoman*, Gene Owens spoke about the late columnist James J. Kilpatrick. The article entitled "Remembering a Voice from the Old South" included several points that stood out to me as being associated with ignorance and prejudice, two bedfellows.

The focus of the article was on the early years of civil rights and the newspaper coverage. Owens recounts how Kilpatrick spoke of the "Northern papers would send in their traveling teams to get all the nasty stories they could about the segregated South, and these people arrived with their prejudices in their suitcases, and never unpacked their suitcases." What struck me about this statement is what is missing. Why these people were considered prejudiced? Was it simply because they were from the North?

The assumption seems to be that the segregated South was doing just fine until these people came down here and started looking at the negative effects of segregation. If that was the bases of these Northerners' prejudice, then what kind of rationale informed the Southerners? Also, notice that no mention is made of their ethnicity.

The next sentence read: "Then a couple of black reporters came down—very literate, very intelligent—and they sat around my office and we yakked for an hour or so. They were two first-rate reporters." Notice that these two reporters were identified as black, but more importantly, they were "very literate, very intelligent." This statement is code for they were almost like white reporters in that they could approximate European Americans in their speech and their thought. The assumption from this statement is that no one expected African American reporters to be literate and intelligent, so when they were both, mention had to be made of it because it was seen as an exception to the norm.

What evidently never dawned on Kilpatrick's mind was the reason that the reporters spent so much time with him in his office was for their own self-protection. Remember, the time was early civil rights years and these reporters were in the South. They had to touch bases with some European Americans of note who could vouch for them if necessity called for it.

The article continued, "I remember saying to my wife that evening—and this may have been part of the awakening— 'If they had been white, I would have invited them to dinner in my home.'" What a bigoted comment to make! The only reason he did not invite them to dinner in his home was because of their color? Actually, their color was not so much the reason for not getting an invite as it was the symbol of the prejudice that was so natural to the South during that time. Would Kilpatrick have been criticized by his neighbors and co-workers had he invited these reporters? We do not know because he did not risk the chance.

What apparently underscores this statement is the ignorance and biased mind-set of Kilpatrick who hadn't the slightest idea of his prejudice. To him, his way of thinking was perfectly in keeping with God and the world. Segregation and discrimination were part of Southern culture. Imagine, having two African American male reporters visiting in the home of a Southern European American at this time in America—what a novel idea! He might have been labeled a civil rights activist and charged with trying to change the social system. He could not afford that, but the thought was nice.

The fact that Kilpatrick would have been willing to invite these reporters into his home had they been white underscores the problem. Ethnic bias or prejudice was the ruling principle in America especially during the early years of civil rights. Kilpatrick tells us of his ethnic ignorance and hence, prejudice:

> "I don't know what attitude I had toward Southern blacks in general. I grew up in a segregated society in Oklahoma City. I spent all my formative years in a segregated society. They [African Americans] were kind of invisible. You saw certain servants…but you never had any relationship as equals."

That says it all. If one grows up in a segregated society through his formative years, what is likely to be his perception of people who do not look like him? If he knew what kind of society he grew up in and the kind of society he lived in, why would he not know that his attitude is one of ethnic superiority?

The focus of the article was to underscore the prejudice of the "Yankee journalist" against the South, and how they went about acquiring their stories. The thought that discrimination and segregation were wrong regardless of their manifestations was never considered. The idea of the Northern reporters making the South look bad was the problem. However, the fact that the two African American reporters were literate and intelligent was special since they spent an hour talking with Kilpatrick.

With due respect to Kilpatrick and Owens, these comments are not meant to ridicule or belittle either man, but to underscore the need for ethnic education in America. Too many Americans feel comfortable with their biases thinking that it is OK to hate your neighbor because of his or her skin color or religion. The article gives us an opportunity to see just how easy some European Americans wear their ethnic ignorance and prejudice.

America needs desperately to be re-educated relative to the power and presence of ethnic diversity in society. America needs to stop using the words race for ethnic group or ethnicity, and black for African American, and white for European American. But first, America needs to know why that change is necessary.

If one thinks that ethnic ignorance and prejudice in America is a thing of the past, one needs only turn on the local news or pick up a paper and the evidence will slap the person directly in the face— Americans wanting to burn holy books, cut off social security to the elderly, stop the poor for receiving food stamps, force unemployed Americans to lose support. And the beat goes on....

Letter Writer Fails to Understand MLK's Words and Actions for America

February 3, 2013

A letter writer by Georgia Sparks, published in the *Oklahoman* on the "opinion" page, "Follow King's Example," (1/26/13) was surely meant to be well-meaning and kind in addressing King's words and actions. What becomes apparent in the letter, however, is the lack of understanding the writer had of King's objective.

Most people upon hearing King's name immediately think of his "I had a dream" speech and all the things he wanted for his children in America. When they think those thoughts, they miss the essence of King's words and actions. If people would take the time to read the entire speech, they would recognize it for what it is—a protest speech. King was angry at America for not living up to its promise of a fair opportunity to all its citizens, especially to African Americans and other Americans.

The Sparks letter stated, "Most people in America are glad that Martin Luther King Jr. was able to help push back the bars keeping minorities from achieving success. He would be glad to see the progress that's been made toward equality of opportunity."

On the contrary, most people aware of King's challenge for the nation would be very upset and angry of the little progress that has taken place over the last fifty years. Since Sparks mentioned specifically "minorities," we might take a look at the progress made by African Americans since King's death. What we discover is that in many cases they have experienced a lack of progress— more African American young men are in prison than in college, the unemployment rate for African Americans is twice that of European Americans, the death rate is higher, the home ownership is lower. So, what would King be glad about? Of course, not only African Americans have experienced set-backs but also many Americans in general for a variety of reasons.

The bars referred to by Sparks that King tried to bring down or push back are still in place, for the most part. They are represented in the bigotry and prejudice still very much a part of the American fabric and manifest themselves in a variety of ways. Many of those ways were apparent during the last presidential election when some state governmental officials tried to prevent many minority citizens from voting. They are present in the laws that many Congressmen want to pass that would place a hardship of many needy Americans.

King would be very upset at the negative attitude of many Americans for wanting to deprive some citizens of much needed help.

The letter continued, "He [King] would not be happy to see how many people who could have succeeded but instead failed because they abused drugs, failed to secure a good education, chose to go into gangs and drug cartels or chose to go into crime and didn't marry before having children." These comments reflect a conception that has not kept pace with reality, but rather remains in a somewhat naïve, but warm and secure cocoon. One of King's primary complaints relative to government's lack of concern focused specifically on the needs of poor people. Sparks seem to suggest that people want to be poor, ignorant, drug abusers, unemployed and work towards those ends.

We know that despite the best laid plans made by people, circumstances occur that disrupt and destroy those plans, and people find themselves in predicaments not of their choosing. Once people find themselves in dire straits, extricating themselves usually proves extremely difficult; some people find it impossible to regain their once enjoyed level of life.

King believed that it was incumbent on society to lend a helping hand, as well as a hand up, to the people who were in need. We have a perfect example of how King imagined the government could benefit people in need by looking at many of the victims of Hurricane Sandy. The people from that experience who were displaced were not displaced because they wanted to be. Most of them are ordinary, decent, hard-working people who had no say in what Mother Nature did to them.

Part of our responsibility as citizens of this great country is to help our fellow citizens when they are in need. Sometime the needs are not as obvious as helping victims of natural occurrences or as immediate. Sometimes the needs include job training and education as well as health care and housing. These are the things King saw as necessary concerns and responsibilities of our society.

Sparks' letter stated, "People who choose to succeed make good decisions. They work hard to prepare themselves for success. They delay having children until they can marry and take care of them inside a family."

Really?

Someone not choosing to be successful might be a possibility, but most people must define success according to the reality of their situation. If all it took to be successful was to choose it and work hard to accept it, certainly more people would be successful. What seems to be missing from Sparks' comments is an understanding of the various levels of the social-economic conditions in America. She has an idea of what the American dream is and it belongs to everyone—the same dream. One way people can be successful according to Sparks would for them to "… work before they play."

Although ethnicity is never mentioned in the letter, one cannot avoid the obvious references that suggest and stereotype groups of ethnic Americans. The mere reference to Martin Luther King, Jr. usually brings to mind African Americans even though King spoke for all Americans.

Sparks again seemed to misplace her focus when she closed her letter with the words about King: "He valued the family structure and took care of his own family. Instead of marching to honor King, I'd like to see people follow his example in their own lives." What a wonderful thought. King certainly would want people to have families if they desired, but more importantly, he would have wanted society to treat all people fairly so they could choose what they defined as life, liberty, and the pursuit of happiness. To follow King's example in light of conditions today would mean people marching in protest every day.

50 Years Later, the Civil Rights Act of 1964 Still Needed

April 21, 2014

The recent celebration of the 50th anniversary of the Civil Rights Act of 1964 (CRA) gives us an opportunity to evaluate a number of concerns relative to that Act, and society in general. Although the process of acquiring the Civil Rights Act was started by President Kennedy, President Lyndon Baines Johnson was the man who championed it through Congress. He paid a large political price for doing so.

Nonetheless, we are thankful for his efforts and success. Today, when we look at the Civil Rights Act, we can identify a number of things that are directly related to society then in 1964 and now.

The first thing we realize by the signing of the CRA is that a need was present for such action. After the Civil War, African Americans were literally kept in slavery via a lack of education, jobs, housing, and political representation. Although segregation, discrimination, prejudice, and bigotry were present and visible in everyday life of America, little was being done to recognize the problems. Americans, both African Americans and European Americans, tried fighting the injustices on a variety of fronts, but the sentiment of the majority population was against social change.

With continued pressure on the Federal Government and the presidents, the civil rights activists over the years since the Civil War were able to acquire an audience with people in power. So, for the first time in American history, Congress and the American people were able to see and accept the fact of injustices visited on African Americans and other ethnic Americans.

As a result, to recognizing the un-American treatment of African Americans and other ethnic Americans, discussions took place relative to how to go about identifying these injustices. With regards to the individual's rights, safeguards must not be placed in the hands of the states, because a lack of uniformity would exist. So, if efforts were to be made, they must come from the federal government.

Under the status quo in society up to 1964, segregation was the law and it existed in every aspect of the African American's life. The sit-ins and marches helped to call attention to the social injustices regarding public accommodations for African Americans. Some success had been achieved in a few areas of education, but the concept of separate but equal was still in effect. So, through the efforts of a number of Civil Rights leaders working directly with President Kennedy and some of his associates, the plan to create a Civil Rights Act that would address some of the injustices experienced by African Americans and other Americans was crafted.

Now that a plan of action was in place, the question was how to get it approved by a Congress that felt no need or urgency to enact a bill that would, in effect, take away some of their power. President Kennedy knew that he would be in for a long and hard fight with certain sections of the Congress in winning approval of this Act, but he was convinced it had to be done. Unfortunately, President Kennedy was killed before he had an opportunity to engage Congress relative to the Civil Rights Act. The task of bringing the CRA successfully through Congress fell to President Johnson. The undertaking for President Johnson would not be an easy one since he was viewed as a Southern politician from Texas and Southern politicians were not very keen on giving equal rights to the sons and daughters of former slaves.

For many politicians, the rights and privileges enjoyed by the European Americans and Caucasians were not to be shared equally with African Americans and other ethnic groups. The concern for so-called white supremacy being negatively affected by passage of the CRA troubled many of the political group known as the Dixiecrats. President Johnson was well aware of this group and their concerns because he was considered part of them prior to becoming vice president. However, Johnson also was aware of the importance of the CRA, since its creation acknowledged the existence of injustices as reflected in the status quo, and the label of hypocrisy of America and its claim of democracy.

Nonetheless, Johnson showed political acumen and courage in getting the CRA through Congress. The passage of the CRA represented the success of the efforts of many civil rights activists who labored many years in this regard. With the passage of the CRA, the federal government assumed control of the protection of the individual American's rights. Rather than representing the end of a struggle, the CRA actually was the beginning of a new sense of democracy where all Americans, regardless of skin color, religion, gender, and ethnicity, could challenge the previously biased conditions.

The challenge came from the mindset of many European Americans who felt deceived by the federal government who gave the minorities the same rights as they enjoyed. Somehow, they saw this as wrong and an injustice to them as European Americans.

Today, as we look back on fifty years of American life with the CRA, we can recognize how that Act has benefited the society in progressing towards that democracy that gives each citizen the rights to life, liberty, and the pursuit of happiness. We can also recognize the struggles that come from making changes in a society based on bigotry. The struggle is still in progress and will be until we educate ourselves and each other of the commitment we made and make as Americans.

In essence, what is the responsibility of each and every American? We find the answer in our pledge of allegiance to our country: "I pledge Allegiance to the flag of the United States of America and to the Republic for which it stands, one nation under God, indivisible, with Liberty and Justice for all."

In this pledge we recognize, accept, and embrace the United States of America as one. We underscore that understanding when we add to the pledge "and to the Republic for which it stands." The remainder of the pledge states what we stand for as a nation. Nowhere in the pledge is there a reference to a state as an independent entity.

As a society, we need to confront those who would like to make America into a nation that caters to their wants based on skin color or ethnicity. The CRA was passed as a measure to confront the injustices of the past and present. As American citizens, we have the responsibility of protecting those rights and privileges.

To witness injustice and not call attention to it is the same as accepting it.

Ayaan Hirsi Ali stated that "tolerance of intolerance is cowardice." To that we add that acceptance of intolerance by Americans is hypocrisy.

Revisiting the March on Washington and the "I Have a Dream" Speech

August 25, 2013

America this week recognized and celebrated the 50th anniversary of the 1963 March on Washington and the speech of Dr. Martin Luther King, Jr. Much attention has been paid to the march and the speech. Unfortunately, most people do not know what either the march or the speech was about.

They believe they know, but their responses to two questions will reveal the extent of their knowledge. The first question is: how much progress has been made over these past fifty years? The second question is: how would Dr. King react to the present-day reality? The answers to these questions are not set in stone, but will vary depending on a variety of conditions relative to the responders—things like ethnicity, age, social status, education, politics, etc.

In response to the first question regarding the progress made during the last fifty years, we must first set the perimeters relative to the march. The organizers proclaimed the objective of the march was to focus Washington of the problem of jobs and freedom for poor and working-class Americans in general, and African Americans specifically, since they were the ones most directly affected. The march was seen by many European Americans as a gathering of minority protesters, especially African Americans to try and get Washington to listen to their complaints; some thought of the march as a nuisance and waste of time.

Many of the African Americans saw the march as an opportunity for all people, especially minorities, to show Washington that they were united in the desire for better jobs, wages, and freedoms in general. They believed that power and strength would be reflected in the large number of march participants to the degree that Washington could not ignore them. So, after years of planning by the civil rights activists and other American citizens, the march envisioned by A. Phillip Randolph, and orchestrated by Bayard Rustin, took place.

Today, when society looks back fifty years to measure the progress made relative to jobs and freedom, the response must be not very much progress has been made. Poor and working-class Americans are still experiencing the same problems that Dr. King and other leaders outlined in the speeches.

The average wage is actually lower than the medium wages fifty years ago when inflation is figured in the assessment. Many citizens are unemployed and must depend on the government for help. Many citizens must work two and three jobs just to try to meet some of their financial obligations. The cost of education and housing has put many Americans in precarious positions that threaten their ability to move forward. But the most important occurrence affecting the poor, the working class, and the ethnic population is the changes in the voting laws of a number of states. The changes made by states like Texas and North Carolina would result in disenfranchising many of the Americans by denying them the vote. So, the answer to the progress question reflects a lack of progress having been made since 1963 relative to jobs and minority freedoms.

The answer to the second question regarding how Dr. King would react to the present-day reality would be anger. He would be angry and disappointed for a number of reasons. Too many African Americans saw the march as a moment and not the beginning of a movement; so much time has been wasted in addressing the needs of the people and not creating solutions for those problems. Much more should have been accomplished regarding all aspects of American life. The people who knew Dr. King knew him to be a non-violent militant; he believed in direct non-violent confrontation. That is why the march on Washington was deliberately a peaceful march.

One major mistake made by the media, the African Americans and the European Americans who knew what the march and speech were all about, did not set the record straight regarding both. Many European Americans then as now think of the "I Have a Dream" speech as a statement of celebration, an expression of all the progress the African Americans had made to that point. So, the march was seen as a celebration of all the good things that had happened to that point.

The problem with that thinking is that it was wrong. The March on Washington as well as Dr. King's speech were elements of protest—not praise. The fact that African Americans and European Americans who had worked so hard to bring these phenomena together did not increase their efforts to have the problems of jobs and freedom resolved represent the disappointment.

Many Americans today still see the march and the speeches as evidence of progress because they continue to embrace the theme of "I Have a Dream." They do not realize that the only reason Dr. King spoke of the dream was because he could not experience the reality, a reality that had been promised by America in its democratic creed of "life, liberty, and freedom for all." When we revisit the objectives of the march and speeches we realize that very little have changed regarding the expressions of liberty and freedoms for all because the concept and attitude of many American regarding America are still grounded in the idea of a "white America." Too many Americans still see America as a "white" society and as long as they can wield the power to keep it that way, they will.

America has been changing since it began, but the changes have been so gradual that some people did not realize that changes were taking place. The eye-opening experience for many of these people was the election of Barack Obama as president. The anger, hatred, bias, frustration and violence directed towards President Obama are not, for all intent and purposes, for Obama personally. All these things are expressions of fear and losing that President Obama represents to their view of America.

Many European Americans fear losing the power to create the perception of America and the privileges that has historically been associated with a "white" identity. Unfortunately, that perspective does not fit with the democratic philosophy that was set in motion at this country's beginning. Unless and until America changes its founding creed, society will continue to move in a democratic direction regardless of the set-backs and slowness.

Fairness and Justice Not Possible in America with the Concept of Races

February 19, 2014

One of the great ironies in America is the fact that people try to act as if ethnic bias only exists part of the time. America has been a nation of bigotry from its beginning. The control of the power and privileges of their ethnic group was the concern of the Anglo-Saxons from the earliest accounts of their life in the new world. The pilgrims and Puritans did not believe in equality and fairness. They believed rather in class status based on wealth and titles. In their eyes, whatever status one was born into, he or she should remain in that status for life. They believed that if God had wanted them to be in a different social class, then he would have put them there at birth.

They had little or no reservations about killing the Indians, whom they called savages, because they believed that God wanted them to clear the land for themselves. America was God's gift to the Anglo-Saxons; they were to be the supreme and superior leaders of the new nation. In addition, while transporting their culture to the new world, they introduced along with American slavery, the creation of race by color and geography. Therefore, ethnic bigotry is one of the basic fabrics of American culture.

Fast forward to today and we find much of that sentiment still exists in the minds of many European Americans. Anglo-Saxon Americans controlled who came to America and who could live here, and that was accomplished through immigration laws. One of the more significant and influential immigration laws based on ethnicity control was the Johnson-Reed Act.

The 1924 Immigration Act also included a provision excluding from entry any alien who by virtue of race or nationality was ineligible for citizenship. Existing nationality laws dating from 1790 and 1870 excluded people of Asian lineage from naturalizing. As a result, the 1924 Act meant that even Asians not previously prevented from immigrating—the Japanese in particular—would no longer be admitted to the United States. Many in Japan were very offended by the new law, which was a violation of the Gentlemen's Agreement. The Japanese government protested, but the law remained, resulting in an increase in existing tensions between the two nations. But it appeared that the U.S. Congress had decided that preserving the racial composition of the country was more important than promoting good ties with the Japanese empire. (http://history.state.gov)

Ethnicity has always been a concern in America; especially with the citizens who call themselves white (European Americans). When these Anglo Saxons realized that the ethnic composition of America was in danger of change, they had to take drastic actions. That action involved bringing into the so-called white race that group of European immigrants that had not been accepted as white were now admitted to the club. The use of a term, "Caucasian," that came into existence just prior to 1800, was called into service: "The idea of a "Caucasian race" represents whiteness ratcheted up to a new epistemological realm of certainty" ("Whiteness of a Different Color," by Matthew Frye Jacobson). The reason for this change was to keep the country from changing its ethnic composition.

Once a lie is told, more lies have to be told to continue hiding the truth. That has been the case for America since the creation of the concept of races—black and white. The truth has been available regarding race for many years. For example, in the Bible, we learn that all people are of one blood"

> 24"God, who made the world and everything in it, since He is Lord of heaven and earth, does not dwell in temples made with hands. 25 Nor is He worshiped with men's hands, as though He needed anything, since He gives to all life, breath, and all things. 26 And He has made from one blood[a] every nation of men to dwell on all the face of the earth, and has determined their preappointed times and the boundaries of their dwellings," (Acts 17:24-26 KJJV)

On numerous occasions the scientists and scholars from the U.N. have made it known that the term 'race' is not correct or accurate because it has no basis in fact. Science—modern genetics in particular—has constantly affirmed the unity of the human species, and denied that the notion of 'race' has any foundation. In the words of Article 1 of the Universal Declaration on the Human Genome and Human Rights, "the human genome underlies the fundamental unity of all members of the human family, as well as the recognition of their inherent dignity and diversity." This Declaration was adopted unanimously at the 29th session of UNESCO's General Conference on the 11th of November 1997, and then by the United Nations General Assembly on the 9th of December 1998, as part of the celebration marking the fiftieth anniversary of the Universal Declaration of Human Rights. (UNESCO 2001)

We can even go the recent science where we learn from DNA that DNA studies do not indicate that separate classifiable subspecies (races) exist within modern humans. While different genes for physical traits, such as skin and hair color, can be identified between individuals, no consistent patterns of genes across the human genome exist to distinguish one race from another. There also is no genetic basis for divisions of human ethnicity. People who have lived in the same geographic region for many generations may have some alleles in common, but no allele will be found in all members of one population and in no members of any other. (geonomics.energy.gov)

What we discover is that America continues to live in denial about the myth of race, and until it can debunk that myth, the lie will continue. But even more, as long as the concept of races exists in America, fairness and justice are not possible, because everything is seen through the prism of race. Every American lives daily in an atmosphere where bigotry is so common that it is presumed not to exist. How can we talk of fairness and justice when we have not divorced ourselves from the concept of black and white races?

Go study.

SOCIAL CONCERNS

*"Where justice is denied, where poverty is
enforced, where ignorance prevails,
and where any one class is made to feel that society
is an organized conspiracy to oppress,
rob and degrade them, neither persons nor property will be safe."*

FREDERICK DOUGLASS

Changing America's Social Conditioning a Challenge for All Ethnicities

November 25, 2013

Americans are ethnically conditioned to discern other ethnic groups with one exception; that exception would be recognizing European Americans. Read any newspaper or magazine article and if the subject of the article is European American, that information is usually not stated, but assumed. If the subject of the article is other than European American, then the ethnicity is identified.

The primary reason for this activity is based on the influence and control European Americans have had on Americans for several hundred years. During American slavery and shortly after the Civil War, emphasis was placed on the irrational conception of race by color; that is, society created two dominant races, one black, the other white. Ever since that creation, fruitless efforts have been made to try and make the myth reflect reality. Nonetheless, what American society has been able to do is promote the concept of multiple biological races with relative success.

Along with the concept of multiple biological races came the acceptance of the European American as the only normal representative of human beings. In effect, European Americans were conditioned to see themselves as not belonging to a race or ethnic groups because they were the model of mankind. So, the inclusion or exclusion of the European American ethnic identity in the print media simple reflects that concept of normalcy.

The concept of European American as being normal manifests itself in a variety of ways daily in society. The majority of models used to sell goods and services are European American. When models of other ethnic groups are used to sell what is generally viewed as normal goods and services, they attract attention because they are not seen as normal based on how they look.

For example, beauty products aired on television usually employ European American models, male and female. Today, when an ethnic American model is used in advertisement the recognition of the difference is almost immediate. Again, the reason for this recognition is based on the conditioning we as a society have been exposed to regarding what is seen as normal and what is not.

One of the great challenges we have in America today is discontinuing the misguided practice of discerning ethnic groups and then stereotyping them according to what are considered to be social norms. For each of the major ethnic groups in America today, society has a stereotype of some sort used to characterize that group. These stereotypes lend themselves to separating and dividing Americans rather than uniting them.

Take, for example, the celebrations of Thanksgiving and Hanukah, occasions that serve to honor events in American and Jewish history respectively. As a diverse society, America recognizes and supports the rights of the Jewish people to celebrate some of their history just as America celebrates part of its history. In effect, we are more alike as human beings than we are different. We need to learn to accentuate our similarities rather than focus on our differences. First, however, we must become aware of how we continue to separate ourselves.

A recent headline from *USA Today* identified the movie "The Best Man Holiday" as having a race theme. That assessment was probably due to the fact that the cast was predominantly African American. The suggestion implied from the reference to race is that because of the color of the majority of the cast—the movie's theme had to be about race.

A number of concerns are presented with the assumption of a movie being associated with a race; first is the acceptance of the false assumption of multiple races, and second is the assumption that skin complexion determines a so-called race. We need to clear the air on the two false assumptions.

If a statement is made about a movie being a race-theme production, then the idea of either a black or some other colored race is intended, because movies using European Americans are considered normal. The faulty logic in a statement referring to a race theme movie is that no such race exists. If the reference is to a so-called black race, then any movie with a cast of people of color, regardless of their geography or culture would be considered black.

For example, a movie made in Nigeria, with a Nigerian cast, or in South Africa, with a South African cast, or in Brazil with a Brazilian cast would all be considered a race theme movie, because of the skin complexion of the cast members. However, a movie made in England with an English cast, or Germany, with a German cast, or France, with a French cast, would simply be a movie because of the skin complexion of the cast members. We can readily understand just how ridiculous the concept of race by color is confusing and useless.

Because Americans are conditioned to see race based on color, they also accept the idea of so-called racial differences associated with the stereotypes. In essence, a so-called race theme movie would depict the elements of love, hate, happiness, and the range of human emotions based on the idea of some specific so-called race. Therefore, following that logic, Shakespeare's Romeo and Juliet performed by African Americans would be a play with a race theme. How stupid are we?

We, as a society could eliminate a large part of the ignorance and stupidity by forgoing the use of the terms black and white and their reference to so-called races. We know, but need to accept, the fact that only one human race exists, and we are all part of it. Every American belongs to the human family regardless of his or her ethnicity. We readily acknowledge the cultural differences that economic, education, geography, and social standing represent, but all those things are man-made. When we take the time to observe and examine our differences, we learn quickly that we are more alike than different and that movies, regardless of the skin complexion of the cast, are about human beings and the challenges they face learning to live with one another.

America and Re-Segregation

April 24, 2011

When the Supreme Court made its decision in Brown v. Topeka Board of Education, the ruling underscored the fact that the schools in America were not equal, that is, the schools attended by European Americans and African Americans were separate and unequal. Many European Americans believed that the goal of desegregation was to bring the two ethnic groups together for the purpose of socialization. The African Americans were concerned only with having their children receive a quality education.

Since that court decision in 1954, the progress made in America providing a quality education for all its children has not been good, fair at best. Why? Simply because education in America is connected to economics, which is connected to ethnicity, which is connected to geography.

Any family with the financial means can provide a quality education for its children. Unfortunately, not every family in America has financial means to give its children a quality education. That was the situation in America after the Civil War when African Americans were allowed to receive an education at public expense. Segregation and Jim Crow laws ensured that the African American children would receive an inferior public education. This fact was made certain simply because the European Americans controlled not only the schools, but the monies that they received. Even more important than the control of the schools was the control of the economy which meant jobs.

African Americans were not able to earn a living comparable to that of the European American because of prejudices and bigotry. For example, in the 1940s and 1950s, skilled African American workers were denied the opportunity to join unions, so when they worked, even alongside their European American counterparts, they earned considerably less money. Also, the type of jobs that were available to them did not pay wages high enough to guarantee their children a good education. After 1954 the chances of African Americans getting an education equal to that of European Americans began to quickly disappear because of white flight.

When the law to desegregate was made, European Americans who could afford it moved to the all-European American suburbs where they could again control the schools and who attended them.

When the middle and upper class European Americans moved to the suburbs, they took their money, schools, and teachers along with them. The lack of money and teachers had a direct negative impact on the inner city public schools. The school equipment, facilities, and employees that departed the inner cities resulted in the quality of education slowly diminishing. This departure also changed the demographics of the inner cities. They began to reflect a greater ethnic minority presence.

A significant number of European Americans remained in the inner cities for a variety of reasons—lack of money, transportation, jobs. However, because there was a greater ethnic minority presence, the per capita income of the school districts changed as well. The differences among the European American schools and those of the African Americans showed just how important money was to a quality education. So, in an effort to address the problem of inequity in the schools, the federal government established commissions to help deal with the problem. The most dramatic program for addressing the educational inequity was bussing. Bussing was a two-headed monster because of what it took and what it gave.

One of the most detrimental things to happen to the ethnic communities during desegregation was the loss of neighborhood identity, integrity, and input into the schools. Most people confuse desegregation with integration; they think they are the same. In desegregation, a minority is taken into the majority with no changes to the majority. In essence, when African American children desegregated to a school, the only thing that changed for the majority students was the addition of new faces of color. For the African American children, the changes were significant; they went from being in a normal environment to being like a small turtle in a fishbowl. Their main objective was to try and get an education and adjust to a way European Americans conducted themselves in school.

In integration, the environment shares elements of each group even though a majority and minority still exists. Unfortunately, for African American children the cultural references, comfort zones, and sincere concerns for their education were left behind when the busses took off. The new teachers could not relate to the concerns and challenges of the African American students because they were ignorant of their plight; that is, teachers were not educated to consider the problems of ethnic minorities except to have their stereotypes underscored. Much has changed since '54, but much has also stayed the same.

Over the years, integration has made its way into some of the curricula, but much of the attitudes against desegregation still remain. As a matter of fact, a number of states have begun the process of reintroducing neighborhood schools and doing away with bussing. If that takes place, the end result will undoubtedly be re-segregation.

Drive through any city or town of thirty thousand or more and the areas of income levels will manifest themselves like raisins in a bowel of milk. What determines these residential boundaries are income and education—the more money and education a family has, the better the quality of living and schooling. If children are made to attend school in their neighborhood, and the level of income and education is low, then the education those children receive will not be comparable to that received by the children living in the upper income and educated area.

In an article published by *The Christian Science Monitor* January 25, 2008, re-segregation is taking place in many places in America. One place singled out is Charlotte, North Carolina: "Charlotte is rapidly re-segregating,' says Carol Sawyer, a parent and member of the Charlotte-Mecklenburg Schools Equity Committee."' The article states further that "It's a trend that is occurring around the country and is even more pronounced than expected in the wake of court cases dismantling both mandated and voluntary integration programs, a new report says. The most segregated schools, according to the report, which documents desegregation trends, are in big cities of the Northeast and Midwest."

Why is this re-segregation occurring? One reason offered by some critics is due to the fact that the Supreme Court is reviewing some cases of ordered desegregation and in overturning them they have taken race out of the equation without replacing it with ethnicity. In so doing, it makes the assumption that everything—jobs, income, and education are all equal, so neighborhood schools should be re-established regardless of the harm it might cause to some ethnic group students. In effect, the court has said that the problem of separate and unequal schooling is solved, so go back to segregating yourselves. This problem is causing enough attention that many national civil rights groups are becoming directly involved.

And here we thought we were making progress.

America's Public Education a Far Cry from Integration

September 30, 2012

When the Supreme Court ruled that separate public schools were not equal, the law was changed to desegregate the schools. While that order seemed to be the appropriate approach to take at the time, what has not changed over time and has been a stumbling block to progress in American public education, is the attitude of European American normalcy. In essence, while ethnic minorities have been given permission to attend school with the European American students, the subject matter as well as the control of the perceptions has been that of European Americans as the model of normalcy.

When the schools were segregated, prior to 1954, the African American students attended school where they were the norm. No doubt existed relative to their self-worth and abilities to achieve an education. Once desegregation came into existence, subjects like African American history were discontinued. Since the majority of the new teachers had no background or knowledge of African Americans from an historical perspective, they could not share that information with the students. So, although African American and European American students attended the same school, they did not receive the same educational experience. If the African American students attended a predominantly European American school, the feeling of self-worth, security, familiarity, and normalcy disappeared. For the European American students, nothing changed but the introduction of unfamiliar students in their school.

Today we live under the misconception that our schools are integrated. America's schools have never been integrated! Let us be clear about these terms. Desegregation of the schools meant simply that African American students were allowed to attend the predominantly European American schools; that is all that happened. Nothing in the European American schools' curricula, attitude and perception of African Americans changed. If the African American students were to experience success, they must adapt to the environments of the schools; no special accommodations were made for them.

Integration is a term that carries the same meaning in science or social environments; it means the process of mixing or combining. If we take a look at our public schools today, we cannot miss the mixing of students in many schools, while we can also notice the lack of mixing of student in others. Unless we are mistaken about the court ruling, the purpose of the ruling was to eliminate the separate and unequal education the students were receiving. Although the impact of the ruling fell on the African American students as victims, the European Americans were victims as well because they had been deprived of information concerning their fellow Americans.

One easy way to check to see if American education reflects integration is to examine the text books being used in the public schools. If they present an accurate and factual picture of ethnic Americans as participants in the making of this nation, then we can answer affirmative to integration. If not, then we cannot claim to have integrated public schools and admit that much work needs to be done, namely, rewriting the American story to include the contributions of ethnic minorities. To date, the history of America as told in the text books is the history of European Americans. In addition to the story that is being told, not all Americans have a say in what is presented to the students. In effect, a form of censorship is practiced that affects and influences the students and teachers alike.

In an article by Gail Collins, "How Texas Inflicts Bad Textbooks on Us," published in "The New York Review of Books" (6/21/12), we learn that "No matter where you live, if your children go to public schools, the textbooks they use were very possibly written under Texas influence." What that means is a few people in Texas have used their power to control the content of many textbooks. We are told that people in Texas are not the only ones to have a say about the content of textbooks, but the influence exerted by Texas comes from its size and system for electing State Board members:

"The difference is due to size—4.8 million textbook-reading schoolchildren as of 2011—and the peculiarities of its system of government, in which the State Board of Education is selected in elections that are practically devoid of voters, and wealthy donors can chip in unlimited amounts of money to help their favorites win."

In her article, Collins details just how Texas and other states, like California, can influence the content of books simply by the volume of sales. The influence of the group in Texas comes from 'the right,' and much of their concern with the textbooks comes from their religious beliefs. For example, the article noted,

"In 2009, the nation watched in awe as the state board worked on approving a new science curriculum under the leadership of a chair who believed that "evolution is hooey." In 2010 teachers were supposed to "work in consultation with 'experts' added on by the board, one of whom believed that the income tax was contrary to the word of God in the scriptures."

To the earlier point that America's public schools are not integrated the article noted the following:

In 2011, the Thomas B. Fordham Institute, a conservative education think tank, issued an evaluation of US history standards for public schools. The institute was a longtime critic of curricula that insisted that representatives of women and minorities be included in all parts of American history. But the authors, Sheldon Stern and Jeremy Stern, really hated what the Texas board had done. Besides incorporating "all the familiar politically correct group categories," the authors said.

The document distorts or suppresses less triumphal or more nuanced aspects of our past that the Board found politically unacceptable—slavery and segregation are all but ignored, while religious influences are grossly exaggerated. The resulting fusion is a confusing, unteachable hodgepodge.

The article provides much more information then could be included in this blog. However, when we stop and take a good long look at education, we realize that much of the perception and attitude relative to what and who is important to our students is still controlled by a small number of narrow-minded people who do not understand or accept democracy.

Desegregation was to be the first major step after segregation on the road to democracy. Today we also realize that we still must face the challenges of ethnic bias, low social and economic status, preschools, curricula and a host of related areas. After taking a realistic assessment of our situation, we find that we have only just begun to see the challenge in education for our society.

American Education Perpetuates Discrimination

August 7, 2010

From the first day children enroll for school, they are placed on the track to discrimination. On the application for enrollment under race/ethnicity when the child's parent or guardian writes "white" or "Caucasian" the element of race enters their world. For too many years America has turned a blind eye to the problems created by the use of racial terms that should have been jettisoned years ago. But today, since these words are still in use, they continue to create problems relative to ethnicity and diversity. Most ethnic Americans can explain the term they have selected to identify their ethnicity and culture—hence, Asian American, African American, Hispanic American, American Indian, etc. However, the terms "black," "white" and "Caucasian" do not lend themselves an easy explanation for children and adults as well.

What do European American parents or guardians tell their young children when they are asked about their ethnicity? If they answer, "you are white," the children have no base of reference from which to make an association other than their skin complexion. If skin complexion is used as the qualifier, then would all people with fair skin complexions be considered white? Are all white people Americans? Do they all speak English? What if one parent is white and the other is another ethnicity?

The same situation falls also on the African American parents or guardians who tell their children that they are black. What makes them different from other people with the exception of their skin complexion, if that can be considered? Not all people who are dark complexioned are Americans. If the children are not given a clear and accurate explanation of who they are, they will answer to whatever they are called.

What we discover in trying to use skin complexion as the qualifier for a so-called white race or black race is confusion and bias. Historically, the word "white" has been used to identify people, European, European Americans, as belonging to a specific biological racial group; the same thing can be said for the words "black "and "Caucasian." The problem with using those terms is that they fail to identify ethnicity or culture as do the other above-mentioned ethnic examples. Also, when an explanation is offered for the use of these terms, the elements of bigotry, discrimination, and prejudice must come into play, thus creating barriers between the children of the black, white, Caucasian groups, and all the others.

America's educational systems, on all levels, have made little or no attempt to address this issue of ethnicity/race. As a matter of fact, they treat both terms as though they are the same thing; they are not. When we teach our children that all people are the same and then turn around and refer to some as belonging to a white/Caucasian race or a black, brown, or red race, and other ethnic Americans as belonging to other races, we become hypocrites. If we are all the same, then we belong to the same race, the human race.

But that is not what American teaches. Let us be clear on this matter of race and ethnicity.

In the early 1940s some international scientists came together under the auspices of UNESCO and came to the agreement that the term race was no longer correct or acceptable when making reference to other human beings, *Homo sapiens*. The word race and its derivatives no longer met the condition for which they were being used. Ashley Montague, the American representative to the group, wrote in 1945, in his book titled "Race, Science, and Humanity," that we use the words "ethnic group" instead of "race." His reason for the change is:

> "'Ethnic group' represents a different way of looking at populations, an open, non-question-begging way, and a tentative, noncommittal, experimental way, based on the new understanding which the sciences of zoology, genetics, and anthropology have made possible."

Montague makes clear that "ethnic group" is not a substitute for "race;" it is a totally different word with a new conception. He adds that

"It is important to be quite clear upon this point, for the new conception embraced in the phrase 'ethnic group' renders the possibilities of the development of 'ethnic group prejudice' quite impossible, for as soon as the nature of this conception is understood it cancels the possibility of any such development."

The point made in using "ethnic group" is that it is not subject to discrimination because all human beings are included. Race no longer becomes a factor, because all humans belong to one race, but not necessarily the same "ethnic group." When the term "ethnicity" or "ethnic group" is used, the word race is irrelevant and its use discontinued. Races of people do not exist on planet Earth—one race of human being exists. Now, how does this information affect American education?

The state of education in America today is on track to create more ethnic bias, prejudice, and discrimination among its youth. Instead of preparing them to deal with the present and the future, we are shackling them with the biases of the past. American education is stuck in the past and continues to prevent our students from making progress toward a new sense of self and community. American education promotes divisiveness, prejudice, and bias from first enrollment, through the material presented, to the ill-equipped teachers and instructors.

When children are brought to school for enrollment, their parent or guardian must fill out an enrollment form. The problems began with the section of this form that pertains to "race" and "ethnicity." For some reason, most American public schools are still operating in the distant past with respect to those forms. The schools do not know the difference between race and ethnicity. This lack of information becomes apparent simply by looking at the form and seeing words, race and ethnicity, used incorrectly. Although this might seem like a minor problem, let us take a closer look at several of these enrollment forms for a better grasp of the problem.

Three local public school districts have sections of their enrollment forms that show a total misunderstanding of the terms "race" and "ethnicity." Oklahoma City and Edmond, Oklahoma Public school forms are similar; they both ask under the rubric of "Ethnicity" to indicate the selection of Hispanic, Non-Hispanic, or Latino. This feature would be acceptable and correct if not for the fact that all the other "ethnic groups" are listed under the rubric of "Race." To make matters worse, for European Americans the only choice is "white." The other selections are not specific because if a check is made in a box, the reader does not know which answer applies. For example, one box offers "American Indian/Alaskan Native." If that box is selected, which term identifies the student?

The third enrollment form is from a small school district, Millwood Public Schools. This form asks two questions. The first, about Hispanics and Latinos and provides two choices for a response of yes or no. No rubric regarding ethnic group is used. The second question asks the question: What race is your child? Five options are listed for response to this question.

In every instance relative to these enrollment forms, the students and their teachers are placed in a position to view the students as belonging to a specific race, not ethnic group with the exception of the Hispanics. Why? Our schools should know better; indeed, America's entire educational system should know that the very term "race" unites and separates. Corrections should be made immediately if the problems associated with so-called racial biases and discrimination are to be addressed. More comments on this topic next time.

American Education Promotes Discrimination II

August 14, 2010

The selection of the three school districts, Oklahoma City, Edmond, and Millwood, was not to single them out for criticism, but to show how uninformed the American educational system is in general in dealing with so-called racial discrimination. Each school district made the same mistake in requesting ethnic group identification from its students.

We know that once an identity is checked on the enrollment form, the children will carry that label with them throughout their public educational experience and possibly their entire lives.

The teacher is the first person to read the enrollment form with expectations for the children. The identity will be used to manage the children in the school environment. Some children will be placed in certain groups based solely on their ethnic identity. What most teachers do not realize is that prior to starting school, children have formed a value based on color from their everyday experiences. More specifically, they have already established values of white bias from society, home, and media. When their enrollment form is checked black or white, that label serves as an official stamp that determines their place in society. They already know that a fair skin equals a positive value, and a dark skin equals a negative value.

An example of the negative value of a dark skin or reference to black occurs when all criminals or suspects are identified by the media by their ethnicity or color, with the exception of whites (European Americans). Most reports assume that if no color or ethnic identity is reported, then the person is white. In essence, European American children hear fewer references to their color in a negative context, while African American children usually hear a reference to black in a negative context. All children are subjected to and influenced by the sounds and images presented by the media, and they learn to discriminate from many of those experiences.

In school, their stereotypes of so-called races are presented if even in a subtle way. For example, when children read picture books that involve children of ethnicity and diversity, the children are usually identified by their color and often by name. The European American children need no special reference because they are viewed as normal. Whether the teachers realize it or not, the fact is that the mere experience of being singled out reinforces for the children the stereotype of white value versus black value. The children are usually too young to know how to register a protest or realize what is happening to them and their self-image.

Educators, instead of debunking the false conception of race simply ignore it. So when the students began to study social science, history, literature, and other subjects where references are made to color, the students are allowed no opportunity to confront the myth of race because the teachers and the learning materials perpetuate it.

For example, when students learn of the United States Constitution are they taught the significance of Section I that identifies slaves as three-fifths a person? Most Americans today are so indoctrinated with the idea of slaves being black that they think every reference to slaves is of blacks, even in the Bible. So how are the students taught to understand and appreciate who they are if they are never fully educated? Their educational experiences reinforce the concept of race rather than the concept of ethnic group.

Often, multicultural and diversity materials simply serve to underscore the so-called racial differences instead of bridging the gap across the divide of race and ethnicity. So, as our children progress up the educational latter, their education continues to make clear the separation of black and white along with their symbolic values. Educators and educational institutions spend much time identifying the cultural differences rather than focusing on the similarities all students have in common. Certainly, cultural differences are interesting and valued by the students who possess them, but students need to learn that cultural and ethnic differences are not biological differences—they need to not identify a race.

What seems to be the case regarding the problem of race today is a general acceptance of the status quo. The attitude of "why rock the boat" prevents society from making positive progress in understanding who we are and why we are in the situation we are in regarding race and ethnicity. Because we are seemingly comfortable with the status quo, our children are growing up believing many of the same myths about race and ethnicity that their parents and grandparents grew up with; that is a tragedy.

Why is it that educators, entertainers, the media, and leaders in general continue to use the language that restricts society from breaking away from prejudice, bias, and discrimination? Why do they not understand that using the words race, black, and white keeps society tied to a past that prevents social and humane growth?

Many people do not like to talk about race because when they do, they realize how little they know and how much they depend on their environment and community to inform them. Unfortunately, too often the environment and community are at a loss to benefit its people with a new and accurate perception and conception of humanity.

The labels children get stuck with early in life can and do have a definite influence on their development. The role that their educational experiences play in that development is too important to leave to chance. We need to help our educational institutions and educators step up to the plate and get it right.

Great Expectations, Giving Credit Where It Is Due

June 10, 2012

An article appearing in the "Point of view" section of the *Oklahoman* (6/6/12) entitled "Innovations produce more effective teachers," was written by Roger Webb, president emeritus of University of Central Oklahoma, and focused on the many contributions of the late Charlie Hollar. The article celebrated both Hollar and the program he sponsored, "Great Expectations," which continues still today. All the accolades and honors given to Hollar are well deserved and should be appreciated by the people of Oklahoma. Lost in the article were a number of important pieces of information that need to be inserted.

The article stated that "Charlie Hollar believed schools could never be better than the teachers who taught our children. He said 'Teachers should be celebrated, encouraged and given the access to the quality of professional education that was available to business executives.'" We were told, "He worked with many of the top state and national education leaders and developed Great Expectations."

The article continued by noting that "Since its inception in 1999, more than 40,000 teachers have been trained under the program." Actually, the program was started in 1990 and although the program for Oklahoma was under Hollar's guidance, the genesis of the program was created and implemented first by Marva Collins as early as 1975. The article leaves the impression that the program from start to finish was created and developed by Hollar. No criticism is intended of the program Hollar developed for Oklahoma educators. We just believe that if one develops a program about gravity, Sir Isaac Newton's name should be mentioned.

Marva Collins, an African American educator, taught in the Chicago Public Schools for some fourteen years after which we are told in an article about her that "Displeased with both the public and private schools in Chicago, Collins took five thousand dollars out of her pension to start the Westside Preparatory School in 1975

on the second floor of her home." The program was so successful
that she received national attention from schools named Harvard,
Yale, and Stanford. In 1982 "60 Minutes" did a show honoring her;
that show was followed by a movie entitled "The Marva Collins
Story." (www.BlackPast.org)

In an effort to make the point of Collin's influences and
contributions we looked at the comments of one elementary school
teacher from a school in Oklahoma, Debbie Vaughan, who stated,
"[I] have practiced Great Expectations for fifteen years in my
classroom and had the honor of meeting Marva Collins and visiting
her school in Chicago."

Another statement in the article seemed to cast aspersions at
educators when it stated that "It is interesting that a non-educator
could have a greater impact on Oklahoma's schools over a twenty-
year period than any elected or appointed educational official." The
fact of the matter is that Hollar, a non-educator, had to work with
equally dedicated educators just to get his program implemented.
In addition, the efforts of someone not working in the educational
system would more than likely experience greater success than
someone trying to work within the system because the structure
inside the system sometimes makes changes difficult—if not
impossible. People outside the educational system, like Charlie
Hollar, are not limited as to how to raise funds for programs
whereas educators are restricted by a plethora of rules and
restrictions.

If we remember correctly, Collins was displeased with both the
public and private schools in Chicago for not meeting the needs
of the children. As an educator, she knew what would work and
what would not work: however, working within the system could
never get her to where she needed to be. So, she went outside of the
school system to accomplish her goal.

Our comments are not intended as criticism of the Great
Expectations program or Charlie Hollar. Oklahoma educators and
children are blessed to have such an opportunity offered by this
program. The efforts of Hollar should continue to be commended
and appreciated as the article recorded. Our concern was with

some of the information in the article that needed addressing regarding the genesis of the program and giving credit where credit is due.

An often used saying informs us that knowledge is knowing that a tomato is a fruit; wisdom is not putting it in a fruit salad.

Naomi Schaefer Riley's Comments Show a Need for African American Studies

January 1, 2013

Back in April 30, 2012, a former writer for The *Chronicle of Higher Education*, Naomi Schaefer Riley, wrote a blog article entitled "The Most Persuasive Case for Eliminating Black Studies? Just Read the Dissertation." The blog caused considerable debate because of statements to the effect that Black Studies no longer served any useful purpose and should be discontinued as an academic discipline. Shortly after the blog's publication a controversy ensued and Ms. Riley was fired.

Anyone with a working knowledge of American History would have detected a number of defects in Riley's comments as well as an attitude akin to arrogant ignorance. The article displayed a lack of knowledge and understanding of American History, African American History, and an attitude of biased superiority.

Most educated people today realize that the only difference between American History and African American History is the point of view; both are American History. The fact that the discipline is known as "Black Studies" places a stigma on it as not being of equal value as other traditional subjects. The stigma comes from the negative value and the lack of information relative to the experiences of African Americans presented through education as well as because of some people's conception of the "Black American 'experience'" which most history books and classes overlook.

Riley's comments relative to the choice of topics of the graduate students for their dissertations showed her lack of knowledge of general American History when she labels all three "so irrelevant no one will ever look at them." When we looked at the subjects, we got a different reaction.

The first dissertation subject Riley commented on was one by Ruth Hayes: "'So I Could Be Easeful:' Black Women's Authoritative Knowledge on Childbirth." Hayes' study looked into the history of African American midwifery because she found that "nonwhite women's experiences were largely absent from natural-birth literature." According to Riley, "How could we overlook the nonwhite experience in 'natural birth literature,' whatever the heck that is? It's scandalous and clearly a sign that racism is alive and well in America, not to mention academia." Obviously, Riley has no idea or concept of what life was like on the slave plantations nor the role African/African American women played in midwifery to both the females in the master's household as well as the female slaves.

Although Riley might not want to learn about some of those experiences, her ignorance indicates a lack of knowledge of its importance historically. Even after slavery, many African American women continued to serve as midwives to both the European American and African American community. My grandmother was such a person, and the one who helped facilitate my entry into this world.

The next dissertation topic Riley selected to denigrate was one written by Keeanga-Yamahtta Taylor entitled: "Race for Profit: Black Housing and the Urban Crisis of the 1970s." Riley shows her complete ignorance of contemporary American History with her comment relative to Taylor's study: "Ms. Taylor believes there was apparently some kind of conspiracy in the federal government's promotion of single family homes in black neighborhoods after the unrest of the 1960s. Single family homes! The audacity!" Unfortunately, Riley adds insult to her ignorance when she states: "But Ms. Taylor sees that her issue is still relevant today. (Not much of a surprise since the entirety of black studies today seems to rest on the premise that nothing much has changed in this country in the past half century when it comes to race..."

Her ignorance is compounded when she states, "...Shhhh. Don't tell them about the black president!)" Riley shows complete ignorance of government sponsored segregation and discrimination in public housing. This blog discussed this very same topic in two recent publications, one dealing with "Good Times," and the other with "All in the Family." Evidently, Riley's education has not served her very well.

The third dissertation Riley selected to discredit was written by La Tasha B. Levy and dealt with the topic of "Black Republicanism, especially the rightward ideological shift it took in the 1980s after the election of Ronald Reagan." Riley adds, "Ms. Levy's dissertation argues that conservatives like Thomas Sowell, Clarence Thomas, John McWhorter, and others have 'played one of the most-significant roles in the assault on the civil-rights legacy that benefited them.'"

What Riley fails to grasp in this work is the fact that these men mentioned are African Americans who, having benefited from the opportunities afforded them through civil rights advances, now want to undo those advantages for others. In essence, the benefits were fine for them, but not for other African Americans.

This topic was also treated recently in this blog and underscored the fact that most African American Republicans today belong to that party for personal attention and gain, not for what the party offers the African American community. The fact that many African Americans belong to the Democratic Party is owing to what the party has to offer them in comparison to what the Republican party offers.

So far, Riley has struck out in her assessment of these dissertations as well as her knowledge of American History. Her comments and assessments are proof enough that courses in African American Studies should be required for all students. Her comments and evaluations of these works show a gross lack of information relative to the African American experience in American History as well as a general lack of knowledge that the influence both had on the other. How she managed to write for as long as she did being so ill-equipped is amazing.

What was the final insult to injury in Riley's blog was the bigoted, better-than-thou attitude of European American superiority she exhibited throughout the piece. In all her splendid ignorance, she felt secure and comfortable in denigrating the work and scholarship of graduate students and simultaneously saying to their institution and mentoring professors that they were all illegitimate scholars. She alone had the intelligence to pass judgment on what should be considered quality academic work based, it seems, on the color of her skin. Rather than dismissing these works as "a collection of left-wing victimization claptrap," Riley should have consulted with someone more knowledgeable in the subject-matter. In fact, that is what most people do when they do not know what they are doing.

Fair Housing Laws Alone Cannot End Bigotry

January 22, 2012

Prior to 1866 African Americans, as well as other Americans, could not live where they wanted to or could afford to live for a variety of reasons. However, after the Civil War, Congress passed a series of laws to implement the 13th Amendment which had the objective of banning slavery and eliminating its vestiges. One law in particular, the Civil Rights Act of 1866, "banned discrimination in the sale, transfer, lease or use of property, real estate and housing. All citizens were granted the same rights enjoyed by white citizens in the use, purchase, lease; transfer, etc., of real estate and property" (National Association of Realtors).

The key phrase in this law is the reference to all citizens having the same rights as white citizens. In essence, the law recognized the preferences and powers given so-called white people. While the law looked good on the books, there was a problem—no provision was given to enforce the law. So, the law for all intent and purpose was ignored.

Fast-forward one hundred and two years later, where we learn that "On April 11, 1968 U.S. President Lyndon B. Johnson signed the Civil Rights Act of 1968, also known as the Indian Civil Rights Act of 1968. Title VIII of the Civil Rights Act of 1968 is commonly known as the Fair Housing Act." One of the reasons for this act was to supply the enforcement provisions that were lacking in the 1866 act. We know that:

> "The 1968 act expanded on previous acts and prohibited discrimination concerning the sale, rental, and financing of housing based on race, religion, national origin, and since 1974, gender; since 1988, the act protects people with disabilities and families with children."

Other provisions of the act protect civil rights workers as well.

So, one might ask, why the history references to Fair Housing? Well, evidently, some people still believe these laws were not meant for them. Since they identify themselves as white citizens, they should be able to ignore the laws and discriminate at will.

Fortunately, better informed citizens became involved in a particular incident to help resolve the problem in part. The story involves "A Cincinnati landlord who claimed a black girl's hair product clouded an apartment complex's swimming pool." She "discriminated against the child by posting a poolside 'White Only' sign." We learned that the Ohio Civil Rights Commission voted 4-0 in favor of the child, recognizing that she had experienced discrimination.

According the article in the *Associated Press* (1/13/12), "The parents filed a discrimination charge with the commission and moved out of the duplex in the racially diverse city to 'avoid subjecting their family to further humiliating treatment.'" The landowner's reason for posting the sign was: "I was trying to protect my assets." When we take a moment to examine her comments we discover that she was being very clear about her actions and motive.

In her mind, African Americans do not belong in the same swimming pool as European Americans. The reference to some chemical in the child's hair causing the water to be cloudy is too weak an argument to support logic. The child would have had to have an enormous head and an equal amount of chemicals to make the water in an entire swimming pool cloudy. We see that argument as silly. Her motive, on the other hand, tells us that she believes that her ability to earn a living because African Americans in the complex swimming pool might negatively affect her business. Which raises the question of why did she rent to them in the first place if she thought they would be bad for business. Maybe she thought they would not use the pool. In any event, she felt she had the right to post a "White Only" sign on the pool gate to resolve her problem.

She was wrong.

While the landowner was misguided in her attempt to allow admission of African Americans in the swimming pool, she truly believed that she was in her rights. Most likely many other European Americans would support her today given the tenor of the times. When a society tells someone that he or she is special and privileged because of his or her skin color—white—and then pass laws underscoring those ideas, chances are the person will believe what they have heard and been told.

What happened when the Fair Housing laws were passed regarding citizen rights and privileges, they were identified as those privileges and rights already enjoyed by the so-called white citizens. In effect, the laws never said that the original laws were incorrect, only everyone would now be able to enjoy "the same rights as the white citizens."

Many European Americans have never been confronted with the idea that they were misled into believing that their skin color was only a ploy used by the elite to control them, and have them serve as a buffer to deflect legitimate criticism regarding political, economic, and social power the elite controlled. Even today, all a politician has to do to gain support from a certain segment of society is to complain that some so-called unworthy people (read as African Americans, minority and poor) are receiving benefits for free that real Americans (European Americans—whites) must work to receive. This statement will be interpreted as a call to join the speaker in protecting the loss privileges and rights by those who still hold on to that idea of specialness based of color.

Enacting laws that seek to change past injustices does not mean the attitudes and beliefs of the people negatively affected will change for the better. For the most part, they probably feel victimized; when in reality they have enjoyed exclusive rights and privileges for many years.

Flocabulary, a Fad or Effective Teaching Tool

October 3, 2010

Recently a number of teachers in the Oklahoma City school district voiced some concern about a new program introduced into the school system. The program is called Flocabulary and uses rap, its main ingredient, as a teaching tool. The program is used primarily for at-risk students in grades 3-12. The program is designed using hip hop and rap music as a way to help students learn facts.

As with any new program, disagreements will exist questioning the program's merit and this one is no different. Some teachers find some aspects of the program positive, some find parts negative. After viewing the promotion video and listening to some of the sample raps of the program, more questions are created than answered concerning the program's merits. These questions involve the teacher, the student, and the parent.

For the teacher, any program introduced into the classroom will naturally address three specific areas—time, creativity, and control. Depending on the subject-matter and the students, the teacher must budget the time to try and complete the objective established for that period. If the program that is being used consumes a large segment of time that conflicts with the period, then both the students and the teacher are deprived. The teacher must decide if the investment in the program is worth the value the students receive. Since time is the most valuable element at the teacher's disposal, it must be used to the students' best advantage.

The next concern for the teacher deals specifically with teaching and creativity. If students could acquire the necessary skills without a teacher, then there would be no need for one. However, we all know that teaching is an art and each teacher has his/her own special way of approaching their students and objectives. A knowledge of each student's strengths and weaknesses always factors into the teacher's teaching technique.

The teacher must decide for the students' benefit if a program meets the needs of all the students or just some of the students.

Programs alone cannot challenge students; only teachers who are aware of their students' capabilities can accomplish that undertaking. The very nature of most programs is objective and not student specific. The teacher must decide if using a program diminishes his/her ability to utilize the skills and talents needed to address the students' needs. Programs like Flocabulary might serve as a form of entertainment for some students after the object material has been presented by the teacher, but not as a substitute.

The third question the teacher must deal with involves control of the students, the material, and the atmosphere. For most, if not all, of the students today, the Hip Hop name and sound reflect a form of entertainment. If a teacher introduces such a program into the learning environment, he/she must know that the students' behavior will be affected immediately. If the teacher is to control the students' behavior during this time, he/she must prepare the students in advance. In addition, the teacher must be conversant with the material to be presented in order to ensure that the object is being met in the manner expected—that is, the students understand that the Hip Hop program is a teaching/learning tool and not simply a form of entertainment. If the teacher fails to control either of these elements, losing control of the environment is a certainty.

Before teachers choose to participate in a program such as Flocabulary, they must ask and answer the questions concerning the program's ability to stimulate, motivate, and continue the students' learning. How will the program stimulate the students to learn or address the objective? If the program's objective is to simply challenge the students to recall information instead of incorporating the information into a development form, then the students are being underserved. In addition to the program offering material that stimulates the students, it must also serve to motivate the students to accept more challenges. If the program fails to motivate the students to go further, then it does not meet its objective.

For the program to have merit, the teachers must recognize the effective qualities of the program and how and if they benefit the students. If the students are not left with a desire to continue their investigation, search, or inquiry relative to the program's objective after the program has concluded, then the program served only as entertainment for the student.

One of the teachers dissatisfied with the Hip Hop Flocabulary program stated that she believed the teachers, students, and public have been cheated in the use of the program. While we cannot speak to the specifics of her concern relative to the program, we can acknowledge that the parents as well as the public should be aware of the program's objectives, the expectations for the students, and a sense of the outcome of the program's use relative to the students who participated in it. The students should not be used as guinea pigs relative to the program.

For example, does the program seek to promote correct grammar and word choice? Does the tone of the speakers engender respect and appreciation for the material? Will the students be prepared to transition from the program to a traditional teaching format and atmosphere? What is used to determine the success of the program; is the emphasis on the success of the students or on the success of the program? Does the program benefit all students exposed to it or is it designed as a tool for some special students?

The chairperson of the Oklahoma City School Board as well as the Superintendent both registered concerns relative to the program and promised to become better informed before allowing its continuance in the classroom. If a mind is truly a terrible thing to waste, then this word to the informed is sufficient.

Race and Baseball in America

December 30, 2009

About ten years or so ago, I wrote an article describing my concern for what I saw was a lack of African Americans playing baseball. Their absence could be discerned from Little League to the professional ranks. My article was based on personal experience, observation, and experience. I conducted a survey via sending questionnaires to both NCAA Division I and Division II Baseball programs. The results of that survey, I included in the article. The references to players and their respective experiences were witnessed by this writer. Comments from coaches were the result of interviews. Other information, namely statistics relative to employment were obtained directly from NCAA publications and its office. Additional information relative to African Americans players recognized in high school baseball was acquired directly from the newspapers from the cities referenced in the article.

Finally, having coached Little League Baseball for a number of years in the 1990s, I had a prime opportunity to observe and experience many of the areas of concern addressed in the article. The point of the article was to register concern for the lack of African American males playing baseball and some of the reasons, in my opinion, why that situation existed. My hope was that a positive change would occur eliminating the problem.

Unfortunately, that change did not happen as witnessed by the reactions of C.C. Sabathia when reporting to training camp in Florida in 2007. The *Associated Press* characterized the reaction in the headlines: "Sabathia pitches for more African-Americans in game." What Sabathia wanted to know was "There aren't very many African-American players, and it's not just in here, it's everywhere. It's not just a problem — it's a crisis."

This article was not meant to be a research project where care was taken to show documentation for every word of number, although that information can be provided on request. The article was simply written to point out a problem that apparently exists not only in my opinion.

Baseball, America's game— or is it?

Baseball, as American as apple pie and hot dogs; the American past time; the game all Americans love; the game that represents what America is all about. So go the clichés. While we Americans like to think that those clichés are true, the real fact of the matter is that they are only clichés. Baseball, for all the good things it offers, also has a negative side. The negative side reveals the sad fact that many young ethnic American males are being selectively excluded from the game of baseball. This exclusion experience is very subtle and almost undetectable if one happens not to be ethnic American.

Many majority individuals might suggest that the claim of exclusion is just another in a series of complaints lodged against the majority society by disgruntling citizens with chips on their shoulders. Although that suggestion might not enjoy credibility in some instances, when one examines the statistics relative to this concern, some credence must be given to the claim of exclusion.

This writer invites a closer look into the claim of ethnic American male exclusion from baseball by examining the process of exclusion. The process begins in Little League and continues through college. How this exclusion can be possible when we see kids all over America playing baseball, one might ask. The answer is that we do not question, generally, what we see. We usually focus on the game, and not on the players. Our concern for individual players comes much later.

Most Little League teams today are formed in the suburbs. European Americans represent the majority population in the suburbs. The teams, in essence, are representative of the community. In Little League baseball, the teams are usually coached by volunteer parents from the community. The teams usually consist of the coach's son, the son's friends, and his schoolmates. Team positions are generally given to the coach's son and his friends first. Children of the coach's friends are also given a priority for positions on the team. If more team members are needed, they are usually acquired from the league pool of players not assigned to a team. Hence, if an ethnic American kid is not a friend of the coach's son, he will get on a team from the pool of players unassigned. A player joining a team from the pool does so with the understanding that he is not a core player; he is just a member of the team. The coach decides the player's value to the team later.

The number of ethnic American boys living in the suburbs today is limited, but growing. While this writer could focus on ethnic Americans kids in general, we can more clearly make to point of exclusion by focusing on African American boys in baseball.

Generally, an African American boy will not hold a starting position on a team unless a number of factors exist: his father is one of the coaches, his father is a good friend of one of the coaches, he is a friend of the coach's son, or the boy is an exceptional athlete—sometimes, even if the boy is an exceptional athlete, he might not start. If none of those conditions exist, the chances of the African American boy starting are little to none.

Why, one might ask, does this condition exist? Again, the answer starts with the coach and his decision to play his son and the friends of his son first. The African American player usually comes from a player pool, so if all the positions are not taken, he gets a chance to play. All the boys get a fair chance to practice, but getting to play in a game is another story. Other possible answers are many and varied, but the results are unmistakable: African American boys do not get the experience of playing ball, therefore, their development as players is affected. If they are not allowed to develop, they will not be able to compete.

A few examples might serve to underscore the essence of some African American boys' Little League experience. One 9-year-old player, Jack Roberts, the only African American on his team, never started a game for his team. As a matter of fact, he played, at most, one ending out of every three or four games. When he played, it was always in right field. A big irony with Jack was that often other teams would play weekend tournaments and invite Jack to play. Jack usually found himself serving as leadoff batter, second baseman or shortstop, and if needed, pitcher. However, on Monday with his old team, he would find himself back on the pine.

Why did he not simply join the tournament team, one might ask? Because these teams did not want him as a regular member, only for tournaments.

Another example shows the lengths to which a coach-father will abuse and exploit his power over a team. Coach Rusty Green took over the coaching task from another father. This team was composed of the same boys who had been together for around three years. When Coach Green took over the team, he made it known through his actions that the most important player on the team was his son. He constantly demonstrated this by having his son play every minute of every game. Unfortunately, his son was not physically developed enough to deliver the baseball from the pitcher's mound to home plate. That fact, however, did not affect Coach Green's decision to play his son every minute of every game in spite of the fact that a number of other players sat on the bench and got little, if any, playing time. Two of those boys were actually very good players, but also happened to be African American.

Once, Coach Green and a couple of team families went on a three-week vacation. The team was left in the hands of two team fathers. During this three-week period, the team improved from a losing record, to a winning one. One reason for this turn-around was that more boys were given an opportunity to play because of the absence of Coach Green's son and several other players; their absence had a positive impact on the team.

When Coach Green and the others returned, however, he reorganized the team again around his son, and a renewed losing record became a consequence of that effort. The African American players who had been enjoying some quality playing time in Coach Green's absence were forced to sit on the bench once again. If anyone questioned the coach's decision, he would simply dismiss them because he was the coach and could not be overruled.

Another example involved a 10-year-old African American, Alvin Byrd, who was known for his foot speed, and who was on a team where he was well-liked. He quit the team after playing only one season because he rarely got a chance to play a position of bat. He was used almost exclusively as a base runner. He realized that his lack of playing time was negatively affecting his overall development. He also realized that nobody cared except himself and his family. Because of his early disappointment, he gave up on baseball and turned his attention to track and football.

Generally, African American players, and European American players held in not so high esteem, are usually not assigned positions. They are generally sent to the outfield. The other players on the team are assigned skilled positions and practice those positions, some include positions in the outfield, where the other players get to watch the "chosen ones" practice. Therefore, if an African American player, and the European American players with him show any improvement, it goes unnoticed.

From the experiences encountered by African American players, one finds little difficulty in recognizing how it is that some African American players do not get playing time from their Little League experience. One also recognizes how it is that some of these boys miss development opportunities in baseball. As a matter of fact, very few African American boys have enjoyed the opportunity to play in Little League all-star games. Some, but not many.

Once the African American player leaves Little League and makes the big move to junior high school, he does so with a feeling of hope. He hopes at this level that the coaches will judge him on his ability, hustle, enthusiasm and hard work. Little time passes before he realizes that the coaches are not really interested in him, because the same boys who played skilled positions in Little League are usually the same boys that will play them in Jr. High. Undaunted, however, he perseveres, hoping that he will impress the coaches. Little does he know that they will not be impressed by him. Their minds are usually made up about him. If he stays on the team, he will receive some playing time, scant though it may be, because the coaches in most public schools try to avoid the look of impropriety.

John Jeffers, the only African American player on his junior high team, played second base during fall practice. The coach had him practice and play that position on a daily basis. However, after football and basketball seasons were over, and other players came out for baseball, John was immediately moved to the outfield. When John questioned the coach about playing second base like he had practiced, he was told that he was no longer needed at that position, although he was better than the player who replaced him. John often inquired of the coach about getting to play at any position. He was told something to pacify him or that the team always needed good pitchers. Armed with this information, John began to work on pitching both on his own and during practice. Even after showing the coach how well he controlled the ball with his slider, fastball, and change-up, he still got little playing time. Sometimes the coach would tell him before a game that he was going to play, only for him to discover at game time he was to warm the pine. Still, John persevered.

What happened to John was no different from what happens to many young players—African American and European American. However, what happens to European players and what happens to African American players happens for different reasons. If one were to assess the skill and talent level of the players, one would notice a difference in comparison.

In essence, stereotypes began to influence choice of African American players who play and those who do not play. One stereotype looks at an African American player's power, size, and speed. If all three qualities come in one package, the coach feels great because he can justify his use of this player. If the coach only selects African American players who possess these qualities, the process in known as 'stacking.'

The other stereotype looks at African American players who do not possess the three above-mentioned qualities in excess as not wanted or needed. Therefore, if an African American player does not excel in two or more of the three areas, he will not play in junior high except as a token payment for hinging around. If the parents of the African American player attempt to talk to the coach, whatever excuse the coach bothers to offer must suffice because the school's principal, and usually the superintendent, give the coach full freedom to do as he wishes relative to his team.

If the African American player continues his objective of playing into the high school level, he must confront new and different challenges. One challenge comes in the form of summer leagues. In some areas of the country these leagues are sponsored by the American Legion. The leagues are actually booster clubs made up of the parents and friends of the players on the team. The teams are usually the same players as the high school team with a few exceptions (some players whose schools do not have a legion team are usually assigned to schools with legion teams in their school district). But, generally, the teams are composed of the high school players from the school team in the district. The coach of the legion team is usually the school coach or assistant coach. Most of the players are familiar to the coach. Therefore, if the African American player did not get much playing time while on the school team, not much will change in legion ball, except he gets to pay for the privilege.

Since the focus of this article is on the suburbs, one might rightfully ask about African American boys playing baseball in the city/inner city. Many civic-minded organizations and individuals contribute their time, money, as well as services to provide a forum whereby African American boys might enjoy playing baseball during the summer months. The predominantly African American public and private schools excluded, the baseball played in the city/inner city is generally for recreational and entertainment purposes only. An African American player wanting to play at the high school or college level would generally want to play competitively. The competitive baseball programs for the African American city/inner city players are very few and far between.

For example, Joe Carter, a now retired African American professional baseball player, attended a predominantly African American high school, Millwood, in Oklahoma. His school did not have a summer baseball program, therefore, Joe had to play with a neighboring suburb school's American Legion team for the summer—if he was to play at all. Although he was a distinct minority on the team, Joe played; he possessed all the qualities of speed, size, strength, and power. He was also a multi sports letterman.

Two factors are represented relative to Joe: his having to seek competitive baseball outside his home school, and the fact that he was an exceptional athlete. Had he been simply an above average to average player, one wonders if he would have gotten a chance to play. Regardless of the programs provided for playing baseball, one fact still stands out above all others, the statistics. The number of African American males playing baseball reflect only a token participation at all levels of competitive baseball.

Two more challenges to the African American player are time and money. In summer baseball the parent or parents must make a commitment that obligates them to financially support the team, as well as provide transportation for their child to each and every game, regardless of the game's location. If the parent cannot be responsible for these concerns, the player should not seek to play on the team.

While American Legion teams are focused on developing the school's players, in reality the only players to really develop are the ones the coach has selected for special attention. Of course, not all the players on the team want to play. Some are just happy to get a uniform; some just want to hang out with some team members. Generally, these players are satisfied keeping stats or running after foul balls. These casual players, and the unfortunate African American, do get some playing time, but not enough to make a difference in their game. If an African American player or his parent were to complain to the coach about playing time, the coach has a ready reference to the casual European American players who also do not get sufficient playing time.

In essence, because the team has to have a certain number of players to exist, the casual players basically subsidize the team with their membership.

If the African American players receive outside help—outside the team, like attending camps or working with knowledgeable individuals—in his development, his improvement makes little or no difference to the coach. Usually, the more progress the African American player makes, the less likely he is to play. What becomes obvious to the players at this time and at this level is the coach's decision to work with and play certain players, and not others.

Many African American parents experience instances of
anger and/or frustration when they are approached by European
American parents of team members and hear the comment that "it
is a shame the way the African American kid is being ignored by
the coach." When the European American parents are asked, "Why
not share that sentiment with the coach?" the response is usually
something to the effect that: "If I say something, he might stop
playing my son." If the African American parents had doubts about
the feelings of neglect experienced by their son not playing, those
doubts disappear when European American parents validate their
suspicions. The African American players, at this time, have been
denied the opportunity to develop into quality baseball players
because of their coach's decision not to work with or play them.

If an African American player survives to his senior year, he
might begin that year with enthusiasm and hope, but these will
soon disappear when he realizes he will not play enough to create a
single statistic.

For example, Robert Graham was a very good pitcher. He
had demonstrated his talent and skills the previous year on the
junior varsity where he had pitched against many of the rival high
schools. However, once a senior and a member of the varsity,
he found himself constantly being bumped by the coach for
underclassmen he brought up to varsity. On those few occasions
when he did get into a game to pitch, he was not allowed to bat
like the other pitchers got to do. A number of times he entered
a game for an inning, to play right field. If his spot came to bat
during this time, he was not allowed to bat. Once he confronted the
coach about not having a chance to bat; the coach told him that he
was not an effective hitter. Robert reminded the coach that he was
one for three at the plate in the three times he had gotten to bat;
however, he reminded the coach that one of his starters was zero
for twenty-two. The coach simply walked away from Robert.

Bill Williams, another African American player, was a pitcher
as well as a short stop. When Bill complained to the coach about
not being allowed to practice at or play short stop, he was told that
his pitching was all the team needed, if that. The coach let Bill
know in no uncertain terms that he was not valued as a member

of the team. Bill realized that his chances of getting some quality playing time—when statistics are kept—were gone.

Not all the coaches on every team will fit the profile of the coaches mentioned to this point. Many coaches are fair-minded, and treat the players equitably, but they are far outnumbered by the others. Also, not all African American players are excluded from playing ball, but too many are left out.

The majority of African American players who are recruited for and play in college, usually come from rural America, not the big city or suburb. Our statistics show that in ten of the largest cities in America, the number of African American players to make All-City large school teams is 2.0 percent. One reason for such a low number is due to the lack of African American players and the lack of playing time afforded them on their varsity high school teams. If a player accumulates no statistics, he has nothing to recommend him to a prospective college coach or scout. The college coaches rely on statistical information in assessing a prospective player's value to his team. No stats, no play.

A retired European American high school football coach, Lonnie Gee, who taught at a predominantly European American school recounted an experience when he counseled a young African American football player not to go out for the baseball team. The coach advised the young athlete to go out for track instead. When questioned about his motives for recommending track over baseball to the player, the coach said that he did not want to see the kid waste his time sitting on a bench. Participating in sports at the college level was more a possibility for this student if he ran track and played football than if he wasted his time trying to get a chance to play baseball. The coach evidently knew something the athlete did not. The recommendation was a gesture of kindness rather than a lack of confidence in the athlete's ability to play baseball.

In gathering information for this article, this writer solicited information from a variety of sources. One of those sources was local newspapers in large metropolitan areas. More specifically, the sport directors at these newspapers who were asked to provide the number of African American players on their All State Baseball teams for the years 1996-1997 and 1997-1998. Two of the papers to respond were the *Oklahoman*, from Oklahoma City, and the *Dallas Morning News*. The *Oklahoman* listed two (2) African American players for both years; the *Dallas Morning News* listed one (1) and (2) respectively. Both cities represent areas of considerable African American population and concern for baseball; nevertheless, each average two African American players or less per team. Those African American players might get a chance to play at the college level.

The only avenue of approach left to an African American player without statistics but with hopes of playing college ball is the "walk-on" or "try-out." On some rare occasions, a walk-on will make the team, usually, an African American player will not be considered because the coach will have selected the African American player or players for his team prior to a "try-out." The general attitude of many coaches toward African American "walk-on" is something like "If I don't come after you, don't come after me, because I don't want you." Also, "walk-on," if they make the team, generally will not play ahead of a recruited player.

Arguments could be made to the effect that many European American players face the same or similar experiences as African American players, and those arguments would be valid to a certain extent. However, when we look at the statistics on a variety of levels, we notice one remarkable difference: European American players dominate baseball rosters in college on two NCAA division levels. The average number of African American players on the top ten Division I teams in the nation is approximately one-point-three (1.3).

Sources show that for NCAA Division II's top ten teams, the average is very difficult to ascertain because the number of African American players reported to the NCAA from 1996 enrollment information is vastly different from the information this writer received directly from the schools.

For example, in 1996, Central Missouri State reported to the NCAA that it had eight (8) African American student-athletes receiving aid for baseball. However, the information this writer received from the school for1997 was zero (0). For the year 1998, the number was one (1). This example is not an isolated one; it is representative of all the teams. The average percentage number of African American players on Division II teams based on the 1997 and 1998 information this writer received from the schools and NCAA is less than zero-point nine (0.9).

One of the myths in fashion today is that young African American athletes do not go into baseball because they are lured away by the possibility of making big salaries in football and basketball at a younger age and in a shorter amount of time. Actually, young African American baseball players are not afforded an opportunity to play and develop in the sport at an early age, so they go where the opportunities are present.

The old adage that an African American athlete has to be twice as good as his European American competitor comes close to being valid in baseball. The apparent assumption of some former players—in some instances, European American as well as African American—is that a coach will play an average European American player over a very good African American one. The coach's philosophy regarding this action is to give the European American player an opportunity to develop skills the African American player already possess. However, if the African American player is average and the European American player is good, then the coach will play the European player for the good of the team. Therefore, one will hardly, if ever, find an average African American baseball player playing at the college or professional level.

Common sense dictates that in order to address a problem or concern, that problem or concern must be identified and recognized. Regarding the exclusion of African American males in baseball, this writer has found few baseball coaches at the high school and college level willing to admit that a situation exists. They also reject the act of "stacking" mentioned earlier. Each coach speaks to his unique perspective on selecting players. That perspective, according to the coaches, does not include a player's color or ethnicity.

However, if a predominantly European American team has
an African American player, the coaches seem to need to qualify
his presence by identifying the player's particular talents or skills
via the stereotype of strength, power, and speed. Nevertheless,
the numbers indicate only a token representation of African
American baseball players on teams from high school to college to
the professionals.

When one realizes the cumulative effects of excluding young
African American males from playing baseball, the magnitude of
the problem becomes evident. In a recent two-year study conducted
by the NCAA, race demographics of NCAA member institution
athletics personnel, April 10, 1998, we find a wealth of information
that underscores our concern. For example, for the year 1995-1996,
in Division I baseball, the total number of schools—historically
African American institutions excluded—reporting to the NCAA
was 249. Out of that number, 243 team coaches were European
American. No African Americans were listed as coach, however,
six (6) were listed as assistant coaches, but the six was from a
number of 451 schools reporting. In year 1997-1998, some progress
was made in that one (1) African American coach was hired. The
number of assistant coaches, however, decreased to four (4).

Similar numbers are recorded for the two remaining divisions.
All the numbers reflect the sad state of affairs for African
Americans wanting to get into baseball. If something is not done to
stop the perpetuation of exclusion, the problem exacerbates. If we
do nothing, we become part of the problem.

What we see is not always what we get, especially when it
comes to America's game of baseball. The African American
players we know and generally like at the professional level are
outstanding players. They represent the exception rather than the
rule.

Today many potential African American baseball players
will never have a chance to realize their potential for lack of an
opportunity to play, an opportunity that usually begins in Little
League. Please understand that the focus of this article concerns
African American males, not males who happen to be of color

from different cultural and ethnicities. That is altogether another story.

At some point our society will realize that the inclusion/ exclusion games played with the lives of our young people by so-called responsible people, are very dangerous and damaging. The biases manifested through subtle but definite means to influence the participation of ethnic American males in sports will be exposed. This writer hopes that once the biases are recognized, reasonable people will work towards eliminating them not only for the individuals involved, but also for the betterment of society. After all, if baseball is America's game, it should reflect America's people.

Observance of MLK, Jr's Day Misunderstood

January 17, 2011

Mention civil rights to most Americans and they will tell you the first image that pops into their minds is either Martin Luther King, Jr. or African Americans. Why? Because they have been programmed to believe that American civil rights are the concerns of only African Americans. Too many Americans do not know the significance of the civil rights movement and the tribute made to them by honoring Martin Luther King, Jr. with a national day. For many Americans, Martin Luther King, Jr.'s day is just another day off. That attitude needs to change.

Many Americans associate American civil rights with Martin Luther King, Jr. and rightly so, because it was King who was the spokesman for the cause. What many people do not realize is that King did not wake up one morning and decide to become a civil rights leader. After the arrest of Rosa Parks in Montgomery, Alabama in 1955, and the introduction of the young Martin Luther King, Jr., the pastor of Dexter Avenue Baptist church where organizational meetings were held, a number of leaders from a variety of civil rights organizations met and decided that instead of each organization making public speeches and demands, they should unite and combine their efforts and speak with one voice.

The voice they chose to represent their concerns was the young African American preacher named Martin Luther King, Jr. Since and after Montgomery, until his death, King was the public civil rights leader, not the only civil rights leader. The civil rights organizations with leaders such as Roy Wilkins, James Farmer, and Whitney Young were all part of this movement and they were not all African Americans, a myth that some Americans viewed as true until a number of European American civil rights workers were murdered in the line of duty.

The gains made in America through civil rights acts were gains not for African Americans alone, but for all Americans. Certainly, African Americans were in the forefront of the battle because they were the primary victims of civil rights abuse. However, if some Americans care to remember, prior to the 1964 Civil Rights Acts certain jobs and professions were generally reserved for males and they were usually European Americans: postman, fireman, and policeman. Many professions were simply male-dominated like doctors, lawyers, dentists, judges, politicians, and others. Because of King and the other civil rights leaders' efforts, those jobs and professions now include among their ranks a variety of Americans. The titles have been changed to reflect a more inclusive identity: postal worker, firefighter, police officer.

What happens today in America relative to Martin Luther King, Jr. Day is unfortunate in that the emphasis of most celebrations focus on King and generally his "I Have a Dream" speech. Americans need to be educated to the fact that King's speech and his life was not the end of civil rights concerns, but a means to a call for justice and fairness for all Americans. The March on Washington in 1963 was a protest march to apply pressure and make demands on America to live up to its creed to honor each person's right to life, liberty, and the pursuit of happiness. The subsequent passage of the 1964, 1965, and 1968 Civil Rights Acts is proof to the positive efforts of King and others.

Without their efforts, America would not have experienced the social changes that have taken place because of these Acts. This information is somehow lost during the celebration and because it is lost, many Americans, especially European Americans pay little or no attention to the day let alone join in the celebration. What must be emphasized is the continuing influence these Civil Rights Acts have on society today.

Most American women, especially European American women since they represent the majority, should be at the forefront of any celebration honoring Martin Luther King, Jr. and the civil rights movement because they are the biggest beneficiaries of it. We are not just talking about jobs in the work force, but the opening of doors in schools, medical, law, and a host of other opportunities. Dare we mention where women athletes would be today without Title IX of the 1964 Civil Rights Act?

The many opportunities and advantages enjoyed by American females are due in large to the work of King and the organizations he represented. America should take note of this and build on it instead on focusing on King's "I Have a Dream" speech, as if that was the only contribution he made worthy of honor.

The fact that many schools across the nation chose to give their students a day off while making King's day an in-service day shows either a lack of respect and appreciation for the work that King and others have done, or ignorance and bias for not using this day as an opportunity to educate themselves and their students. Americans should be given the opportunity to understand and appreciate the fact that although Martin Luther King, Jr. was the spokesperson for the movement, the movement did not die with him nor did the efforts of other concerned Americans. America was changed for the better because of King and the civil rights movement, so let us celebrate those changes while we pay homage to King's memory and continue the work he helped to champion.

We Americans should come together as a country and recognize that we owe a debt of gratitude to many who came before us and, through their efforts, helped to make our lives better. We need to know what they did, why, and how they did it, because if we remain ignorant of their sacrifices for us, we will indeed have nothing to celebrate.

Knowing the name Martin Luther King, Jr. is as important as knowing what he stood for and what he represented, but just knowing his name is not enough.

Our Changing Society Demands a New Sense of Value for Each of Us

September 23, 2013

We read or hear on almost a daily basis, accounts of the shooting death of a young African American. We have experienced this sort of news so frequently that it almost seems routine. Of course, we know that the deaths of young people are never routine. The public, in general, seems to accept the news as something of little importance. Why?

Maybe the reason for a seemingly lack of interest by the public is based on learning and past experiences. What seems to be the case relative to the shooting and deaths of young African Americans is a public that does not see value in African American lives; this lack of value for African American lives is part of the legacy of American history beginning with Reconstruction after the Civil War.

Once the Civil War was over, the former slave masters and people in the slave business were no longer concerned with the value of former slaves; they were now free. The 13th Amendment to the Constitution stated: "Neither slavery nor involuntary servitude, except as a punishment for crime whereof the party shall have been duly convicted, shall exist within the United States, nor any place subject to their jurisdiction." So, once freed, the African American did not carry the same value to society that the slave carried.

Under the laws of the states, especially in the South, the concern and focus was not on the value of the African Americans, but on the avenues of approach needed to recapture their labor as cheaply as possible. In essence, laws were created to exploit the newly freed African Americans for whatever purpose the European American society felt necessary.

The laws created by many of the Southern states to control the African Americans came to be known as "The Black Codes." These laws tried to recapture the powers of the slave masters that were lost as a result of the Civil War. The first set of these laws came from the state of Mississippi. History tells us:

"The first such law was enacted on November 22, 1865. It directed civil officers to hire orphaned African Americans and forbade the orphans to leave their place of employment for any reason. Orphans were typically compensated with a free place to live, free meals, and some type of nominal wage."

In addition, we learn that "other white employers were prohibited from offering any enticement to blacks "employed" by someone else."

Mississippi passed other laws that restricted the movement of African Americans; some laws even required them to carry papers to provide information of their employment. The objective was to recreate the master-slave relationship, but with the protection of the state laws. History shows that "within a few months after Mississippi passed its first such law, Alabama, Georgia, Louisiana, Florida, Tennessee, Virginia, and North Carolina followed suit by enacting similar laws of their own." The Congress recognized what these Southern states were doing and passed the Civil Rights Act of 1866. This Act did little to change the attitude of the European Americans and the social value of the African Americans until the first half of the 20th Century.

In America, the laws passed by the Federal government did not change the mindset of many Americans concerning the value of the African American. As late as 1970, Peter Loewenberg, in an article, "The Psychology of Racism," made the comment that "In the unconscious of the bigot the black represents his own repressed instincts which he fears and hates and which are forbidden by his conscience as it struggles to conform to the values professed by society." Loewenberg continued by stating, "This is why the black man becomes the personification of sexuality' lewdness, laziness, dirtiness, and unbridled hostility. He is the symbol of voluptuousness and the immediate gratification of pleasure." Loewenberg referred to the experience encountered by biased European Americans as a form of projection. He added, "These feelings are easily associated with low status or tabooed groups such as negroes. Blacks are pictured in the unconscious imagery of the white majority as dark and odorous, aggressive, libidinal, and threatening."

Many of the changes that have occurred in American society toward valuing all human beings since 1964 have been on the shoulders of the African Americans. One of the major changes by African Americans to see themselves differently from how European Americans viewed them was to change the connotation of black from negative to positive. The cultural references of the late '60s and '70s reinforced the positive value of being a black in America with phrases like "Black and Proud, or "Black and Beautiful," as well as a host of others. Nevertheless, the changes that affected the African American population did not place any stress or feelings of commitment of change with the European American community.

We have a tendency to forget that the public schools were desegregated, not integrated. So, the curriculum did not change to include the many positive contributions of African Americans in building our great society. The history taught was the same as before Brown v. Topeka, the only difference was African Americans were allowed in the classrooms. The norm for the European Americans did not change simply because the laws did.

If nothing happens to change the way Americans look at each other, then the same old negative stereotype that has been associated with ethnic Americans will still be in place. Education has done little to change the way European Americans view African Americans as well as other ethic Americans. That has to change if we are ever to value one another.

When Barack Obama became President of the United States, many Americans seemed to have lost their sense of respect for the office of the president because it was occupied by an African American. The negative attitude of not valuing non-European ethnic Americans continues today because we as a society have not worked hard enough to eliminate the ignorance associated with race, ethnicity, and diversity. Through ignorance and bigotry, many Americans have failed to recognize the truth of who we are as human beings and to value each other.

Laws cannot change attitudes, but people working together can effect change. Chances are that when we start viewing each person as a valued member of society, we will start treating them differently. Whether we like it or not, America is changing into a more ethnically diverse society, and the sooner we realize that we cannot go back to the 1800s, and accept the reality of our diversity, the sooner the madness of hatred and bigotry can start to decrease.

We, as a society cannot afford the luxury of sitting back waiting for others to make the first move toward creating a better society where young Africans Americans are not shot every day; it's time we act.

Christian Church that Rejects Mixed-Ethnic Couple Not Racist, Just Ignorant and Biased

December 4, 2011

Many people upon hearing about the church in Louisville, Kentucky rejecting a couple of mixed ethnicity, probably thought the appropriate term suited to describe the church's behavior is racist. They would be incorrect because all the people concerned are human beings—the same race. For those not familiar with the story, the *Associated Press* reported, "A tiny all-white Appalachian church in rural Kentucky has voted to ban interracial couples from joining its flock, pitting members against each other in an argument over race." The article continued by pointing out, "Members at the Gulnare Free Will Baptist Church voted Sunday on the resolution, which says the church 'does not condone interracial marriage.'"

The problem started when Stella Harville, a European American (white) female brought her African fiancé, Ticha Chikuni, to church with her. We are told that on one visit, Chikuni sang a song for the congregation. The church board member who offered the resolution, Melvin Thompson, made the statement: "I am not a racist. I will tell you that. I am not prejudiced against any race of people, have never in my lifetime spoke evil about a race." In his mind and heart, Thompson believes he has done nothing wrong or un-Christian. How can that be?

First, we need to make clear a number of points. First, Ticha Chikuni is an African, not a black. Although the article did not mention his cultural identity, we know that he is not African American. Chances are he would be the first to correct anyone making that mistake. Next, we are dealing with people who take their religion seriously. Finally, we are dealing with some people who are still living in the 1800s relative to their beliefs and behavior.

Because of the confusion and the false information regarding the concept of race, many people still identify some people's ethnicity on the bases of their skin color. Make no mistake, that concept of regarding race by color has been in existence since slavery, and as noted in the article, it still exists today.

The church is regarded by most observers as the most segregated institution in America. One reason for that segregation can be traced back to some clergy who were warriors for segregation, discrimination, and bigotry. They used the Bible and their biased interpretations, along with some creativity, to underscore their point. One clergy in point was Josiah Strong (1846-1916) who believed, preached, and wrote about how "God, nature, science, and history all legitimated white supremacy over black people."

Many other prominent clergy, scientists, and doctors promoted the concept of the so-called black race being created differently from the so-called white race. The arguments were presented so well and so often that most European Americans did not question the legitimacy of the information, and like their religion itself, they internalized the concept of race as truth. Although religion is based on belief and race is available for scientific investigation, when the concept of race is presented as if it were a religion, argument is fruitless.

Thompson can state that he is not a racist because he does not see any problem with rejecting someone not of his so-called race. His biblical teachings and the word from many clergy would free him from any sense of wrong-doing. The fact that he has been taught that being white made one superior over nonwhites, underscores his ability and right to refuse to worship with any non-white person. Rather than his religious beliefs keeping pace with the changing times, socially and historically, Thompson and those who supported him possibly feel comfortable and protected in their religious beliefs even when it goes against the general precepts of Christianity. Part of the problem with being identified as a racist is the fact that race has not been defined clearly other than in scientific terms. Rather than clarifying the confusion of race, society continues to add to it.

The media referred to the couple in its articles as being "interracial" or "mixed-race." Neither term is accurate or correct in trying to identify the couple. When the couple is identified by color, that description is incorrect because Chikuni is African, not black; that he is not black, unless one conceives of all people with dark complexions as blacks or of a black race. If Harville is identified as white, then one must assume that white is a race as well as African; that is the only way the couple can accommodate the descriptions.

What the media has to understand is that a racist cannot exist in isolation. When a person is called a racist, he or she has to be viewed as a representative of a larger group known as a race. If mankind consists of only one race, then no other races exist for comparisons. The problem still involves ignorance and bigotry. If the people who are aware of the fallacy of the race conception continue to address people who are ignorant and/or bigots as racist, they are, in effect, supporting and promoting the fallacy.

When a bigot is called a racist, the mere word underscores his beliefs in so-called racial supremacy, and offers security and protection within his so-called racial group. However, when one is referred to as a bigot, then the full impact of the charge falls squarely on the individual, not a group. A bigot would prefer to be called a racist because that gives aid and comfort to his beliefs. What reasonable and knowledgeable people must understand is that they are part of the problem if they do not recognize and correct the fallacies of race, racist, and racism.

Many Americans are discovering since the election of President Obama that the social progress thought to have been made since the 1960s in some cases is just an illusion. Who would have thought that today in America a so-called Christian church would refuse to accept children of their God simply because one child does not look like the rest of the people?

That makes one wonder what heaven will look like.

Colorblindness in a Biased Society is Impossible

October 16, 2011

On any number of occasions, we have heard someone say something to the effect that when they look at someone they do not see color. In other words, they consider themselves colorblind when looking at other people. Actually what they are saying is not that they are colorblind, but that they do not regard color as essential to that person's social value or that they are not biased relative to a person's color. While that might sound OK, the fact of the matter is that being colorblind in a society that bases ethnic identity on color is impossible.

When we look around society we recognize the part that bias plays in our lives. We see that so-called black Americans with college and university educations are unemployed two times that of so-called white Americans. In addition, while so-called blacks represent a small percentage of the population, around 12-13 percent, their representation in prisons is disproportionate to that of so-called whites. The statistics are not much better if we look at the biases of Latinos in comparison with so-called whites. The point being made is that color is a primary element of ethnic bias in American society today.

Some people have tried to use the election of Barack Obama as President of the United States as proof that color bias is no longer a determining factor in valuing all Americans. Sally Lehrman, in an article (2003) "Colorblind Racism," states: "While many Americans agree that open racial bigotry is generally a thing of the past, stark disparities in daily life persist, as documented by academic researchers, the U.S. Census Bureau, and the Institute of Medicine." More specifically, Lehrman notes that "when blacks and Latinos are hospitalized with a heart problem, they are less likely than European Americans (whites) to receive catheterization, be sent home with beta blockers, or even be advised to take aspirin to protect their health."

When a society continues to use color as part of an ethnic identity, escaping the consequences of ethnic bias is impossible. The problem does not rest with color, it rests with the concept of race. The fact that during slavery in America, color was viewed as something of extreme value, especially if one was considered white, and it still has meaning in today's society. People are still being recognized by their ethnic identity and the amount or degree of so-called whiteness they have. Since color that characterizes ethnic identity is not a constant entity, the question arises of how amounts and degrees of color are measured in people.

Fortunately, we have an answer to that question. The answer comes from the Human Genome Project that reported that race has no biological foundation as a way to categorize human beings. In other words, a person's color is insignificant when it comes to being identified as a human being.

America has known for many years that color is not a factor with respect to a person's intelligence, physical and mental well-being. However, because of the social value placed on color historically, many people find it impossible to accept the fact that all human beings belong to the same family. When some people who do accept that fact try to express it by saying they are colorblind, they misunderstand the reason for the bias being present. The problem is not with the person of color; it is with the person who tries to disregard color. Unless a person identifies him or herself without a reference to color, in other words, African American and European American, color still remains are part of their perception. As long as the government allows people to identify themselves as blacks and whites, the social and historical significance of color will remain a part of the bigotry in society.

When one hears someone saying they try to be colorblind, the statement rather than being interpreted as a compliment on their good character of the person of color, actually reflects on a sense of superiority of the speaker. This superiority is based on the judgment rendered in ranting the people of color some social value. In other words, if they do not consider color a detriment in society, then the person of color is acceptable to them despite his or her color. Anyone making the statement does not understand the problem; they are, in fact, blind to it.

The problem is and will continue to be the false concept of race and the association of color with ethnic identity. Prior to the '70s, the color white had significance in society relative to privilege and special treatment. Today in our culture of greed, the only color of primary value is green—the color of money.

The fact that the color white is being eroded strikes fear in the minds of people who rely on that color as a source of their importance and social value. When color as part of ethnic identity no longer has significance in society, so-called racial bigotry will be forced to find another home.

Having colorblindness was supposed to signal a sensitive and compassionate feeling towards those of color by someone whose color was seen as superior. The irony of colorblindness comes from the fact that if the essence of color is not a factor in judging another, why would there need to be a reference to color and blindness at all? If the person making the reference to colorblindness places no value on color, then the statement actually shows ignorance, arrogance, and bias because a person's color is a factor in his or her physical identity and, as such, should be respected and valued—not ignored.

Accepting people as human beings with no reservations to their physical appearance is the objective; after all, we're all human.

Cheerios Commercial a Positive Sign of Growth in America Accepting Its Ethnic Diversity

June 9, 2013

All the negative comments concerning the ethnic Americans in the Cheerios commercial are signs of growing pains in American society. The pains come from both African Americans and European Americans having to deal with the ignorance, segregation, and bigotry that have been part of the social atmosphere since slavery. The commercial is doing double duty by forcing society to see what is happening in the real world while challenging those ignorant, isolated, and bigoted people to reevaluate their perspectives.

Many Americans today still believe in the concept of multiple biological races with the so-called white race being special and different from all the so-called other races. That being the case, any examples of race mixing involving a European American (white) with any other ethnic American diminishes the strength of the white race.

Therefore, all races mixing involving so-called whites are frowned upon. Because of the social value placed on the European American by European Americans, for one to be intimately involved with an ethnic American is a sign of low self-esteem and self-worth. Although most Americans know that to hold and express those beliefs is an indication of ignorance relative to America's social environment today and a far cry from reality.

For some people, the so-called white identity is the only thing of value they have, so to have that threatened is of major concern. For some people, losing their white identity would be devastating because they have no idea of who they are without that identity. They choose not to accept the truth and progress of America's diverse society, and like children not wanting to hear something they already know, stick their fingers in their ears thinking that if they do not hear what is being said, it will not exist. Such is ignorance.

Segregation and separation of ethnic Americans present opportunities to create stereotypes that living in an integrated or even desegregated society could easily debunk. After World War II ended and the troops came home, the government found that housing was a problem, so it created help for the veterans through the GI Bill and FHA. While these programs were great for the country, they provided little help for the African Americans. The new housing additions that were created were segregated. The housing additions led to the creation of segregated communities that included churches, school, and public facilities.

For example, in Oklahoma City before 1954, African Americans could visit the public zoo only on Thursdays; state parks were off limits for African Americans also. So, without direct interaction with other ethnic Americans, European Americans were free to create any stereotype they desired. To be sure, African Americans living in a segregated society and communities also held stereotype of European Americans.

The belief that European Americans were superior to other ethnic groups was part of the educational package taught to all students while the negative stereotypes were constantly underscored in the newspapers, movies, radio, and television. The idea of the African American knowing "his place" had to do with the African American knowing that the European American had more social value than he and that he must respect that superiority regardless of the social and economic status of the European American and that of the African American. For some Americans that concept of European American superiority still exists and should remain forever.

So, when a commercial presents a mixed ethnic American couple and their child, some people who live segregated lives, fear the change because of what they believe they will lose as a group.

One of the primary reactions to the Cheerios commercial can be identified as ethnic bigotry. A large segment of the European American population born and raised in America, entered this world that was filled with ethnic bias against African Americans. All the social institutions promoted the concept of American being a European American country that permitted other ethnic Americans to live here. But make no mistake about it; they believe that America belonged to only them. The concept of democracy, equality, fairness, and freedom for all is fine as far as lip service goes, but when it comes to actual change in the direction of diversity, the game changes. When they see or witness things that go contrary to their beliefs, they become upset and angry.

What the commercial has done is bring a touch of reality and changes in society to the forefront. The fact that American's diverse population is growing and gaining more power is reflected in the commercial.

Another thing that was not so obvious, but well supported, was the fact that the old European American standard of beauty is under attack. Most reasonable viewers would consider all the actors to be attractive, handsome, or good-looking. In essence, if the European American female finds the African American male handsome, then the concept of European American standard of beauty is being ignored. That fact alone is enough for bigots to feel threatened and fearful. At one point in American society, the color of one's skin determined if beauty could even be considered let alone recognized and appreciated. Now, along comes this commercial that throws a monkey wrench into the entire concept of so-called race and separation.

Whether it was intentional or not, the Cheerios commercial brought to public scrutiny a major problem many Americans must face—a changing society and world. The problem is not the fact that people from different ethnic groups form relationships, because diversity has always been a part of the American experience. The problem is that the diverse relationships had always been kept in check through segregation and out of the public eye. When an example of a diverse ethnic couple came to public view, it was always viewed as extraordinary, unusual.

For years legal segregation and biases created boundaries that made miscegenation unacceptable to society. After the Supreme Court ruled in 1954 that public facilities must be opened to all Americans, other laws soon followed that made it possible for different ethnic groups to interact with one another in public. That interaction today is a common occurrence and generally accepted as normal behavior.

So, for those folks who found the Cheerios commercial negative and uncomfortable, they need to realize that their idea of America needs to catch up with reality. Society changes whether we want it to or not. If we choose not to accept the reality of change, we will be left angry and frustrated wondering what is the world coming to. Recognizing the changes does not mean our readily accepting them, but it does mean that they exist and have been validated by at least a significant segment of society.

So, here's to Cheerios– eat up! They're good for your heart!

Being Poor Signals a Lack of Power with the Police for Ethnic Minorities

September 2, 2012

Is there any doubt about why most ethnic American communities, especially the African American, American Indian, and the Hispanic, have problems accepting the police as being "servants of the people" when the majority of the experiences involving the police in these communities are negative? Unless the readers are ethnic American, chances are their experiences with the police are quite different from those who are. One only has to watch the local and national news to learn about how many ethnic Americans are treated by the police departments in given situations. They, generally, get no respect. Two recent examples of disrespect to African American families come to mind– Trayvon Martin and Robin Leander Howard.

Most people know the story of Trayvon Martin being shot and killed within sight of his family members' residence. His family was not notified for several days that their loved one had died from a gunshot wound. When his family inquired of Trayvon's location, they were not given any answers. When Trayvon's father went to the police and requested a missing person's complaint, he was not told about his son's death. The police listed Trayvon as "John Doe," since, according to them, he did not have any identification on him.

The fact of the matter is that the family of Trayvon was not given any detailed information until they obtained the services of an attorney. Even then, the information requested by the family attorney was not readily forthcoming.

The situation was somewhat different with respect to the victim in the case of Robin Leander Howard. According to the newspaper report (the *Oklahoman* 8/15/12), "Officers said Howard led them on a chase that ended in the 1400 block of Monticello Court, about 150 yards from the small home he shared with his mother. What happened after police caught up with Howard is a mystery" Reports indicate that medical assistance was first called to the location, but later refused.

The article did not indicate who refused the medical attention. However, we are told that the police took Howard to a hospital where he later died. His family was able to retrieve the mother's vehicle from the impound lot, but when inquiries concerning Howard's location were made the family received no helpful information. Finally, after four days, the family was notified by the police that Howard was dead and that he had died in the hospital.

Still unable to obtain detailed information concerning Howard's death from the police department, the family hired an attorney to assist them. A few days later, the city's police chief made a public apology to the family for not notifying them of their loved one's death in a timely manner. However, the family still did not receive any information relative to why and how Howard died. The family decided to seek the assistance of national organizations to help in this matter so maybe they can receive the information they want.

The object of this topic is not to cast aspersions towards the police and/or the police departments in general, but to focus on how the families of ethnic minorities, especially African Americans are treated by many law enforcement agencies. To say that they are treated with disrespect would be an understatement; they simply are not valued. Why?

Part of the answer lies in the attitude of the establishment regarding minority ethnic groups that is expressed in the number of incarcerations. Two researchers, Richard Wilkinson and Kate Pickett (The Spirit Level), state that "Racial and ethnic disparities in rate of imprisonment are one way of showing the inequalities in risk of being imprisoned. In America, the racial gap can be measured as the ration between imprisonment rates for whites and blacks."

Wilkinson and Pickett further noted that "Twenty-five percent of white youths in America have committed one violent offense by age seventeen, compared to 36 percent of African Americans, ethnic rates of property are the same, and African American youth commit fewer drug crimes." However, we are told that "…African-American youth are overwhelmingly more likely to be arrested, to be detained, to be charged, to be charged as if an adult, and to be imprisoned."

In addition, these researchers indicated, "The same pattern is true for African American and Hispanic adults, who are treated more harshly than whites at every stage of judicial proceedings." Also, we learn:

> "Facing the same charges, white defendants are far more likely to have the charges against them reduced, or to be offered 'diversion'—a deferment or suspension of prosecution if the offender agrees to certain conditions, such as completing a drug rehabilitation program."

While the information pertaining to the treatment of African Americans and other minorities is important, it does not give a reason for it happening, the cause. The reasons are spelled out, however, in the following statement by Wilkinson and Pickett:

> "People nearer the bottom of society almost always face downward discrimination and prejudice. There are of course important differences between what is seen as class prejudice in society without ethnic divisions, and as racial prejudice where there are. Although the cultural marks of class are derived inherently from status differentiation, they are less indelible than differences in skin color. But when differences in ethnicity, religion or language come to be seen as markers of low social status and attract various downward prejudices, social division and discrimination may increase."

If we translate the language of the researchers, we find that the reasons for the lack of respect shown to the African Americans relative to the various police departments is due to their perception of African Americans having little or no economic, political, or social power—poor people equal no power. The attitudes of both the police and the ethnic communities are generally based on the experiences encountered by each segment. Approximately 90 percent of the police encounters in the minority communities are negative. The communities, then, assume that the only values police officers associate with them are negative. So, the assessments go both ways.

If the practice is to stop, work has to be done by the local police departments in improving their images and relationship with the ethnic communities and the communities must help to create better positive relations with the law enforcement agencies. The best way to ensure continued negative results and poor relations between both sides is for each side to ignore the problems.

African Americans and Law Enforcement Agencies' Relationship

August 26, 2014

The relationship of the African American community and law enforcement agencies has never been good, and at times, simply tolerable. Some people say this lack of a positive relationship between these two groups has to do with the majority society's ignorance, stupidity, and bigotry. In essence, the law enforcement agencies reflect the mindset of the majority society—European Americans. In some instances, the actions of the law enforcement agencies seem to manifest a fear and anger towards the African Americans. Why? What would be a reason for European Americans via the law enforcement agencies to hate African Americans?

Historically, European Americans have been conditioned by society to see themselves as superior to all people of color. They generally do not view themselves as a race, but as the model of the human race. The reason for this view is based on the efforts of society to create the concept of the European American as "normal."

For example, when a European American woman walks into a department store and asks for stockings that are "nude" in color, she is given stockings that match her complexion. Maybe she wants facial make-up, so she goes to the cosmetic counter and asks for a "natural" shade, she receives make-up that matches her skin complexion. What these two examples suggest is that the skin complexion of the European American is the model of normal, natural, and nude skin. Where does that leave the rest of society— the people of color?

When people believe that they and the people who look like them are normal, then the people who do not look like them will appear abnormal or less-than-normal. What society knows, but chooses to ignore, is the fact that 80 percent of the world's population is people of color; that means that only 20 percent of the world's population is of fair complexion. Using those facts and common sense, the people of fair complexions would seem to be the less-than-normal at 20 percent. However, if those with fair complexions in the minority can convince the majority people of color to view themselves as less-than-normal, then they have an advantage.

The advantage grows when positive social and personal attributes are associated with the fair-skinned people while negative and degrading qualities are associated with people of color. Add to this concept the idea that every gain that people of color make towards being "normal" is viewed as a deduction from the fair-skinned people's sense of superiority and power. This idea of having something taken away from them creates fear, anger, and even hatred of the people making the advances.

So, the African Americans represent the enemy. This picture is a reflection of what has taken place in America over the last four hundred plus years. The irony of it all is that the reference to a superior and inferior group of people based on skin complexion is pure conjecture—illusion; only one race of people exists on the planet and it comes in a variety of shades.

The fact that the concept of race is a myth has not been communicated to many of the European American communities or if it has, they choose to ignore it. Unfortunately, what cannot be ignored are the changes taking place in society—changes like those stated by Ronald R. Sundstrom, in The Browning of America and the Evasion of Social Justice (SUNY Press, 2008).

The United States is undergoing the most profound demographic changes in the country's history so that in a few decades, if not sooner, persons identified—and identifying themselves—as white and tracing their ancestry to Europe will have become part of the nation's racial and ethnic plurality, no longer its numerically dominant racial group. This historic development portends others equally historic and transformative, among these the gradual— possibly even dramatic — displacement of white people as the dominating group politically, economically, socially, and even culturally.

These changes are not what the majority European Americans expected or anticipated relative to their tenure in America, so the changes must be discarded whenever and wherever possible. In effect, President Obama cannot be accepted as the president because that takes away the superiority from the biased European Americans.

The ignorance and bigotry against the African American is reflected in the treatment of the African American community by the law enforcement agencies. Because of the social conditioning of the law enforcement agencies, they show little or no respect towards the African Americans. They feel empowered to act this way because of the general lack of power the African Americans and poor people have in the society and the "us versus them" attitude of the agencies. Our society is not viewed as unified, but separated by color and socio-economic status. Taken together, the attitude and treatment of the law enforcement agencies towards the African Americans leaves little or no room for trust in fairness and justice.

An example of how this lack of trust in the system works can be seen in a recent story printed in the *Oklahoman*, "More victims are possible in sex crime case against officer" (8/22/2014). The story involved allegations of a series of sexual attacks by a police officer while on duty in a largely African American community. The article noted that the officer was accused of "stopping women—some as they walked through neighborhoods—and threatening them with arrest.... Police said ... [the officer] forced women to expose themselves, fondled the women, and in at least one instance, had intercourse with a woman..."

The officer is European American.

Why did these alleged crimes go on so long? We might suggest that the officer believed that his word, as an officer, would override the word of any African American female. And in most cases, he would be correct because of past experiences of officers in situations regarding African Americans. Many of the women who filed complaints held little hope that this officer would be stopped.

More than likely the mere number of complaints to the department finally got someone's attention, so some action was finally taken.

The number of women reported in the article was seven and their ages between 34 - 58. The lack of trust comes from the repeated experiences of lack of respect and negative treatment by people who are paid to enforce the law, serve and protect, but who often assume to be the law, judge, and jury.

We must come to the understanding that we are all family— the human family, and our society and world must change for the better for everyone. At some point in our changing society, we will realize "that the twisting kaleidoscope moves us all in turn."

People of Color Want Just and Fair Treatment from the Law

July 20, 2014

Eric Garner of Staten Island, New York, an African American man, was put in a chokehold—a procedure against NYPD policy—for allegedly selling single cigarettes. He was physically subdued and taken into police custody July 2014.

Luis Rodriguez of Moore, Oklahoma, a Hispanic American, was physically detained for questioning by the police outside a local theatre relative to a domestic matter involving only his wife and daughter. He was physically subdued and taken into police custody Feb. 2014.

Oftentimes, when African Americans or Hispanic Americans complain about the unjust treatment of the police in relation to them, some Americans think that those claims are far-fetched. Usually, those not thinking the claims are unjust and false are European Americans whose relationship with the police is different—nonviolent and generally positive. The recent incident of New York Police's actions involving an unharmed, African American man, Eric Garner, created a variety of questions about the police, their training relative to people of color, and society.

Because of past experiences involving the police—not just in New York—and people of color, we know the importance of eye-witness and video accounts of these incidents. One fact is certain involving the police actions; without creditable eye-witness and video accounts of an incident, the police's word is accepted above and beyond what any citizen has to say. Even with eye-witness and video accounts, most cases where police extreme force is alleged and death or injury to a citizen occurs, the police actions are usually found to be justified.

Evidently, the only actions evaluated during these types of incidents are those of the policemen; the citizens are usually presumed to be at fault. Why is it the case that police use more force in encountering people of color?

The recent case of extreme force in New York involving an African American man shares a number of similar things with a recent case in the Oklahoma City area involving Luis Rodriguez, a Hispanic man. In both cases, numerous policemen were involved in the physical altercation. The first thing these two cases have in common involves the apparent haste by the police to physically subdue them. What seems out of reasonable thought is the lack of patience by the police to converse with the citizen when little or no threat of harm is imminent. Common decency would suggest that the police would want to get information relative to the situation before initiating any physical action. That was not the case with the two incidents in question. Rather than trying to become informed about the situation, the police, as the videos show, simply order the men to submit to being arrested and placed in handcuffs without any stated cause for their actions.

In both cases, when the men try to speak to the police in an effort to understand the police orders to be handcuffed, the police apparently interpreted their actions as refusing to obey a command and begin immediately to physically subdue them. Why? Are the police taught during their training that physical restraints are necessary for all subjects regardless of what their offense might be? Why do the police not take more time to discern the situation before resorting to physical action against a subject? Is there a time limit involved in making an arrest? The actions of the police appear to be a rush-to-judgment rather than the use of rational judgment as in these two cases.

In addition, the lack of patience and communications demonstrated by the police in these two cases—the use of physical force as seen on the videos— is appalling. We must keep in mind that the two victims did not have weapons nor were they attacking the police—they were trying to get information as to why they were being arrested. However, as soon as the order was given by the police, if the victim did not act immediately in compliance with that order, he was physically restrained.

What seemed appalling during the physical restraint by the police was the lack of resistance from the victim. One notices that not two or three policemen are involved in the restraining but usually four or more. The actions of the police involved in the restraining resembled something like a scene from a National Geographic video where some lionesses have just made a kill, and the rest of the pride comes in to take part in the feast.

What was generally missing from the total incident was the rationale for treating the victim like a wild animal, rather than a human being. Once the victims are on the ground and under control why press their heads into the concrete; they have been subdued, and are not fighting, why keep applying unnecessary pressure and pain? What seemed out of place to most objective viewers of these incidents were the inhuman and unjust actions of the police. Where does the mantra of to "Serve and Protect" enter the minds of the police?

All the police seem to be in agreement when subduing a subject and applying unnecessary force, because not a single one finds the action not in keeping with proper conduct or try to prevent or discourage the others from their action. The actions of these officers are more a disservice to the police force than a service in that the impression one takes away from viewing these videos is one of callous disregard for the feelings of a human being.

In each incident, the victims told the police that they could not breathe. In each case, the words, and pleas of the victims were disregarded. Once they stopped breathing, no immediate medical assistance was offered. Both victims died.

The irony of their deaths is that neither of these men had committed a crime that warranted arrest; at worse, had they been treated with respect and dignity as a human being, they probably would have been given a citation. In effect, the only crime, if we can call it a crime, these men are guilty of is not responding immediately to the policeman's order to submit to being arrested.

The cases of Garner and Rodriguez, two men of color, follow a long list of other victims of unjust and unfair treatment by some members of police forces across the country. Why is it that a herd mentality seems to take over when some police confront people of color?

We suggest that in addition to honoring the mantra "To
Serve and Protect" that police receive training in recognizing
the challenges involved with treating human beings with respect
and dignity regardless of how they look. The officers should be
trained to think of themselves as being in the subject's place. The
phrases "We are Family," and "Patience is a virtue," if considered
by police, would go a long way in helping police do a better job in
closing the gap in their relationship with people of color.

The Department of Justice Report
on Ferguson and America

March 6, 2015

The Department of Justice just recently published its report on the city of Ferguson, in an effort to get a clear picture of the community relations involving African American citizens. Since before the death of Michael Brown, the African American citizens had been complaining about the unfair and abusive treatment they have received from the police department as well as the municipal court and jail.

Many outsiders questioned the complaints made by some of the African American citizens because of the trust and expectation for justice that has always been a part of common belief relative to these entities. The DOJ's report should give some credence to the African American citizens' complaints.

A typical example of what the report indicated regarding a community 67 percent African American and the percentage of African Americans stopped by the police. The report indicated that over the past two years, the police conducted traffic stops where 85 percent were African Americans. From those stops, 90 percent of the African American citizens were issued tickets. In addition, the record shows that 93 percent of the total arrests were of African Americans. Finally, 95 percent of the stops made by the police were for Jaywalking. The report further indicated that African Americans were two times as likely to have their autos searched than European Americans (whites) and if arrested, African Americans represented 95 percent of citizens kept in jail more than two days.

Other aspects of the report serve to underscore the systemic discrimination and abuse perpetrated on the African American citizens of Ferguson by the municipal and police agencies. Because of the amount of monies generated from the citizens' arrests, fines, and incarcerations the report indicated that it constituted 21 percent of the city's budget. The DOJ sees the means for collecting that money as a violation of the citizens'

First and Fourth Amendment rights. In effect, the operation of the city of Ferguson, in part, is dependent on the unfair and unjust treatment of its African American citizens.

To those American citizens who had doubts relative to the reports of African American citizens who raised complaints regarding the treatment they experienced by the police and other public agencies, the report should be sobering, to say the least. However, if the reaction of those Americans who do not feel that this DOJ report reflects only on the people of Ferguson, they are sadly mistaken. If they choose not to realize that ethnic bigotry and discrimination is an American problem, then they are living in an illusion.

Some police and local governmental officials can no longer use the excuse that only a few "bad apples" create the problems that the entire department or agency must bear. When we look at the numbers in the report, we must conclude the possibility of a number of things: one, the problem of bigotry is part of the system, or two, only the "bad apples" do most of the work.

If the arguments of only the "bad apples" create the community relations problems involving the African Americans, and the police and municipal government know this as a fact, why have they let it continue without recognizing the injustices and moved to correct them?

One reason has to do with the community being conditioned to see the police as "never at fault" in making an arrest or using deadly force. The number of African American men killed during police interaction in the past two years is proof that something is not working in the African Americans' favor. When one public official from Ferguson was asked about the large percentage of African American arrests, he shifted the responsibility to the people being arrested by saying that they should not have committed an offence or they deserved to be arrested.

While the DOJ report is important and informative, the conditions in Ferguson will not change unless and until some definite action to address and correct the problems are pursued, and soon. To many of the European American officials in Ferguson, the problem is minor and simply involved hiring a few people of color and maybe dismissing a few employees.

Unfortunately, they do not realize that they are part of the problem—their mindset does not encompass the systemic presence of bigotry. They are not exceptions, many European Americans do not understand, accept, or appreciate the presence of ethnic bigotry in America. We must await the reaction from the citizens of Ferguson to the following statements in the article, U.S. NYT, "Now Ferguson Police Tainted by Bias, Justice Department Says," by Matt Apuzzo and John Eligon March 4, 2015:

> "The Justice Department on Wednesday called on Ferguson, Mo., to overhaul its criminal justice system, declaring that the city had engaged in so many constitutional violations that they could be corrected only by abandoning its entire approach to policing, retraining its employees and establishing new oversight."

That statement did not call for the hiring or firing of a few individuals, but "to overhaul its criminal justice system." Obviously, simply replacing parts of the present system will not suffice. Chances are the officials in Ferguson do not view the problems in the same context as the Justice Department. The problems as the DOJ sees them are systemic, not modular. The next statement is more specific and direct relative to the experiences encountered by the African Americans citizens of Ferguson:

> "In one example after another, the report described a city that used its police and courts as moneymaking ventures, a place where officers stopped and handcuffed people without probable cause, hurled racial slurs, used stun guns without provocation, and treated anyone as suspicious merely for questioning police tactics."

Many European Americans do not see ethnic bigotry as a systemic problem affecting all Americans; rather they see it as separate instances involving individuals with personal problems. That might explain the Ferguson police department and municipal authority's initial reaction to the report. Ferguson is not an isolated example of the refusal to accept ethnic bigotry as an American problem.

However, if Americans do not recognize and accept their responsibility as part of the problem, then little positive change will take place. They need to see bigotry from their inside out, rather than from the outside only. The problems of Ferguson are America's problems; America needs to address them.

Walter Scott's Video Underscores Police Creditability Problem with People of Color

April 10, 2015

Once again a video shows a European American policeman shooting an unarmed African American in the back and killing him. Unfortunately for the policeman, someone captured on video the action that compromised the officer's account of what happened. What the video does in this case is call into question the officer's account of fearing for his life.

In the majority of cases involving the shooting of an unarmed African American by a European American officer, the words of witnesses and especially those of the people of color are usually discounted. Since slavery, the words of a European American trump those of the African American citizen if they contradict the law enforcer, even in the face of creditable evidence. With the Walter Scott video, Americans have cause to pause and question the practice of taking for granted the police's word as truth.

Since the Scott video showed the actions of the policeman while contradicting his report, he was arrested and charged with Scott's death. While this arrest might signal a problem in the system of criminal justice for African Americans, the fact is that nothing lasting will change for the benefit of the African Americans and people of color until the system is changed. The system was what gave the police officer the ease to write a report that turned the victim into the villain without question. The system is what allowed the acceptance of the officer's story without investigation, before the video appeared. The point is that because of the system that supports the actions of the officers, usually without question, the greater percentage of shootings by European American officers of unarmed African American men creates little or no concern relative to the officers' actions.

The way the criminal justice system works now is when an officer stops a citizen, the citizen loses all rights. In many cases violence is introduced by the officers. However, when the citizen asks questions or hesitates to comply, in the officer's opinion, with the officer's order, he or she is charged with some offence. From this point on until the citizen is arrested, or worse, shot, all citizen rights have been forfeited. Whenever an officer says his or her life was being threatened, we are led to believe that the life of the citizen is worthless. In essence, citizens have little or no rights when engaged by an officer because their lives have less value than the officer's.

All too often we hear that the negative actions of the law enforcement agencies are caused by a few bad apples. With all the instances of these bad apples shooting unarmed African Americans, it almost appears that the good apples are the exception in law enforcement.

If the system is going to change, then the good officers are going to have to take the lead in seeing that their actions comport with the value of all citizens. The excuse of a few bad apples in the force causing all the problems has run its course now to have any creditability. Structural changes are needed in order to begin to address the systemic changes needed.

One of the primary changes that needs to be addressed is the practice of the law enforcement agency investigating itself. How can that not be viewed as a conflict of interest? We need to forgo the idea of a guilt-free and truthful band of law officers, never at fault for any negative actions. We have proof in the Scott video that some officers have a totally different perspective of how they do their job. If only the people who serve with them get to investigate their actions, well, the outcome is generally obvious.

Until recently, it appeared that only the people affected by the action of the bad apples complained for justice to be served, and their cry usually fell on deaf ears. The system needs changing.

Although the practice of self-investigation by law enforcement groups needs to be changed, the culture of that system must be first addressed. From the evidence reported via media and other sources, the law enforcement agents do not value all citizens fairly. Certainly, the unfair treatment of African American citizens and other citizens of color by law enforcers is constantly called into question. The fact that no apparent repercussions for the ill treatment of African American citizens by law enforcers is ever evidenced, seemingly, encourage the officers to continue the practice. When all the law enforcers see and treat all the citizens that they are employed to serve fairly, then positive changes will happen. Unfortunately, that is not the case presently.

Most citizens understand the need for policing and protecting the public, and that this job requires officers to experience life-threatening situations from time to time. However, how can a traffic stop for a minor law infraction, like a broken tail light or an unfastened seat belt, lead to death?

If officers are afraid for their lives when serving in areas inhabited by people of color, they need to request a change of service location or seek other employment. No one is forced to wear a uniform or carry a badge to protect and serve the citizens. If stereotypical negative concepts color or dominate an officer's behavior towards people of color, then he or she needs to find employment in a community that suits their needs or try another profession.

The Walter Scott video shows without doubt that a problem exists in police community relations, especially involving people of color. One sure way of knowing that structural changes will not occur is when the administration officials fail to understand that their concept and perspectives help to create the environment that produced this outcome. Adding faces of color to an existing police force will not solve the problem because the problems exist in the way the community and the police view the citizens of color. Unfortunately, too many European Americans cannot see the problem as it relates to human value or recognize that they are part of the problem. So we wait for the next video to appear.

Fighting a Corrupt Justice System is a Waste of Time; Replace It

December 31, 2015

For the past year America has witnessed the spectacle of young, mostly male, unarmed, people of color being killed by law enforcement agents. In all instances, the use of deadly force by the officers was employed when other options were available and appropriate. The result of the actions by the law enforcers in these deaths were few or no repercussions for the law officers; in essence, the victims were responsible for their deaths.

In most of these cases when video was available and compared with the officers' written reports of the incidents, they did not correspond. The videos told different stories from the ones in the official reports. Never-the-less, the outcome of these events showed the public that justice and fairness does not look the same when law enforcement views it alongside society in general. What seems justified in the eyes of the law does not reflect fairness and justice to many Americans in general, and to people of color in particular.

Two things can be ascertained from the experiences involving the deaths of people of color at the hands of European American and other law enforcement officers: 1. the present system of jurisprudence is corrupt in dispensing justice to people of color and 2. the system must be replaced, not revised or re-developed. The reason for these facts can be observed in the reactions of the public and the citizens directly involved with the system.

Americans have been conditioned to accept the words and actions of the law enforcement agents without question because of the trust that has been placed in their hands. In the past, records concerning citizens' deaths were not kept to any appreciable degree by law enforcement agencies and so that information relative to the number of African Americans and other people of color were not available to the public. Furthermore, the public did not seem concerned regarding those deaths because of the mental social conditioning.

However, when videos of officer shootings became available to the media and were aired, people began to pay closer attention to and take an interest in what was being presented.

The corruption of the justice system relative to the prosecution of officers can be seen in the method in which the cases are handled. The entire process is handled in the law enforcement community; no one from outside or from an independent agency plays a role in assessing the criminal concerns of the officers.

The only possible group of people to play any role in hearing accusations against an officer is a Grand Jury. Unfortunately, the only person to appear before the Grand Jury is a prosecutor. Since the prosecutor works closely with the law enforcement agencies, which might include many of the officers in question, his or her perspective is generally skewed towards helping the officers. The results, as we have seen, favor no charges being brought against the officers. Because of society's conditioning of not questioning the findings of an officer-involved proceeding, little thought is given to the fairness and justice of the cases until recently.

We are compelled to question the system of justice when day after day we see and hear contradictory information relative to the deaths of a people of color and no one, except the victim, is held responsible for a crime.

A question comes to mind when discussing the occurrence of a European American officer killing a person of color on a force that includes officers that are also people of color. Why do we not hear or see officers of color involved in the killing of European American citizens? If all the law enforcement officers experience the same or similar training, why is it that European Americans are the primary killers of people of color, yet officers of color rarely, if ever kill a European American?

One response focuses on the culture of the law enforcement community and its corruption. The nature of the corruption can be seen in the silent code of group unity—backing one another right or wrong. The group identity represents a serious challenge to justice and fairness.

What most Americans do not realize or understand is that the ethnic bigotry that sees African Americans as inferior beings and of little social value is normal for European Americans; that bias is also part of their social conditioning.

When a European American becomes a member of the law enforcement group, that bigotry is not checked at the door and left out. The fact that society conditions European Americans to see African Americans and dangerous, evil, threatening, etc., helps to fuel the attitude of these officers not only when they join the group but also when they come into contact with African Americans and other people of color. No question remains about the corruption of the system; we only need to check the records.

The system of social injustice and unfairness exhibited primarily by law enforcement agencies cannot be fought or defeated using the tools of the system. The system must be replaced in order for justice to be available to all citizens of America.

Time and again the Federal Government has stepped into the workings of a police department in one or two large cities when a lack of justice and fairness has been documented. A study is usually conducted and after a period of time, all parties gather and review the findings of the study. Certain requirements for change in everything from policies, to procedures, to training, etc. are made and a time frame is given to accomplish these objectives. When we look at the history of success involving these experiences, we realize that little has changed—a new suit might appear on the officer, but the undergarments are the same as before.

What has to change is the culture of bigotry that has long been part of the American psyche, generally without many Americans realizing it. When a European American sees an African American or another person of color and not see that person as a social equal, class concerns aside, that is called bigotry or social conditioning. No amount of training can remove that bigotry; it has to be replaced through education.

The law enforcement agencies represent only a part of the cultural structure that promotes, sustains, and defends bigotry. Change is slowly taking place now through the efforts of civil-minded people and groups who recognize that America is not the kind of society they want to live in or have their children and grandchildren inherit.

So, they must continue to PROTEST, PROTEST, PROTEST in order to call attention to the injustices being committed. They must continue to PROTEST, PROTEST, and PROTEST in order to make the changes that are needed to replace the system. They must PROTEST, PROTEST, and PROTEST until the changes are made. The American Revolution began as a protest, and we see what that got us—freedom.

The Criminal Justice System Must Be Replaced for Justice to Become a Reality for All

September 25, 2016

By now most of America should realize that the continued shooting of African Americans and people of color by police officers is not just a random act of an inexperienced, untrained, misguided rookie cop. The plethora of excuses for the killings does little to avoid the conclusion that the problem is systemic—part of the culture of law enforcement nationwide.

The idea of a few rogue cops committing these killings does not stand the test of validity for dismissing their actions as random while protecting the force. The fact of the matter that law enforcement culture views African Americans and people of color as the enemy or less valuable than European Americans is more than evident by the mere number of incidents that have occurred recently as well as historically.

Holding town hall meetings, public panel discussions, firing a few officers, hiring a few officers of color, making speeches and the like will do nothing in addressing the problem. The problem is the culture that views the African Americans and people of color as having less human and social value as the European American citizen.

According to some former police officers, European Americans are conditioned to view African Americans with fear and trepidation. Norm Stamper has said that as an officer he experienced the fear that European American officers had for African American men. This cultural view is held by European Americans as part of their view of reality and normalcy in America, i.e. European Americans have been conditioned to not see their bigotry as a problem, but as the normal way to see society.

Until they are able to see and understand that their view of reality is bigoted, the problem will persist.

The recent deaths of Terence Crutcher in Tulsa, Oklahoma, and Keith Lamont Scott in Charlotte, N.C. should serve as proof sufficient to underscore the charges African Americans and other people of color have made against the various police forces for many years. European Americans have been conditioned to view police and other law enforcers as public servants whose character project honesty, truth, justice, loyalty, dedication and integrity, and certainly, many officers do project those qualities. What the African American community has been saying for years is that they are not viewed or treated by law enforcement the same as European Americans and therefore their relationships are not the same. Now that America and the world can witness via video just what happens in many of these cases, the call to replace the system and culture of criminal justice in America should be readily acceptable to all.

What we witness in the Crutcher and Scott cases goes totally against the picture of law enforcement presented to the general public. The fact that the police not only lie about their actions but also create false reasons for their actions; these faults constitute deceit. The tacit of trying to find something considered socially unacceptable in the African American victim's background to make him or her appear in a negative light is below contempt. The result is that the element of trust in law enforcement is no longer possible.

We are not indicting all individuals who have taken the oath to serve and defend, but when time and again the result of any actions involving the killing of an African American with little or no repercussions for the officers, we have to ask, where is the justice?

The protests that we witness around the country are not against police officers, but the system and culture in which they work that discriminates against African Americans. These protests must continue and include more citizens of all ethnic identities, especially European Americans. The media presents most protests involving African Americans as an African American protest when in fact it is a protest by American citizens because the problems being underscored by the protestors are American made. All Americans should be affected by the videos of unarmed citizens being shot by police officers and the subsequent lack of appropriate justice for their acts.

The American criminal justice system must be replaced, not adjusted, expanded or tweaked because the core of the system would not be affected. The core in place presently views African Americans in a negative and uncomplimentary perspective, and because of that view, they are treated with a lack of respect. That view must be replaced with one that views all people as valuable human beings worthy of respect and deserving the protection and service given by law enforcement.

To fully address the problem of injustice, European Americans must be educated to observe, speak, and behave in a way that includes them and all human beings in the family of mankind. In order to begin the process of replacement, all citizens must be educated to the fact that the concept and belief in a system of biological races is a myth, false, made up. No one's skin complexion gives him or her preferences of any nature over another human being, except by man-made laws. The protests today are focused on getting rid of those unjust laws.

The social conditioning received by European Americans relative to skin complexion has been so overwhelming that separating the fact from fiction is a monumental challenge. However, society is rapidly changing its demographic profile to the point that the social value of white versus black skins will have little to no value. Some Americans turn a blind eye and deaf ear to the protests now happening in society thinking that since only African Americans are involved, that they are not affected by whatever the problems might be. They will learn that they are directly implicated in the problems and must become a part of the change or remain a part of the problem.

If Americans who view the videos showing the treatment of African American citizens by law enforcement want to become involved in making positive change, they should not only voice their concerns to local authorizes but also seek out organizations and/or civic groups where they can become active participants. If no such groups are readily available, they can start one to focus on the problems that need changing. Words without action are just hot air.

The Jury's Not Guilty Verdict of the Philando Castile Case Sent a Message to America

June 20, 2017

With the jury's finding of not guilty for the officer who killed Philando Castile comes the implied—but blatant—statement from law enforcement that the justice system overwhelmingly favors their agents, the police. The ruling says that in spite of you forcing us to use dash cams, body cams, and surveillance cams, you, the people, cannot prevail over us because justice is what we say it is.

Most people of sound mind can usually tell right from wrong, but somehow lawyers, prosecutors, judges, district attorneys, and others in the justice system cannot when a member of law enforcement is involved. We the people cannot continue to allow this miscarriage of justice to take place and assume that all is right with the world because it is not. So, what can the people do to replace this misguided system?

Although a disproportionate number of police victims have been people of color, the corruption is not exclusive to people of color, so, all people who want justice to serve everyone should be concerned and involved in bringing about a system that serves everyone. We know that many people are angry and concerned about the lack of justice simply by looking at the makeup of the protesters. While the protests serve a purpose in bringing the problems to public awareness, it should also serve as an opportunity to organize groups to study and develop plans of actions directed at replacing the system. Nothing will happen to replace the system if the people do not get involved and execute specific plans of actions.

Also, change will not happen overnight. The first order of business is to organize and develop a plan of approach to addressing the problem. The need for this process is important because it saves time and energy.

For example, developing a plan to replace the chief of police, if effective, might bring about some relief, but would not solve the problem because the chief is simply one part of the total organization. Any plan to be effective must understand the system and its organizational structure in order to replace it completely. Some of the tools available to the people include political power—finding suitable candidates for the various offices and supporting them to victory; political pressure—the people putting pressure on current politicians to introduce legislation written to address many of the current problems in the justice system; the law—suing the city, police, Fraternal Order of the Police for as much money as possible so they get the message that injustice also comes with a price. Whatever approach taken must involve all concerned citizens, not just the vocal ones, and it must start at the local level.

We have heard all the excuses offered by law enforcement to justify their actions; excuses like "I felt threatened," or "I felt my life was in danger," or "I thought he was going for his gun," or "I was afraid for my life." All of these excuses and others have been offered as reasons for using deadly force, and yet, in spite of their fears and feelings of trepidations, many of these officers remain on the force. If they are in a state of constant fear or insecure feelings, they should not be in law enforcement. How can they "serve and protect" when they are under constant stress?

In addition to the individual excuses we hear the all too often, references to the "bad apples" in the department or the "need for more training," or "the need for more officers," or "our lives are on the line every day." While all those reasons might be valid in some cases, none of the excuses explain why departments do not do a better job of vetting future officers or explain why some officers think it is fine to knowingly use excessive force, or officers using common sense and a degree of patience before resorting to deadly force, or spend more time educating departments and officers on the meaning of all people living in a diverse society rather than training in military combat tactics. Enough with all the excuses; ways and actions speak louder than words ever will.

We, the people, are tired of the unjust actions of the criminal justice system and its agents as well as the over-used excuses to try to justify and maintain the system. We are not trying to appeal to a sense of Christian fellowship, valuing our common humanity, or democratic principles when we protest and ask for fairness for ourselves and fellow citizens, but to human decency and to a simple attempt to know the difference between right and wrong, and to seek to do what is right.

We should not take lightly the necessity for change in the system of justice as it continues to wreak havoc on the lives of people of color in general and show disregard for the rights of many of its citizens. To seek a replacement of the unjust system is not a suggestion, but a responsibility as noted in the Declaration of Independence: "But when a long train of abuses and usurpations, pursuing invariably the same object evinces a design to reduce them under absolute despotism, it is their right, it is their duty, to throw off such government, and to provide new guards for their future security."

The founding fathers believed that replacing a corrupt and abusive system was not simply a choice, but a "duty" of the people. The focus is not replacing the government, but the abusive system. We should not look to violence as part of a remedy for injustices, but the legal tools that are available and most of all, the people.

Change and replacement of the criminal justice system will not come easy or quickly because of the long years of its entrenchment, but it must come. Any plan for replacement must begin at the local level and involve as many people possible—strength in numbers. People wanting to join in the effort should look for groups and/ or organizations already active in the process. Joining efforts with other individuals and organizations does not mean one has to agree with everything the group or organization represents but agreeing on replacing the justice system should be the primary focus.

All American Society is Implicated in the Deaths of African American Men by Police

July 8, 2016

The recent video showing the shooting death of two African American men, Alton Sterling and Philando Castile, by European American police officers in Minnesota and Louisiana simply underscores the point that anywhere in America, the value of an African American's life is little to none existence. Calls for changes in the police departments will do little to remedy the problem because the problem does not reside in the police departments per se; the problem is the culture of American society that does not value African Americans. The law enforcement agencies and its representatives only reflect what society empowers them to embody—a lack of value for people of color, especially African Americans.

We know from past experiences that videos will not be sufficient to promote justice for the African American victims. The culture of bigotry is part of the system that permeates law enforcement nationwide and although videos have been produced to show the actions of law enforcement, they do little to convict officers who are involved in the action.

One reason for the lack of justice is because the entire community is not directly implicated in the injustice. Rather than the African American community of Minnesota and Louisiana protesting, the entire cities should protest to show that they understand the culture of bigotry they promote and sustain through the police force and say it is not acceptable.

Real and sustainable change will not occur in America until the culture of ethnic bigotry is replaced with a system that values all people. We need not legitimize prejudices by listing conditions and by giving names to them such as ethnicity, gender, color, religion, etc. If all Americans should enjoy the same right, liberties, and freedoms, then no qualifications are needed—all says it all.

To understand the culture of bigotry as exemplified by law enforcement we need to look at what serves as its base. Simply stated, the answer is anger and fear of the African American by the European Americans acquired through social conditioning. In their homes, neighborhoods, communities, schools, and churches, European Americans from early childhood learn and are shown how to behave toward African Americans and people of color in general; unless they are employed or serve the European Americans in some non-threatening position, they are to be avoided.

Because the African American lacks little social value in society when compared to European Americans, any social improvement acquired by African Americans appear as a threat to the supremacy of the European Americans. These social improvements serve to anger the European Americans because they are often viewed as encroachments on their rights. The worse possible experience for a European American is having to view an African American as an equal; that goes totally against the social conditioning under which they were reared.

So, until the total national community can accept the injustice committed against an African American as wrong, replacing the system of injustice will not occur. The problem is not just between the police department and the African American community; it involves the entire national community. The focus should be on the injustice committed against any person and not finding fault with the parties involved; we are all involved and we need to accept our role in fighting against injustice or promoting injustices by our silence.

Fear of the African American comes from the ignorance and myths associated with the invention of races and the concept of European American supremacy. The fear of losing that concept of supremacy serves as the motivating element to inflict physical violence against African Americans. Anger and fear of African American men are joined together at the heart of the American culture. We can and do readily observe it through the actions of law enforcers.

In my recent book about the system of European American Supremacy the following reference focused on the subject: A former police officer, Norm Stamper, (Breaking Rank, Nation Books, 2005) clears up any misconceptions European Americans might have about law enforcement and African Americans: "Simply put, white cops are afraid of black men. We don't talk about it, we pretend it doesn't exist, we claim 'color blindness,' we say white officers treat black men the same way they treat white men. But that's a lie." Stamper noted that while bigotry and fear are part of the police culture and a significant fabric of their thoughts, most European American officers will not admit to the bigotry in themselves and others.

We know that anger, fear, and bigotry exist in the culture of law enforcement nationwide and we have statistics to support the degree to which men of color are killed by law enforcement agents. The question now is: what can be done to eliminate it?

The first order of business is for the Europeans Americans to recognize that valuing the lives of people of color is necessary. For European Americans to act like the murders of African American men have no more than a passing effect on them is to approve of the injustice. They can no longer stand passively on the sidelines and shake their heads saying how sorry they are that this or that tragedy occurred. They need to join forces with all the members of society in protest and actions to change the system from the top to the bottom.

The law enforcement agencies work for the people, all the people. Unfortunately, the police unions and other criminal justice elements work to protect the officers, not the citizens. If that statement is thought to be presumptuous, one needs only to check and see how many officers shown on videos killing unharmed or legally armed men have been convicted. The officer has only to say that he or she felt their lives were threatened and all the focus falls on the victim for somehow forcing the officer to shoot him.

The laws need to be changed to protect the citizens from the police in that all citizens should be given the right to exercise their rights. Many of the African American men who were killed never had an opportunity to be asked questions or respond before they were shot. As a society, we can put a stop to these senseless killings, but we must do so as a society, not just people of color and a few European Americans. All Americans should be outraged at the display of injustice regarding the shooting of men of color—outraged to the point of action.

Changing America from a Racist Society Will Require Time and Patience

September 8, 2013

Turn on the television, the radio, or even the internet and we find the common use of the word race in a variety of ways. We have been told that racism is a belief that people of various biological races have different qualities and characteristics that make them inherently superior or inferior to others.

In America, we have what is known as white racism. That means people believe that a white race exists and that this race is superior to all others. This belief came into existence in America as early as the middle 1500s when the Spanish would hunt, capture, and sell Indians into slavery.

The words racism and racist, as well as a host of others, are derived from the word race. In the America of the 1600s, the word race was meant to indicate social and economic status and not color because the slaves in America during this time and later were of various skin colors. Counted among the slaves were Indians, Europeans, and Africans.

The demand for slaves created a problem for the ruling Europeans who quickly embraced the importation of Africans to fill the labor gap. With the introduction of the African into the system of slavery, the ruling Europeans decided to create a buffer among the slaves by giving special privileges to the European or white slaves. We are told:

> "In 1705, masters were forbidden to 'whip a Christian white servant naked.' Nakedness was for brutes, the uncivil, and the non-Christian. That same year, all property—horses, cattle, and hogs—was confiscated from slaves and sold by the church wardens for the benefit of poor whites."

This was done to create a bond between the wealthy whites and the poor whites as well as create a distinction among the slaves. We learn that "by means of such acts, social historian Edmond Morgan arguers, the tobacco planters, and ruling elite of Virginia raised the legal status of lower—class white relative to that of Negroes and Indians, whether free, servant or slave." (See America's Race Problem: A Practical Guide to Understanding Race in America)

So, the element of color became a major factor in America's system of slavery as well as society in general, because all the Africans living in America were not now, nor had ever been, slaves. Color and Christianity became the criteria for discriminating against people. The problem of free Africans and Indians living in society alongside Europeans was a problem for the Europeans. Making a contrast based on the physical appearance of the African and Indian became the primary criteria for creating biases. American society decided to create two biological races, one black and one white, based primarily on color of skin. We wonder why they did not create a race for the Indians.

The white race was made to be superior to the black race in every respect. In essence, this was the beginning of racism based on color. Because the ruling class of Europeans had the power and control to create such a fabrication as race it became accepted by society.

Regardless of the truth of a concept, according to scholars, if it is repeated constantly for the benefit of some people, they will after a while ignore the fact that the concept is a fabrication and accept it for fact or truth. That has become the case with the belief in two races, both supposedly biologically different with one being superior to the other. Because of the acceptance of such a belief, America and Americans became a racist society.

Some two hundred years after the introduction of slavery in American, we can see how thoroughly the biased and false concept of two races had affected America. When we examine the words of President Abe Lincoln in 1862 as he spoke to a group of free men of color, we recognize the conviction of his belief in race by color: "You [African Americans] and we [European Americans] are different races. We have between us a broader difference than exists between almost any other two races." The broader difference Lincoln speaks of is basically, color; other differences existed because the slaves and free African Americans were prevented

from experiencing those things written in the Declaration of
Independence the Constitution about rights, freedom, and justice.

What makes race so confusing in America is that it was
illogically conceived using color as the base for determining
superiority and inferiority. How can a society base superiority
or inferiority on color and at the same time have slaves and free
men of the same color exhibiting totally different characteristics
attributed to differences of the condition and status of each
individual? Logic does not enter the thinking process when one
has accepted as truth or fact that races based on color really exist.
Nonetheless, President Lincoln firmly believed that the two races
should be separated because they could not live together in peace
because of their color. Fortunately, Lincoln later changed his mind
about the latter.

So, what is the point of this discussion?

When we examine the past objectively, we can understand
many of the things taking place today, and why they are taking
place. When American came into being, it came as a society that
believed in race by class and economics; later, color was added to
the mix. One thought dominated the general thinking, however,
and that was the supremacy of the whites. In effect, America
wanted to be known as a white society with different classes of
whites. Other non-European ethnicities were not considered suited
for citizenship, but were allowed to live here.

For over four hundred years or more, the most cherished
beliefs among many Americans are their white identity and that
America is a white country—their country. The concept of race has
undergone new analysis and the results reveal that only one race
of human being exists in spite of color. So, the theories and beliefs
that were created to separate various human beings from each other
because of color are being debunked.

Unfortunately, as a society we have not pulled away from our
use of the word race and all its derivatives that keep us tethered to
the biased past. So, we continue to use words like racist, racism,
etc. as if they are valid and accurate. In America, an African
American cannot be a racist, if we accept the definition of that

word, because in America, African Americans have never had the power or control to create the concept of race superiority and maintain and promote it. He can certainly be biased and prejudiced because those feelings are purely related to the individual, not a group or so-called race.

America has been a racist society for a long time, so some patience is required while change is taking place. Progress for some people is very hard.

POLITICS

"Let us not seek the Republican answer or the Democratic answer, but the right answer. Let us not seek to fix the blame for the past. Let us accept our own responsibility for the future."

JOHN F. KENNEDY

The Emotional Challenge of European Americans to President Obama

March 31, 2010

From the moment Barack Obama was elected President of the United States of America a whirlwind of emotions was set in play for people the world over. For the first time in its history, America had elected an African American as president.

Naturally, the feelings about these phenomena were mixed, but little thought was given to reactions of the losing political party and the people who voted against Obama. The accumulation of negative reactions to Obama and his administration has caused some concern because of the seriousness and violence included in the reaction.

In an effort to understand just what is at the heart of the matter, my thoughts took me back to an Ethnic American Literature class I taught in the early '90s. Having observed over a period of time the negative reactions many of the European American students had to the literature, I finally wrote an article examining the emotional challenges they were encountering so they might understand just what was happening to them. All the students were required to read the article and participate in a discussion of the material. For the students, understanding what was going on in their minds made a big, positive difference.

What many European Americans are experiencing since the election of President Obama is akin to the loss of a very close and personal friend. What accompanies such a loss is known as grief which, as we know from scholars who have studied and published in this area, occurs in stages. Knowing and understanding those stages can help some individuals cope with their emotional challenge.

What has happened to many European Americans as a result of Obama's election is called an emotional crisis. For the many European Americans who identify themselves as "white," the challenge is extremely serious. All their lives they have relied on the myth of being special, valued, and privileged by virtue of their skin color. Part of their personal value was that they were led to believe they were better or superior to all non-whites. What was even more apparent to them was that they would always be superior to African Americans. Unfortunately, the center could not hold.

When President Johnson signed the Civil Rights Act of 1964, many European Americans believed that the country had turned its back on them. They believed that African Americans were never to have an equal status in society with "whites." Naturally, they were upset and angry, so they took out their frustrations any way they could, but especially through politics.

These European Americans thought they could regain the level of privilege they enjoyed prior to 1964 if they controlled the vote, and they did manage a degree of control in slowing down justice for many African Americans. Unfortunately, when Obama won the Presidency, their hopes were not only dashed, but also destroyed, because now they had to face the reality of having to be superior to no one. The idea of having to pay homage to someone who they and society treated as underclass since slavery was too much of an emotional challenge. What these European Americans are experiencing now I call the Seven Stages of Emotional Confrontation.

These seven stages are fairly akin to the stages of grief, but different. Stage One is shock; Stage Two is denial; Stage Three is anger; Stage Four is rejection; Stage Five is examination; Stage Six is understanding; Stage Seven is acceptance. Since the emotional confrontation occurs in stages, any person can find him or herself at any one of the stages. The important part of this confrontation is to get through it and not get stuck in it.

Although all seven stages are challenges to the emotions, they are not all based in the same area of concern. For example, Stage One has as its base the element of surprise. The next three stages are based in fear. The remaining three stages depend on logic or rational thought that helps to influence the emotions. A brief example of each stage should create a picture that helps to explain what many European Americans are experiencing and their reactions.

When the news of Obama's election victory was made known, that information was a shock to many European Americans who felt secure in the idea that it would never happen. The news was jarring to their mind and emotions—Stage One.

Once the news of Obama's victory was verified, some European Americans refused to acknowledge the truth of the information. At the base of their refusal was the fear of having a central part of their self-image destroyed– the part that made them superior to African Americans of which Obama was a representative. Relinquishing that place of privilege must be resisted, hence Stage Two, denial.

The stages are numbered to indicate the progress of the emotional journey; that is, each stage can be examined separately, but must also be considered as part of a process. Continuing the process of the emotional challenge, we come to the most dangerous and volatile place in the process; the fear of losing one's positive perception of self while being forced to accept a new perception of those that were formally despised served to create extreme displeasure that manifests itself in a variety of ways. Some of those ways include rage, indignation, resentment and even wrath—examples of incidents which the media has reported being directed at Obama. The accumulation of fear and loss of self-worth manifests itself in anger, Stage Three.

One has to take stock of the recent history recorded by the Republican Congressmen who have opposed every piece of legislation offered by the Obama administration. What would cause this type of negation to happen?

The manifestation of fear through anger lends nothing to solving the problem of losing the power of ethnic and social privilege. So, some kind of actions must be taken to try and discredit the source of the problem, namely, President Obama. The elements of Obama's character that lend themselves to intelligence, leadership, control, decency, and national unity must be denied because they contradict everything that some European Americans believe that African Americans are not capable of possessing and manifesting. Having a president who represents qualities that are usually admired in European Americans generally becomes a threat in an African American because if he is legitimate, then their views and beliefs about themselves are in danger. Therefore, the challenge to recognize or accept the reality of history must be met with rejection, the fourth stage.

As stated earlier, the final three stages require serious thought without the hindrance of fear. When the reality of our national situation is viewed objectively, we understand that Obama will continue to be president for the next three years regardless of what anyone says or does, generally speaking. Rather than fighting a losing battle, many European Americans decide to weigh the pros and cons of the situation and, in doing so, enter the process of examination, the fifth stage.

One of the benefits of examining a problem or situation is that a variety of pictures are presented to the examiner. For example, taking an objective look at just what Obama and his administration are doing for the good of the country rather than trying to find fault in everything associated with him might produce some surprising results.

In other words, those pictures can help the examiner decide what avenue of approach to take in addressing the challenge; in essence, through careful examination of the situation, the examiner can arrive at an understanding of the challenge, which is the sixth stage.

The final stop on the journey through this emotional confrontation has to do with recognizing the reality of the situation: Obama is president. Whether one likes him and what he is doing is secondary to the fact that he is the president. What impact that information has on the European American whose sense of self-worth and superiority has been challenged, the journey to meeting that challenge must begin with accepting the fact that Obama is President of the United States of America. That acceptance is Stage Seven.

How one manages the journey depends on the individual. A former neighbor was to me the perfect picture of a Christian, patriotic, American citizen, that is, until Obama was elected president. Since that time he has not had a kind or positive word to say about Obama. My question to him was: did your God make a mistake? If so, did He want you to take matters into your own hands in correcting the mistake? Fortunately, I realize that he is on a trip.

Republicans in Congress Fight to Retain Myth of Superiority

April 30, 2010

The Congressional Republicans have demonstrated time and again that they will not support any legislation offered by President Obama and the Democratic Party. Why have they taken such a stand? Can their actions be defended as being good for the country? Let us examine each of these questions respectively.

The fear of losing their belief in ethnic superiority and having to accept an African American as not only an equal but also as their leader is too much for them to accept. Therefore, they must resist as much as possible any semblance of success by Obama because they believe that when he wins, they lose. They believe that as long as they do not accept Obama's leadership, he is not a leader. Their actions are akin to a child not wanting to accept the fact that mom or dad is really the tooth fairy, so he or she continues to place the tooth under the pillow even after being told that it was a myth. To the Congressional Republicans, rejecting Obama is a life-changing proposition they cannot accept.

Can the act of rejecting all things Obama be good for the country? They can be only if the rejections can be seen as logical, emotional, and ethical. The long list of rejections reflects the degree of dedication of the Congressional Republicans in thwarting Obama's leadership. Rather than delving into a list of the rejections, examining one, the health care reform, should serve to underscore our purpose.

The purpose of the health care legislation was to benefit a large segment of America's citizenry in a variety of ways. For certain, the legislation was not perfect, but the option to not support it showed more concern for the Republican Party than for the American people. In essence, rejection of the bill showed invalid reasoning and a lack of sound constructive thinking on behalf of the people.

The level of stress that accompanied the vote on the health care bill was not positive for either side in Congress. The arguments brought out feelings of extreme fear, hate, and mistrust. The American people did not have an opportunity to fully understand or appreciate (not accept) the bill before they were persuaded to one side or the other. Since passage of the legislation would benefit a majority of Americans, passing it would have generated good feelings if the advantages of the bill were known. Unfortunately, we will have to let time inform us as to the wisdom of the decision.

From an ethical perspective, can the continued rejection by the Congressional Republicans be good for the country? If we evaluate the reason for the rejection in the first place, then we must admit that their actions are wrong. They are wrong because they simply put the desires of the party before the needs of the people. If nothing was done to relieve the continuous growth of insurance expense, more Americans would opt not to be insured. Who would that hurt? The Americans with insurance would be forced to pay the tab for the uninsured, so it would hurt the American people. From a humanistic standpoint, as a people are we to ignore the needs of our fellow Americans?

We did not become a strong nation by isolation—each person for him/herself; we became strong by working together and helping each other. We know the difference between right and wrong.

The Congressional Republicans, through their continuous rejection of any Obama legislation, are doing a disservice to themselves and our country. They have placed party concerns and prejudices above the needs of the people and tried to convince the people that they are acting in their behalf.

Obama, an African American, is the president and therefore the leader of the country. That is now a part of America's history. Nothing the Congressional Republicans do today or tomorrow will or can change that. As hard as it may be for them to accept these facts, the logical, emotional, and ethical thing to do is focus on the job the American people elected them to do—take care of the people's business and leave personal and party bias for another time. Rejecting Obama cannot or will not restore or retain the myth of ethnic superiority some in Congress and the nation feel they are losing.

Republican Bigotry Hurts America

May 15, 2010

Congressional Republicans and their bigotry against Obama hurt America. If ways and actions speak louder than words, then the number of bills passed by the House and deliberately not considered by the Senate, as well as the number of appointees for administrative positions being held-up by the Republicans, simply tell the American people that the Republicans value their partisan politics more than the people's business. How do they rationalize the fact that they are denying Obama his administration by holding up appointments and still complain that he and his administration are not doing a good job? Common sense dictates that they cannot have things both ways.

Senator Thomas Coburn of Oklahoma stands as a symbol of the hypocrisy that has come to represent the Congressional Republicans. The best interest of the American people must take a back seat to the political antics that are employed to delay or defeat any Obama or Democratic action. Why? Again, if the actions were for the benefit of the American people, then we should support the Republicans' actions, but when they are merely to prevent Obama and his administration from achieving some required objective, then they should be called to answer for their actions.

In a Washington Bureau article by Chris Casteel (May 5, 2010) concerning Coburn and his Republican colleagues, he writes that "Sen. Tom Coburn fended off Democratic attempts Friday to break secret Republican 'holds' on dozens of President Obama's nominees, and Coburn revealed that he had been blocking votes on six people himself."

What would be the purpose for blocking more than sixty nominees for Federal Department positions? The only logical explanation is to sabotage President Obama's administration. Why? To try and make him appear too incompetent to be president and in doing so justify their bigotry towards him and his administration. But who suffers because of these Republican actions? Certainly Obama loses because he cannot get the people he needs to do the jobs he want done. Unfortunately, the American people are the ultimate losers because the country will be negatively affected by the lack of qualified people in responsible government positions.

The American people will at some point come to realize that the antics of the Republican Congressional leaders serve no useful or beneficial purpose for the country. The argument of doing what the American people want done falls on its face when we realize that if a leader's hands are tied behind his back the complaint of him not doing a good job makes no sense at all. Add to the argument the fact that the House of Representatives has passed numerous bills that await the Senate's action and the picture becomes quite clear—the Republicans want Obama to fail even at the country's expense.

Legislators engaging in meaningful debate over important issues is considered necessary to our form of government. However, when even debate is being blocked by Obama critics, then one must question the motives and objectives of the blockers. Why do they always take the negative approach?

Nothing Obama does seem to be acceptable to these naysayers. Common sense tells us that a broken clock has the correct time two times a day. That is two times more than they give Obama. The perspective changes when we look at things from the positive point of view.

One of the major complaints is that of unemployment. If 9 percent of the population is unemployed then 81 percent must be employed. The difference is certainly not wanted or acceptable, but it is also not a sign of impending doom. Another complaint is that of too much taxing. Well, the majority of working Americans make under $250 thousand a year; they paid fewer taxes last year than the year before. Who's making these complaints?

Plans are in effect to bring our troops home from both Iraq and Afghanistan as promised. More Americans will receive affordable health care insurance now and in the future than ever before. What is wrong with that? Most experts believe that the economy has turned around and is heading towards stability. If Americans start to look for the positive in the current administration, more will become obvious.

When Republicans say they want less government and criticize the Obama administration, they serve as representatives for people who do not realize that politicians play word games for partisan reasons. If one was to stop and ask protesters to give an account of how and where their taxes have increased, they would be hard pressed to come up with a rational answer. If they are asked where they would like to have less government involvement in their lives most would not mention roads, highways, bridges, schools, food protection, police protection, fire protection, the U.S. Military, Veteran benefits, state guards or even the FDIC that protects their savings from loss. They simply mimic the negative things they hear their so-called leaders say without reservation.

We should never settle for less than the best we are able to achieve, but that does not mean we have to concentrate only on the negative. We actually get a different perspective when we look at life from the positive side.

Do the Republicans want the country to fail? Most would answer no to that question. Do Republicans what President Obama to fail? Judging by their actions, the answer would be yes. Do they not realize that by promoting the failure of Obama they are inviting failure for the country?

We know that denial and rejection are part of the process of fear. The Republicans should seek help in trying to deal with their fear of Obama and what he represents. Bigotry is a very serious condition not unlike cancer that if left untreated, can destroy its victim.

House Bill Rejected Out of Fear of Obama

May 29, 2010

Many Americans suffer from a fear that dictates their thoughts and actions without them being cognizant of it. Unfortunately, if someone tried to explain to these people what the problem really is about, they would be greatly offended.

To be blunt, the problem is ethnic prejudice. Placing a label on someone for no good reason is not fair, so let us examine a case in point. The *Oklahoman* ran an article on May 26, about House members rejecting an education reform bill. One legislator in particular, Rep. Sally Kern, R-Oklahoma City, was very outspoken about her decision to reject the bill.

One of the first things we notice about Rep. Kern is her bias against President Barack Obama. Please understand that one does not have to mention Obama's name to make reference to him. All one has to do is mention the words Federal Government or simply the government and the code comes out Obama.

The article, written by Michael McNutt, states that "Rep. Sally Kern, R-Oklahoma City, said she was concerned that some of the standards being proposed to win the federal government's Race to the Top, were developed by the United Nation." In other words, Obama is trying to force foreign standards created in part by the United Nations on the American children. So, because the standards are coming from Obama and the foreign countries of the United Nations, they should be rejected. Anything coming from Obama must be rejected. The fear continues concerning the origin of the standards.

Regarding these standards Kern states, "These are standards that are not American." Just what might she mean? The Ten Commandments are not American, but many American Christians subscribe to them. Can acceptable standards come only from America? Evidently the fact that the government is offering this plan for education reform is not sufficient for Mrs. Kern because, she does not feel safe with Obama as president. McNutt states that "Kern, a former teacher, said she also is leery about the program

because it is developed by Democratic President Barack Obama."
Her fears do not end here.

The prejudice Rep. Kern has for Obama leads her to question
all things having to do with him and the government. She states
that "Race to the Top is Obama's baby." She adds that "with this
money will come strings." McNutt quotes her as stating that "I'm
not willing to sell out our children." Again, because President
Obama supports this bill to help reform education for the nation's
children, it must be dangerous, unacceptable, and therefore,
rejected. What is it about Obama that creates this fear in Rep.
Kern?

The only reasonable conclusion to be drawn from her
behavior is prejudice. So what is prejudice? The American
Heritage Dictionary of the English Language lists a number of
conditions that seem appropriate, but one in particular seems to
fit– "3. Irrational suspicion or hatred of a particular group, race, or
religion."

Some Americans grew up in a society that shielded them from
interaction with an ethnically diverse population, so the only frame
of reference those people have of ethnic Americans is based on
stereotypes, usually negative. The fear expressed by Rep. Kern,
although not stated, seems to come from Obama's ethnicity. The
fact that her precise fear is not stated protects her from being
labeled a bigot; it does not protect her from showing a bias towards
Obama without stated justification.

To many Americans, Obama represents a nightmare becoming
a reality—an African American being President of the United
States. Because of years of feeling and acting superior towards
non-European Americans, the elements of fear and a sense of loss
of control have taken over their perceptions of reality. One cannot
trust someone perceived as having little value in society. America
is in great need of some educational reform, not just for the
children, but society in general.

The education reform bill passed the next day.

The GOP's War Against Obama
Fueled with Hate and Fear

September 16, 2012

When Barack Obama was elected President of the United States of America, conservative elements of the GOP went into shock. All their plans and victories at the local, state, and national levels were now in question because the totally unexpected had happened. Never in their lifetime did these conservatives believe America would elect an African American for president. So, after the shock wore off and even before Obama made it to the Oval Office, they gathered together to plan how to undo the damage to their master plan by getting rid of Obama.

Whether one considers Obama's ethnicity or political party the reason for the GOP's wanting him to be removed, the fact still remained that he must be removed. Part of the problem resided in the fact that Obama won the election, a phenomenon that was never supposed to happen. What went wrong?

Some people believed that the country suffered a brief period of insanity because people in their "right mind" would have never elected an African American president. So what is the reason behind wanting to remove Obama from office? Part of the answer lies in what Obama represents rather than Obama the individual.

When Africans were introduced into slavery in America, the image of the slave as property had to be established, maintained, and promoted in order for the system to operate effectively. The first order of this business was to strip away any and all human and personal worth of the African slave. This effort was made effective by removing any vestiges of the slave's former life and history and remaking him as a less-than-human thing or property. His names, Negro, black, slave, etc. give no indication of a language, geography, culture. All his new names placed him in the system of slavery, and the only value he exhibited was either via work or the market place (auction block). His whole being represented nothing that the majority society viewed as deserving respect or value.

Although the idea of democracy as stated in America's Declaration of Independence 1776, declared that "all men were created equal," nevertheless, America forgot to include the African Americans and other slaves as men in the 1787 Constitution. They were listed as "three fifths," a person. The problem that resulted from these concepts of democracy and slavery juxtaposed created two additional concepts: 1, many Americans knew that African/African Americans were human beings like themselves, but was made less so by society, not God or biology; 2, Many Americans accepted the concept of African/African Americans being less than human regardless of the fallacy. Although Americans in both the North and South shared in both concepts, more Americans in the North accepted the first concept while the majority in the South shared the second. Today, the two concepts are represented in politics with the Democrats identified with the first concept, and the GOP representing the second.

Since the Civil War, the two concepts of the African American have been germane to the progress of American society as represented in the various Civil Rights Acts. Unfortunately, laws do not change individual concepts, so although society through government and science has attempted to correct the injustice and fallacy, many people hold on to the second concept religiously. Their reason for holding on to the concept is based in fear of losing their place of prominence in society. That is, if the African Americans are equal to all people, then they, the people representing the second concept, are less than privileged—they lose value.

So, when Obama was elected president, the GOP felt the immediate blow to their belief system and social status. Damage control had to be the first order of business. The objective they set regarding Obama was to make him appear totally unfit to be president by any means necessary.

The efforts to discredit him as inept did not work, so they took another approach, to make him not one of us—someone alien, not American, a foreigner. That campaign is still in progress. In addition to not being American, these critics accused President

Obama of being a socialist, communist, Muslim, and a host of other things that might cause him to appear unfavorable.

With a continuous barrage of negative charges against President Obama, the GOP believes they can convince enough people to their way of thinking in order to defeat President Obama in the election. The fact that Obama, an African American, is president is a reality the GOP cannot accept, not because of Obama personally, but because of what he represents—a changing America. The change that is taking place in America is a change that takes away the prestige, privilege, and power that was once associated with being European American (white).

The battle now is for the GOP to try and forestall as much change as possible; hence, the phrase "we need to take back our country." Because Obama represents change, he also represents the enemy, and the enemy must be destroyed. Former President Bill Clinton said during his speech at the Democratic Convention words that address the problem: "Though I often disagree with Republicans, I never learned to hate them the way the far right that now controls their party seems to hate President Obama and the Democrats."

Hate seems to be the fuel that propels their actions.

We should not think that the battle against Obama is weakening. Obama's election to president did more than indicate a positive change in America, it also brought to light the many bigots that were hiding behind façades. One irony that was created by the election campaign includes European Americans who say they differ with Obama's politics, but get accused of being biased against him. Their complaint is similar to the African Americans who get accused of voting for Obama only because he is African American. When the GOP declared war against Obama being re-elected, they colored the field with prejudice, so identifying the European Americans who simply differ with Obama's politics get caught in the mix. Sorry.

Many members of the GOP believe strongly that their party will be victorious in this election. One commentary by Victor Davis Hanson compared the election to the classic story "The

Tortoise and the Hare," with Obama being the hare. He stated that "The country is also not quite ready to confess that it went a little crazy in 2008 and voted for the embarrassing banalities of 'hope and change' offered by a little-known senator with a thin resume and little national experience." He continued by offering some scenarios that might befall Obama and Romney and concluded with "Barring a real recovery or sudden war, the steady, plodding Romney tortoise is ever so slowly winning the race against the flashier—surging, yet always fading—Obama hare."

So now the country "went a little crazy" for voting Obama into office because it was duped by his con game. Maybe this time around the country will "go a little sane" and look at the issues and elect the best man for the job. In any event, a change is coming, and any change that diminishes hate is a good change.

Understanding the Bigots' Loss of Power and Control in America

July 31, 2010

Reading, hearing, and seeing all the negative and hatful things associated with President Obama and his administration these past few months have called some things into question. Namely, the issues of bigotry and discrimination. For some reason, many people believed that when Obama won the election that all animosity and hatred against African Americans and other ethnic Americans of color would disappear. That did not happen. As a matter of fact, the disharmony actually increased.

Looking back in history for some kind of explanation for this kind of negative behavior the mystery grows. An attitude of resentment and hatred towards African Americans in particular seems to have no rational bases for existence other than the fact that God made them and put them here, among European Americans. What did African Americans ever do to European Americans to warrant such resentment and hatred? History shows that at different times some European Americans believed that African Americans were unjustly breathing the air that should be reserved for them. Why?

The answer, in part, always goes back to power and control. The ruling class of European Americans knew that using the carrot and stick philosophy with the poor and working class European Americans would always work when pitted against African Americans and other non-European American ethnic groups. So, in an effort to keep the majority group satisfied, they gave them membership in the 'white' club.

The idea of being satisfied meant making up for the lack of self-esteem and self-worth of the poor and working class European Americans when they compared themselves to the wealth ruling class of European Americans. Being white meant having the privilege of feeling superior and better than non-European Americans, and being able to control to a major degree their education, employment, and environment.

The fear, hatred, and resentment we observe today from the right and extreme groups comes from the fact that over the last five or six decades they have been losing their privileges and control. Electing President Obama seems to be the straw that broke their camel's back. Let look at what has happened.

After the Civil War, slavery as an institution was ended, but slavery in other forms came into being. While African Americans could no longer be held legally in physical bondage, they could be prevented from making progress in other ways. Education was viewed as an avenue of approach to improvement for all people, especially the poor and working class. Unfortunately for African Americans, education was unfair and unequal.

This situation was just fine with the bigots because it gave them a reason to feel superior to African Americans. Then, in the 1954 Supreme Court decision Brown v. Broad of Education of Topeka, Kansas declared that segregated schools were inherently unequal and unconstitutional. This action for some European Americans was a slap in their face— losing control of their separate schools. Many battles were fought across the nations by cities and states to maintain the status quo. Some battles are still going on today. One of the most famous conflicts was the Little Rock Central High School incident in Arkansas.

The feeling of loss of control and self-esteem as a result of the Brown decision was renewed ten years later when then President Lyndon B. Johnson signed the 1964 Civil Rights Act. Among other things, this act prohibited discrimination by employers and unions, and established an Equal Employment Opportunity Commission. Any public place and/or program receiving federal assistance came under this act.

This act created one of the biggest rift in American politics because, as President Johnson said at the time, the Southern Democrats would leave the party because they could not stand to have their power, privilege, and control being taken away and given to lesser people. The underlying fear was that first educational control was taken from them, now employment control was taken from them. What would be next?

After the 1954 Brown decision was rendered, a phenomenon occurred in most metropolitan areas known as white flight. European Americans had a choice in this desegregation business; they could move and start their own segregated communities, churches, schools, businesses and all. And so they did. However, another blow was dealt them in 1968.

The federal government said that discrimination could not occur in the sale or rental of almost 80 percent of all housing. The Civil Rights Bill of 1968 took away another privilege from some European Americans, the privilege of controlling the environment. African Americans paid taxes like all working citizens, yet, they could not enjoy all the benefits that their monies helped provide. For example, prior to 1954, many public places forbid and/or limited African Americans access or accommodations to places like libraries, parks, zoos, etc.

Today, many European Americans remember once having control of education, employment, and environment in American society and grieve over the loss of their feeling superior as well as having power and control of other people. Those feelings turned into hate, anger, and resentment when they saw Obama, an African American, elected. His election was yet another slap in their face and the beginning of the end for all the things they were led to believe was theirs for life. For them, the protests are not really about politics, it is about the loss of self-esteem, pride, and power in being 'white.' Now even that is being taken away and European American used in its place. Our understanding the fear, anger, and resentment of these European Americans help in interpreting the meaning behind phrases like "take back our country," restore the American Dream," "restore our freedoms," and "protect our Constitution," among others.

With all these privileges being taken away, old signs like "No niggers need apply," "no niggers allowed in this school" or "any niggers in town after sundown, hold only memories of bygone days. Some European Americans will have to look elsewhere for something or someone to use as a contrast to make them regain those old feelings. From all indications in the media these days, they are not ready to surrender the fight. For the ethnic bigots in

America, President Obama and his rainbow administration is a reflection of how much our democracy has changed, and judging from their attitudes, how little.

The power in bigotry, discrimination, and bias comes from the degree of difference that can be used as a contrast against the so-called normal; the degree of similarity signals a loss of power. So, the more rights and privileges that the African Americans acquire, the more some European Americans feel their loss. They forget that American society is not reserved uniquely for European Americans, that it is an ethnically diverse society of, for, and by its entire people.

Criticism of Obama Based in Bigotry

September 4, 2010

Although many reasons are given by the Republicans and the right for casting aspersions and criticism at President Obama, the most obvious reason is his ethnicity. Two noted journalists, E. J. Dionne, Jr. of the *Washington Post*, and Paul Krugman, of the *New York Times*, wrote in recent articles that the lack of leadership from the Republicans and the right in speaking out against the negative and often less than accurate criticism against President Obama could spell serious trouble for the country. Although previous presidents were the recipients of criticism, none have had to deal with the direct personal and character attacks lodged at Obama.

Two charges assigned to Obama are troubling to say the least. One claim is that he is anti-American, the other is that he is Muslim, both of which are untrue. Under some circumstances some might consider these claims political, but when we evaluate their nature, the focus is more on his ethnicity. The basis of the claims is steeped in bigotry.

In noting his concerns about the attacks on Obama, Krugman observes that "Mr. Obama's election would have enraged those people if he were white. Of course, the fact that he isn't and has an alien-sounding name, adds to the rage." These attacks are not restricted to a narrow segment of society. Krugman continues by adding, "By the way, I'm not talking about the rage of the excluded and the dispossessed: Tea Partiers are relatively affluent, and nobody is angrier these days than the very rich." He goes on to mention a number of the rich– Steve Schwarzman, and the Koch brothers. So, the attacks are serious enough to have the rich and powerful participate. Why is all this happening to Obama?

Rush Limbaugh refers to President Obama as "Imam Hussein Obama," and had called him "the best anti-American president we've ever had." To reasonable people, these references might appear to be the ravings of an entertainer wanting to get attention in an effort to boost ratings. However, Limbaugh has made it clear from the day of Obama's election that he wants him to fail. So, any rhetoric by Limbaugh focusing on Obama's politics is simply a cover for his bigotry. And because he is such a popular spokesperson for the right, thousands of people believe what he says.

Both Krugman and Dionne note that the increase in the extreme language by the GOP and the right has gone unchecked by the so-called responsible Republicans. Dionne notes that "the rise of an angry, irrational extremism—the sort that says Obama is a Muslim socialist who wasn't born in the United States—that was not part of Ronald Reagan's buoyant conservative creed. Do Republican politicians believe in the elaborate conspiracy being spun by Glen Beck and parts of the Tea Party?" He adds, "If not, why won't they say so?" The reason for not stepping up and renouncing the hateful language is because of fear from the rest of the group. No one wants to be the one who points out the ignorance and stupidity of the group.

When we examine some of the claims against Obama, we must admit that they are without merit. For example, if he were anti-American, why would his actions display the opposite effects? What specifically has he done that can be characterized as anti-American?

The people who work with and around him must all be under some spell or other not to recognize his anti-American behavior—or maybe those actions do not exist. One thing is certain on which both Dionne and Krugman agree, and that is Obama, his administration, and party need to get busy and try to deflate the extremist language before it becomes uncontrollable. Too many people are starting to believe the irrational language of Limbaugh and Beck.

To say that these attacks on Obama are based in politics and not on his character would be incorrect. Constructive criticism is generally welcomed because it provides help in working towards the objective. Negative criticism and name calling serves no useful purpose. So, when the Obama critics offer constructive criticism they give him something to build on, but when the criticism is negative, it simple adds unnecessary heat to the atmosphere.

If the GOP wants to attack Obama as the Democratic president regarding some political concern, then that is fair game. However, the attacks have not been about his policies, but attempts in trying to label him as Muslim, socialist, anti-American, alien—none of which are true. The attacks are focused on Obama, the African American, because therein lies the threat of loss. When we give some thought to the nature of the attacks, we note that had Obama not been African American the attacks would reflect more on policies rather than negative name-calling and labels. That, however, is not the case.

We can all hope that the GOP and especially the right will come to understand that the Civil War and Reconstruction are over, that we are the United States. President Obama is president of all the people regardless of how they might regard him. Rather than trying to help Limbaugh, Beck, the GOP, and the extreme right cause Obama to fail, which also means the country fails, why not try to add some constructive criticism to the mix and see what that produces. For certain the negative criticism will yield no good fruit.

Dionne and Krugman are correct in speaking out about the destructive possibilities of the extremely negative comments of the GOP and the need for Obama to address the problem. After all, being patriotic is grounded in taking positive actions that help to build towards a better and brighter future. When the actions taken are meant to do harm or destroy our country that we call anti-American.

Gingrich's Choice of words for Obama Shows Bias and Fear

September 19, 2010

Why would a respected former congressman refer to President Obama as a Kenyan, anti-colonialist, and even a con man? That is actually what Newt Gingrich, former Speaker of the House, said of Obama recently during a televised interview.

Make no mistake about it; Gingrich knew just what he was doing when he selected those words to characterize the president. He capitalized on the negative political atmosphere he has helped to promote. His comments were meant to discredit the president as an American, to spread fear among the people about the president's political philosophy, and to convince the people that they were duped by a confidence man.

When Gingrich referred to President Obama as a Kenyan, he was connecting with the people who claim that Obama is not an American citizen, the "Birthers." In spite of all the evidence to the contrary, many Americans want to believe that Obama is not a citizen, therefore, he should not be president or even eligible for the office. The obvious reason for this attitude is plain and simple bigotry.

Call it politics if you will, but the facts are that these Obama critics are against him because of his ethnicity. No other president's citizenship has been called into question except for Obama. The media has produced newspaper accounts of Obama's birth in Hawaii as well as copies of his birth certificate to prove that he is an American citizen. This information is rejected by the "Birthers." They want to keep the flames of criticism against Obama burning hot and bright. Gingrich knows the power of this negative criticism and decided to tap into it. One reason for this attitude is to continue to keep the doubt in the minds of some of the critics; to feed the hunger of those who consider Obama an alien.

In addition to Gingrich wanting to continue the criticism and fear of some Americans concerning Obama, he wants to underscore the fear of these people by making a reference to a political philosophy—anti-colonialist. Just what this means is never made clear by Gingrich, but the mere suggestion of something not sounding American is enough to set off anyone looking for a reason to reject Obama. Most Americans know that we were once a colony and that our Declaration of Independence shows that we are anti-colonialists. But Gingrich also knows that the people looking for justification to reject the president will latch on to any information to try and prove their point, so he stresses that recognizing this mind-set of Obama helps to predict his behavior. Now the Obama critics are armed with a new (old) term with which to characterize Obama's brand of anti-American politics. How very right of Gingrich to provide that service to his supporters.

The most serious and dastardly criticism Gingrich makes of Obama questions his honesty and integrity; he states "This is a person [Obama] who is fundamentally out of touch with how the world works, who happened to have played a wonderful con, as a result of which he is now president." So now we come to the meat of Gingrich's point regarding Obama, his citizenship, his political philosophy, and now his character. He states that "I think he worked very hard at being a person who is normal, reasonable, moderate, bipartisan, transparent, and accommodating—none of which was true." Gingrich sees Obama as a flawed person who is an alien, anti-American, dishonest, obsessed, irrational con-man who duped literally millions of people to elect him president. Now the Obama critics can sink their teeth into something concrete against Obama when they cry about wanting to take their country back. Newt doesn't say to where the country will be taken or how it will be taken.

Raising the emotions and spirits of angry people is one thing, but an objective must be in place as a focal point to strive to accomplish. What is missing from the nonsense of Gingrich is where is this talk leading the people? The people need to be able to articulate just what the problems are and how they should go about correcting them collectively.

Criticism of the policies of the president at the mid-point of his term makes about as much sense as asking a brain surgeon half-way through the operation if the operation is a success. No one will know until the surgery is complete. People might disagree with choice to have surgery in the first place, but that is why people are in positions to help make those decisions. We can certainly argue the pros and cons of the policy after it has been given time to work, but to complain about it before then is foolhardy.

Gingrich's uncomplimentary comments and characterization of Obama are not the first nor will they be the last to try and create fear and doubt about our president and the direction in which he is taking our country. Instead of relying so heavily on what people say about this or that policy, people need to become better informed about things that will affect them directly, then make an educated decision.

Regardless of one's politics, knowing what is being proposed and its effect on our society in the short and long run of things just makes sense. When people yell that they want the government out of their lives do they really know what they are asking? If they were to start listing the things that our government actually does for us, they might arrive at a different conclusion. Statements that sound like bumper stickers, for example, "take our country back" make no sense since no one knows who is supposed to do the talking, and where it is to be taken. Another statement, "government spending is out of control" does not identify any specifics about government spending.

When the people become responsible for the government, then the government can be made to be responsible to the people. As long as this negative and critical attitude relative to the president and the country exists, and supposedly responsible people like Gingrich continue their campaign of fear and hate, America will not realize its potential of being the land of freedom and justice for all.

Disrespect for the President has Consequences Far Beyond the Immediate Present

January 29, 2012

According to American politicians, one of their major concerns is children. For example, many references have been made regarding the national debt that our children and grandchildren will have to pay or the need for better education and health services for them. While all these concerns are valid, one concern apparently goes unchecked—common decency and respect for the president. Ever since his election, people in general, and many politicians in particular, have set unacceptable examples for our children by not showing proper respect for the office of the president or the individual serving as president.

The attitude and treatment of the president displayed by many of his critics have been despicable to say the least. However, the vocal criticism of the president has been, for the better part of his term, like the five-hundred-pound elephant in the room; everybody knows it is there, but no one calls attention to it. At least not until recently, when CBS News chief Washington correspondent Bob Schieffer spoke out last Thursday on the Evening News.

As Americans we have been witnesses to the lack of respect directed towards President Obama from the very beginning. Some like to think that the criticism of the president comes from his party affiliation; however, the criticism is usually directed at his person, not his policies. The lack of respect for the president that continues reflects more on a matter of perception rather than any policy or action.

For example, even before the president had offered any plan for Congress to consider, the leader of the Senate, Mitch McConnell made the statement that in essence his party's chief object for the next four years was to see that President Obama serves only one term. What kind of message did that statement send to our children?

Later, during the president's address to the Congress, one of the Representatives, Joe Wilson, yelled the word "liar" directed at the

president relative to one of his comments. This incident marked a
first in recent times that a president would not only be interrupted
during his speech but also be accused of lying. Rather than being
disciplined by his colleagues, he was rewarded by some of his
supporters with more than a million dollars in campaign funds.
What lesson should our children learn for this experience?

The lack of respect for the president spilled over into the
military briefly when a magazine article quoted U.S. Army General
Stanley McChrystal making disparaging remarks about the
president. Again, the focus of the remarks landed on the character
of the president rather than concerns about policies or plans. This
general showed little respect for the fact that the president is the
commander in chief, his boss. Fortunately, since the general's
comments became part of the public record, they could not be
ignored, so he was fired by the president. What lesson should our
children learn from this experience?

In every one of these above-mentioned incidents, the disrespect
for the president was shown by European Americans, not that
some African Americans have also made some contributions in
this regard. However, the majority of the atypical behavior seems
to come from individuals who refuse to see President Obama
as leader of the country and feel superior to him. They also feel
at liberty to act on their perceptions. When they execute their
behavior, they evidently give little thought to how their words and
actions will affect the children. The fact that they have not been
called to answer for their lack of decency regarding the president
shows a problem that Schieffer addressed in his comments.

What prompted Schieffer to make his comments involved a
picture of the Arizona Governor Jan Brewer poking her finger
in President Obama's face. The focus of the problem reflected
by this gesture, according to Schieffer, is "not a Democratic or
Republican issue, but a question of how the Office of the president
is treated." He continues by saying "This is just another sign
of the incivility and really the vulgarity of modern American
campaigns. These campaigns have gotten so ugly and so nasty, that
they're tarnishing the whole system." Rather than speaking to the
president's ethnicity as part of the problem, Schieffer says "I think

it also underlines the coarseness of our culture in this age of social media when it is so easy to say anything about anybody and get no penalty for saying it."

He could have easily been making a reference to the comment someone made about Newt Gingrich "putting in his place" Juan Williams, an African American correspondent who questioned Newt about his ex-wife's comments on open marriage. In essence, Williams should not have taken that liberty with Newt, a European American. The statement regarding "putting someone in his place" had never been made regarding any questions posed by other correspondents. No one made reference to the fact that it reflected Newt's ethnically superior attitude towards Williams until much later.

Schieffer's concluding comments brought to mind the impression that the disrespectful actions and words regarding the president might have on our children. He said, "The thing that has always made our system so strong is that whatever we have thought of the office holders, we have held the offices themselves in high respect. We have respected the office." Then he ends with, "I've watched a lot of presidents over the years but I can never recall a president stepping off Air Force One, which is itself a symbol of the presidency and American democracy, and being subject to such rudeness. I think really we're a better people than this little incident illustrates."

We would all like to think that we are better people, but until we start speaking out and teaching our children that being respectful is the only acceptable behavior, we will have to contend with these public examples. And believe it or not, children will learn from our examples, respectful or disrespectful.

Anti-Obama Bumper Sticker Underscores Fear and Bigotry

March 18, 2012

A graphic from MSN, shows a bumper sticker in a red, white and blue rectangle separated in three sections: a white square with two smaller rectangles on top of each other. The top one is blue, the bottom one is red. In the square is the international symbol of "no" or "do not," a red circle with a line diagonally through it from top left to bottom right. A picture is inside the circle that shows a blue sky with a raising three-quarter sun with red and white stripes of the flag completing the bottom of the circle picture. The blue rectangle has white lettering that reads: "Don't Re-Nig." The bottom, red rectangle also has white lettering that reads: "In 2012." In smaller print at the bottom of this same rectangle is a message that reads "Stop repeat offenders. Don't reelect Obama!" MSN shows the graphic with the following message:

Seller pulls website after racist anti-Obama sticker goes viral

This year's presidential race is already one of the ugliest and nasty in recent history. But a photo of a racist anti-Obama bumper sticker that has gone viral across social media, ranks as one of the lowest of many low moments.

The sticker reads "Don't Re-Nig in 2012" in large white script, with "Stop Repeat Offenders. Don't reelect Obama!" in smaller script below. The sticker originated from a site called Stumpy's Stickers, which has since shut down and which also sold several other racist and anti-Obama-themed stickers, including one with hooded Ku Klux Klan figures bearing the phrase "The Original Boyz N The Hood."

Since his election, even before he took office, the cry of President Obama's critics flooded the media. The desire of wanting to "take back our country" was their objective. Many Americans thought the criticism of President Obama was based on his politics or party affiliations rather than his ethnicity. Little doubt should exist now as to why President Obama's critics want him out of office—their bigot his ethnicity.

When most Americans heard the cry of "let's take back our country" they probably assumed the idea was political. That is, the Republicans and other presidential critics wanted to regain power of the White House and Congress. Apparently, that was only part of the objective. The phrase "taking back the country" can now be viewed as a desire to turn back the clock to pre-civil rights times when African Americans and women were controlled by the European American males from pulpit to polling place and schoolhouse to courthouse.

The recent rash of legislation from Republican Governors restricting the rights of women seems to suggest that the fear and anger of losing power has grown from simple fear to near panic. If America could be brought back to a time when the European American male was in total control, the "good old days," then "happy days," would be here again. The problem with that idea is it is long passed for most of society. We cannot turn back the clock of history and relive our story.

The problem facing those critics wanting to "take back the country" is three-fold. First, they see themselves presently as losing ground rapidly. That is, they see themselves losing their power and privilege based on the color of their skin. Since African Americans had little or no social value to them prior to civil rights, the idea of an African American president is anathema to them. They will not accept him as their leader; they cannot accept him as the leader of the free world. They believe by accepting President Obama as their leader, they relinquish their power and privilege and value as European Americans.

Second, they realize that change has already taken place with respect to African Americans and women since the enactment of civil rights requirements. Since they could not prevent changes from taking place earlier, they will try and rescind them now while they have an element of political control. They have a difficult time seeing themselves living with people for whom they feel superior.

Discharged Airman Questioned Obama's Citizenship

August 28, 2011

The *Associated Press* ran a story (8-18-11) about an Air Force Staff Sgt. Daryn Moran, who refused to accept a duty assignment in Germany. His reason for the refusal was that he doubts President Barack Obama's citizenship. The Air Force said it is discharging Moran.

The article referred to Moran as a hero to the birthers and added, "Although the 41-year-old Nebraska man refused to report to duty and had called for Obama's arrest in statements on websites, several other things contributed to his discharge, including his opposition to allowing gays to serve openly in the military." While a discharge of Moran would be in order, the military should consider other forms of action in order to protect itself from others who might want to follow Moran's example.

The very first course of action the military should take against Moran is a complete psychiatric examination. One has to question the mental stability of a 41-year-old Staff Sgt. who, after all his time in the Air Force, questions the citizenship of his commander in chief. What the important concern here is not the doubt of the president's citizenship, but the fact that Moran rejects the competency of all the people who voted for the president as well as the people who vetted all the presidential candidates. He even challenges the competency of the Supreme Court in swearing in Obama as president.

So, if all the people responsible for electing President Obama and having him assume
that role are wrong or mistaken about his qualifications as a citizen of the United States, then who is right?

Evidently, Moran has been greatly influenced by the birthers. That influence came in spite of the fact that "Obama released a copy of his detailed birth certificate from Hawaii in April in an attempt to quell the questions about whether he was born outside the U.S." None-the-less, Moran did not accept this information and like many of the birthers, considered it fake. So, under these circumstances, when someone rejects the actions of people who are in responsible positions to provide accurate information, the rational mental condition of the person doing the rejecting must come into question.

The next action the military should take is a court-martial, because this member of the Air Force disobeyed a direct order. If the court determines that an offense was committed, then Moran should be made to pay for his offense. An important part of the military is the discipline that is required to maintain maximum effectiveness. If a breakdown occurs in the chain of command, then the effectiveness is destroyed. If Staff Sgt. Moran is allowed to refuse the orders of his commander in chief, what is there to prevent other military personnel from doing the same thing?

What is interesting about Moran's action is the fact that he bypassed the order of command between himself and the president to offer his reasons for disobeying his orders. His court-martial hearing should include questions about why he directed his focus on the president and why did he not challenge the past presidents he served under.

As a relatively high-ranking member of the enlisted military, part of Moran's responsibility is to serve as an example for those under him. If the example he serves shows disrespect to the commander in chief, then his example is destructive and detrimental to the military service. When members of the military swear to protect and defend the country, they do not get to add to that pledge "only if they personally find the commander in chief to be acceptable to them." In hearing his case, the court should take into consideration the collateral effect Moran's action might have on the other troops.

The final action the Air Force should take in addition to the discharge is to make it an honorable discharge. For most military personnel, questioning the orders of a commander is extraordinary. One might understand refusing to join the military as a conscientious objector, but that happens at the beginning of military service. What would motivate someone who has risen to the rank of Staff Sgt. to question the status of the president?

Most people in or out of the military would look upon this action as suspicious. Some might even go so far as to think that Moran is using this excuse as a ploy to leave the Air Force. We are told that the birthers view Moran as a hero because "Moran, who has served nine years in the Air Force, drew the attention of the birther movement when he shared his views on Obama's citizenship on websites of groups that believe Obama is not eligible to serve as president or commander in chief."

If the military would allow all its personnel to follow in the footsteps of Moran one wonders what kind of military it would be. One of the byproducts of questioning the citizenship of Obama is not having to say that the reason for refusing his orders from the president is because he is African American. If the reason is not about his ethnicity, then it is about questioning the creditability of the state of Hawaii.

Either way, Moran's mental state has to be taken into consideration because his actions do a disservice to the military and to all those who follow the rules of military command. The military, like society, has established rules of conduct that help to promote order, peace, and justice. When anyone in society decides to break any of its rules, he or she must understand that consequences are also in place to deal with the rule breakers. These consequences are created and enforced in order to maintain order and prevent chaos.

The Air Force or any branch of the military cannot prevent its personnel from having doubts or any thoughts whatsoever, but each person takes an oath of service. Unless Staff Sgt. Moran has forgotten, he took an oath that states:

> "I, (NAME), do solemnly swear (or affirm) that I will support and defend the Constitution of the United States against all enemies, foreign and domestic; that I will bear true faith and allegiance to the same; and that I will obey the orders of the President of the United States and the orders of the officers appointed over me, according to

regulations and the Uniform Code of Military Justice. So help me God."

The bold print was added for emphasis and to underscore the responsibility that Moran accepted when he joined the Air Force. His service is to his country regardless of who represents it. So, since he can no longer adhere to that pledge, then America is better served without him in uniform.

Bigotry Behind Obama Birth Question

May 1, 2011

The people who have for two years or more questioned the birth place of President Obama finally got the proof they requested—the original long form of his Hawaii birth certificate. Unfortunately, that was not really what they wanted. They really wanted to say that he was not an American citizen.

Regardless of what happens, these people will never be satisfied with anything Obama does and says because they are brain-damaged. They lack common sense, common decency, and patriotism.

First, they lack common sense in their supposed quest for Obama's real birth certificate because they never really wanted it. They merely wanted to create doubt in the minds of their fellow brained-damaged associates. Common sense should have informed them that someone in America would have uncovered the problem with Obama's birth place when he ran for Senator a few years ago. Certainly during the presidential campaign someone would have discovered the problem. Since no problem came to light, some people thought they would do the country a service and start a rumor about Obama's birth place just to create some doubt for the people who have not accepted him as president. The plan worked, but only for those with damaged minds because they lack the element of common sense.

Many Americans have graced the television cameras with words of doubt concerning the president's birth place. Why? Their minds are so constricted that it will not allow them to accept an African American male as the leader of America. So, since they cannot allow this image of Obama as president to enter their brains, they must combat it in any way they can and by any means available. They believe that the more people they are able to convince, the more likely it will prove to be an illusion. In reality they know their battle is loss, but they cannot stop fighting because they lack common sense.

Merriam-Webster Dictionary sees common sense as "beliefs or propositions that most people consider prudent and of sound judgment, without reliance on esoteric knowledge or study or research, but based upon what they see as knowledge held by people "in common." Thus "common sense" (in this view) equates to the knowledge and experience which most people already have, or which the person using the term believes that they do or should have."

These same people also lack what is known as common decency because they act as though their actions to discredit President Obama are righteous. They fail to understand their inability to conform to prevailing standards of propriety or decorum and modesty. Their lack of understanding of decency and common sense give them the freedom to say and do whatever they believe is in keeping with their battle. In our democracy, we as citizens have the right to disagree with and, indeed, not like our president. We should, however, respect the office he holds, because it represents the leader of our country.

An example of someone lacking common decency is the Pastor of a small southern church who burned the Koran as a form of protest. What was he protesting? Another example is the pastor and his congregation who frequently protest the funerals of slain American soldiers. People with what is considered normal brain functions would not participate in any of the actions noted above. Those actions are not in keeping with acceptable decent behavior. So, the people who do participate in it must suffer from some brain-damage.

The other element lacking in the people who question the birth place of the president, in spite of all the evidence to the contrary, is a lack of patriotism. Since these people lack the elements of both common sense and common decency, they cannot or fail to see that their actions reflect negatively on America as their country and society. When they show a lack of respect for the office of the President of the United States or the word of a sovereign state such as Hawaii, then their actions suggest a lack of love, care, and respect for this country.

Common sense and common decency tells us that one does not denigrate or try to cast aspersions at the leader of one's country or disrespect the honor and authority of a state if you love and care for it. Most people would agree that protest can be a very positive and constructive form of democracy, because it shows people who want change within the government and are willing to work for it. Actions that lack common sense and decency are negative and destructive. They should have no place in a democracy because they work against it.

What is it about these people who question President Obama's birth place that keeps them in an attack mode? They are in a battle for their minds. They were raised to never accept an African American as an equal because if they do then that makes them no longer the standard for being normal. If everybody is considered normal, then how can they, the European Americans, be viewed as superior to all non-European Americans, and especially African Americans?

Once we understand that their battle is not about a birth place or certificate, but about a false perception created by society, yet believed to be true, then we will realize that the battle will continue under any guise just as long as Obama is held mentally at bay. Common sense and rational thought is not sufficient to satisfy their damaged brains nor is concrete evidence.

These comments are not meant to demean or belittle the people in question. We need to understand why they do what they do in regards to President Obama. The inability to accept reality represents a serious problem for some people, especially the ones who cannot accept Obama, an African American, as President of the United States. So, for that reason, they have to create life-lines for themselves to keep their image of self-worth and superiority alive. In doing so, they forgo common sense, common decency, and patriotism.

Gen. Powell Identifies Concerns for the Republican Party

January 15, 2013

On Sunday (1/13/13) General Colin Powell was on Meet the Press and spoke with David Gregory about some of the problems with his political party, the Republican Party. General Powell, a former Secretary of State in the last Bush administration, is a well-respected statesman as well as an African American. Most people listen when Powell talks because he does not generally engage in idle chatter. If anyone witnessed the interview, then there is no question about the seriousness of Powell's comments. He talked about the Republican Party's identity problem, its shift, its need to be concerned with society's needs.

The first party problem Powell identified was that of the Party's identity. He stated, "In recent years, there's been a significant shift to the right and we have seen what that shift has produced, two losing presidential campaigns. I think what the Republican Party needs to do now is take a very hard look at itself and understand that the country has changed." In what can be considered constructive criticism, Powell makes the suggestion that the party takes a good look at itself and recognize the variety and diversity of its membership to see what needs to be addressed for a successful future. With the failure of the party in the last two elections, something must be done to correct the problem. Powell even pinpoints the problem regarding the party's identity: "The country is changing demographically. And if the Republican Party does not change with that demographic, they're going to be in trouble."

Powell's comments come as no surprise since most news pundits as well as ordinary citizens realized that after the elections the majority of minority and women voted for Obama. A number of Republicans also noted the lack of support of ethnic Americans for Republican candidates. All Powell was doing was underscoring the problem and challenge his party faces. The lack of ethnic diversity in the Republican Party calls attention to itself.

The shift Powell refers to, meaning to the right, is cause for concern also. Many of the party representatives hold views that show a lack of concern and compassion for the well-being of some of our less-fortunate citizens. Their primary concern seems to be in total support of the rich and powerful at the expense of the working and middle class citizens. All one has to do is look at the record of Congress the last four years for verification of this fact. If the party wants to be successful in the future, according to Powell, it must expand its membership and become more receptive to the middle-class and minorities.

With respect to the party's identity, Powell stated that it has developed what he called "a dark vein of intolerance" in its perception. For example, when President Obama was first elected, Mitch O'Connell made the statement that the number one objective of the party was to make Obama a one term president. All the efforts of the party since that statement seem to throw support towards that objective. Unfortunately, the first order of business for many of the Republicans was to show disrespect for the president. This show of disrespect became apparent in a variety of ways.

Although Powell does not say so directly, his examples show that the disrespect was meant to convey a specific message regarding the president's ethnicity. Powell mentions the reference made by ex-Governor Palin regarding his "shucking and jiving," which can only be associated with African Americans and the slavery experience. Another reference made by a Republican official after the first presidential debate to President Obama as seeming to be "lazy," a term generally associated with a negative stereotype of African Americans, as opposed to some other term. To Powell, these references show a negative and mean-spirited attack on the president's ethnicity. The birther movement challenged his citizenship in spite of the documentation shared with the public– birth certificates, newspaper birth announcements, etc.

Powell also included the party's negative actions regarding immigration, voter suppression, and general actions underscoring an attitude of intolerance of minorities. Although Powell's comments were meant to alert his party to many of its problems, the likelihood of some of the people in his party receiving his comments as constructive criticism is questionable. Some will attack Powell because he spoke at all; some will criticize him of pointing out the problems and challenges; some will condemn his as a turn-coat or a Democrat in disguise. In any event, his comments will be met with ungrateful attitudes especially because he is an African American.

Powell sees himself as a mainstream Republican who cares deeply for his party and would like to see it address its many problems. His final comments during the interview underscore that idea:

> I think the Party has to take a look at itself. It has to take a look at its responsibilities for health care. It has to take a look at immigration. It has to take a look at those less fortunate than us. The party has gathered unto itself a reputation that it is the party of the rich. It is the party of lower taxes. But there are a lot of people who are lower down the food chain, the economic chain, who are also paying lots of taxes relative to their income, and they need help. We need more education work being done in this country. We need a solid immigration policy. We have to look at climate change.

Chances are the Republicans will overlook Powell's comments and move ahead with the plans they have in place. After all, they do not have to worry about being re-elected to office since most come from gerrymandered state districts. Some probably see Powell as an unfortunate nuisance.

National Election Shows that Prejudice and Hatred are Alive and Well in America

November 7, 2010

When the leader of the GOP says that their top goal is to make Obama a one term president, we have little choice but to believe him. Sen. Mitch McConnell left no doubt in the minds of the American people that the GOP will do nothing that appears to help Obama, even if their actions will hurt the rest of the country. Whether one considers the reason to be Obama's ethnicity or his political party the GOP's objective is the same—get rid of Obama.

Since day one of Obama's election he has been the target of the GOP. Why?

First, and foremost, is that they do not respect him as a person and especially as the leader of our country. However, to state the reasons publically would cast a light of prejudice on them, so, they resist it. What they do instead is attack everything he says and does in a manner that forces him to defend himself continuously. Of course, if he chooses to defend himself, he simply opens the door for more accusations; the game becomes a Catch-22.

Shortly after Tuesday's election McConnell reiterated the GOP's objective of making Obama a one term president. His reasons for this wish is because Obama does not follow the wishes of the GOP, but chooses to try and run the government in a rational, logical, and practical way that benefits the working and poor Americans. The GOP will have none of this foolishness. McConnell says that

> "…if our primary legislative goals are to repeal and replace the health spending bill; to end the bailout; cut spending; and shrink the size and scope of government, the only way to do all these things is to put someone in the White House who won't veto any of these things."

In other words, the GOP has said that it is their way or no way.

Tuesday's election showed in many instances that the politics of rejection works, even if it works against the people who voted for it. In Oklahoma, for example, the Republican candidates did not have to run on issues against their opponents; they ran only against Obama. They ran the table in winning all the Republican offices from "governor to dog catcher." The state's largest newspaper, the *Oklahoman*, stated that "Republican legislative leaders were ecstatic Wednesday by posting record gains in both chambers after several Democratic incumbents were knocked out of office by a buzz saw named President Barack Obama." Please take note of the statement relative to why the candidates won—they ran against Obama!

The newspaper article (11/5/10) continued by stating that "People were voting against Barack Obama and (House Speaker) Nancy Pelosi," said Rep. Glen Bud Smithson, D-Sallisaw, who lost his bid for a fifth term." The mention of Pelosi was just to fill space. The real reason according to Smithson is that "The candidate really didn't matter. They were voting Republican because they hate our president." So, as far as this candidate was concerned, voting Republican was a hate vote to hurt Obama. Why do they hate Obama? Evidently, the hate does not come from his party affiliations but from his ethnicity. Had it come from his party affiliations then there would have been specific issues presented for addressing. None were mentioned.

So for those who want to downplay the ethnicity issue and focus on the party partisanship, what happens when nothing regarding the arguments on issues is presented? What are we left with as reason for the hatred? The only logical reason comes from slavery's legacy—the African American's lack of positive value.

One of the most important historians of the Reconstruction period was William A. Dunning who saw this period as a failure. His sentiments regarding the freeing of the slaves were based on their being the reason for the war. After the war, the freedmen were used as a form of punishment for the South and its pro-slavery sympathizers. In any event, anger and fear of pro-slavery in the South relative to the freedmen was created and housed in the Democratic Party.

The mixture of fear and anger originated during the Reconstruction period because of the various acts that gave privileges to the Freedmen. Dunning (Essays on The Civil War and Reconstruction 1897) states that, "Enfranchisement of the blacks was to accompanied by disfranchisement of the whites. Not that distinctions of color were embodied by express term in the laws; nothing so invidious would have been tolerated at that date, and nothing of the kind was necessary."

The rationale of the South was that when the freedmen (African Americans) were given something by the government, something was taken away from the Southern European American. To be more explicit about the South and its pro-slavery sympathizers regarding their feelings towards the freedmen Dunning adds that

> "It was thought that the anticipated evils of the black vote might perhaps be mitigated by giving all the whites an equal part in politics; and doubtless some felt that the imposition of negro suffrage and the prospect of negro domination constituted a sufficient punishment for the leaders in rebellion."

The fear and anger of African Americans in positions of political leadership has long been a concern of some European Americans. The South and its pro-slavery Sympathizers felt right after the Civil War that the rights and privileges given to the African Americans was a form of punishment for them. The fear of the Southern European Americans was so great that they created in the various states law known as "The Black Codes" to keep total control of the freedmen. The Republican Party during that time was the champion of the freedmen, along with President Lincoln. They were able to pass the 13th, 14th, and 15th Amendments. The Democrats were more concerned with states' and individual's rights and keeping control of the freedmen.

Everything changed in 1964 when the Democratic President, Lyndon B. Johnson signed the 1964 Civil Rights bill. What that bill did was to remove, by law, anything that could be used by the European Americans as privilege over not only African Americans, but also all ethnic Americans. The Republican

Party took up the mantle of saving the privilege and prestige of the European Americans, so the South began to move to the Republican Party and many of the southern Democrats joined them. In essence, the parties switched roles with the Democrats becoming the people's party and the GOP representing those citizens who worked towards restoring the privileges and prestige the European Americans enjoyed prior to civil rights.

Today, the references to Washington bailouts, Obamacare, out of control spending, and the Democratic Party by the Republicans are all camouflaged phrases that simply means president Obama. The hate and fear are not hidden from the American citizens. What is obvious is as Smithson stated concerning the Tuesday election in Oklahoma, "The candidates really didn't matter. They were voting Republican because they hate our president."

A Lesson from Biases in Obama's Election

December 21, 2010

A little over two years ago, many Americans, especially those on the political right, were filled with anger and madness over the election of Barack Obama. Many Americans believed that never in their lifetime would America have an African American president. The anger came from what they considered a surprise attack from the political left; the madness came from the fact that the attack was successful. They were faced with the question of what to do next. We have discussed many time the lack of value placed by European Americans in African Americans going back to the time of slavery.

Some of the fears were based on the false stereotyped beliefs about African Americans held by many European Americans. For example, will Obama seek revenge for the injustices committed by the European Americans in the past against the African Americans? Will Obama have the leadership qualities necessary to run the government? Will Obama be the president of all the people, left, right, and middle? These questions were generated from the stereotypical beliefs of the African American's lack of intelligence and general incompetence.

Americans have known for over two hundred years that African Americans, as well as other ethnic Americans, have not been treated fairly in employment, education, and housing. With that information in mind, hearing that Obama, an African American was elected president, fear was created in the mind of many that he would somehow seek revenge. They were under the belief that Obama would seek to turn the tables on society in favor of the African Americans.

In the past, African Americans did not have the power and influence to make any kind of major social change. So, in an effort to try and head him off at the pass, Obama critics created a campaign to demonize, discredit, and destroy him. They did this in a variety of ways, but mainly through the media, calling him names, creating pictures of him as Hitler, as clowns, as stereotypical negative caricatures. They challenged his religious beliefs and even referred to him as the antichrist. In essence, they tried to portray his as a devil.

Americans are generally not well informed about cultural ethnicity; they believe and hold on to whatever they were led to believe in their homes and communities. Unfortunately, much of what they received are stereotypes that picture African Americans as lazy, ignorant, stupid, immoral, and a host of other negative features. These stereotypes came to the surface when Obama became president. The critics began to label him by challenging his education and experiences. They paid no attention to his accomplishments, only those things they thought would somehow discredit him. Even today many people question Obama citizenship, refusing to accept the evidence that confirms his identity as American. One would not think that a person's ethnicity could cause such a campaign of hatred and anger, but it did.

Probably the most challenging element in Obama's presidency came in the form of the Republican attitudes of no compromise and no second term for him. However, to Obama's credit, he demonstrated to his naysayers as well as to the world that he was more than capable to govern, negotiate, and take a leadership position in conducting the people's business.

If the people who had misgivings about Obama's so-called defects take a moment and look at what he has accomplished in two short years, they would realize that he has done more in two years than any of the presidents in the last fifty years. He has also done more for the middleclass, working class, and poor Americans than any president in the last several decades.

Many critics have tried lately to predict what Obama would, should, or could do in confronting some of the challenges he has had to face. When he does not fit into the box created for him, the critics complain that he is doing too little or too much or that he is leaning too far left or right. Regardless of what he does, his critics are never satisfied. What these critics fail to realize is that Obama will never fit into their box because he will not conform to their expectations.

They have no idea for what it is like being an African American president. They have no base of reference from which to measure him except the example of past presidents. They, however, provide little information outside of political protocol from which to make comparisons. All humans are unique, and Obama, because he is in an African American and in a unique historical position, will defy comparisons to other presidents.

Some might offer the argument that Obama should be judged by the same measuring stick that all presidents are judged. If Obama's life experiences were comparable to those of the European American presidents then that might be a good idea, but we know that is not the case. Throughout his campaign Obama tried to avoid bringing in his ethnicity as an element for political consideration. His naysayers did the job for him. In a speech to the nation, he made a special effort to underscore the fact that his ethnicity should not be a factor in his campaign. Little good that did for his critics; they continued to try and discredit and destroy him politically.

Whether one agrees or disagrees with Obama's policies, likes or dislikes him personally, when one measures his accomplishments in his short term in office with the expectation of his failure, one cannot argue with his success against tremendous obstacles. We all can learn a lesson from what we as a people are experiencing with Obama as president. The lesson that should underscore Obama's presidency, keeping in mind the fact that he is an African American, is that the sense of value and judgment placed on his ethnicity and color is misleading.

The adage that says we should never judge a book by its cover can certainly apply here. Prejudice and bigotry more often than not creates distortions and a lack of clarity. Ethnicity and color is never a substitute for competency and character.

President Obama, Biracial Versus Black, Not a Problem

November 20, 2012

In an opinion article by Patrice Peck published in the *Grio*, "Biracial versus black: Thought leaders weigh in on the meaning of President Obama's biracial heritage," he asked the question of how to identify the president—biracial or black. What Peck and the "Thought leaders" are doing in attempting to answer that question is the same as beating a dead horse—counterproductive.

The Western world, American society, and especially, African Americans have accepted the concepts of multiple biological races of human being as well as the concept of a black race and a white race as factual. If we are to educate ourselves and our children with accurate, factual, and up-to-date information, then we need to abandon the concepts of races, black and white.

In my latest book, "America's Race Matters: Returning the Gifts of Race and Color," I discuss the problems attendant to continuing to promote the false concepts of race and color. Most educated people know that race is a social construct, made-up like other myths– Santa Claus, Easter Rabbit, and Tooth Fairy. While society recognizes these latter myths as myths, they still want to hold on to the myth of races and color.

Unfortunately, our changing world and society are forcing us to make adjustments to our concepts or become more confused and misinformed. With respect to African Americans, the willingness to accept the color identity given them by a slave-owning society to deny them a positive self-identity is way past due. We will be more specific about that issue later.

If we want to educate ourselves and our children about race, let us be factual—all human beings belong to one race, *Homo sapiens*. If some doubt exists about this fact, the people who subscribe to the Christian religion might want to reference in the Bible, Acts 17:24-26 which states in part:

"God that made the world and all things therein, seeing
that he is Lord of heaven and earth, dwelleth not in temples
made with hands; neither is worshiped with men's hands,
as though he needed anything, seeing he giveth to all life,
and breath, and all things; And hath made of one blood all
nations of men for to dwell on all the face of the earth..."

(The bold print supplied by the writer). So, we are one people
as for as God is concerned; so why not accept that concept?

We are not restricted to what the Bible says about being one
race. The Human Genome Project mapped the Human DNA
sequence in total. What the research tells us is that

"we [human beings] are so much alike, that only our
individuality separates us. For every group [ethnic group]
assumption there are several exceptions that can be shown.
While we [scientists] can identify your ancestry, DNA
tells us that we share so much in common that any two
individuals on earth can trace some common ancestry in
six generations or less."

So now we can recognize that by accepting the false concept
of multiple biological races, we invite the acceptance of additional
false concepts of racism, racial, mixed-race, and yes, even biracial.
So, when the race experts and intellectuals continue to promote
the concept of races, they are not presenting factual, accurate, and
current information. President Obama is neither biracial nor black;
he is African American.

Now the acceptance of the term black or black race or white
or white race falls in the same category as does the term race. The
term race was determined by world renowned scientists in 1945 to
be ineffective as a social term (see UNESCO). In other words, the
word race should not be used as a form of identity as in black race
and white race. Instead, the term ethnicity or ethnic groups would
be more accurate and certainly less confusion.

The Census Bureau has discovered the confusion created by
not defining the words race and ethnicity from the data received

in the 2010 survey. Still, they refuse to drop the term race; so the confusion will not only continue, but also grow.

Part of the problem with using colors to identify people is that it does not work and actually does them a disservice. No one comes to America as a black or white person; they must use their cultural or geographical identity. Once here, they can evaluate the positives and negatives associated with changing their identity. Most European Americans select a white identity; most people of color retain their cultural or geographical identity because they see no value in being identified as black.

Eighty percent of the world's population is people of color, all shades; twenty percent of the world's population would be considered "white" in America. In America the color white has positive social as well as historical value, the color black does not except for the African American community.

President Obama is not black because black is a color, not an identity. To underscore this point we might ask the questions: what language do black people speak, from what country do they reside, what culture do they exhibit, and what religion do they embrace? We can ask the same questions of so-called white people as well. What we discover in the responses is a lack of certainty and understanding relative to race. Technically, all people are of African ancestry, but those people of color living in American with African ancestry are more correct in referring to themselves as African Americans rather than black. The people who identify themselves as white can more accurately refer to themselves as European Americans.

So, if Mr. Peck is fortunate enough to have children, he should tell them that President Obama is an African American, not a biracial or black person. They, his children can identify themselves in a manner that suits them, except for black or white, because the colors say nothing about who they are; they are merely colors, and not accurate colors at that. Society does not care what African Americans call themselves, so it is up to the African American community to start divorcing itself from the term black which was given them during slavery. Although the cultural revolution of the sixties and seventies did much to change the negative concept of the term black, it did not change anything in the European American community. The time for updating identity is here. America is rapidly turning brown and when it does, color will be insignificant.

Playing the Race Card is Not a Winner

January 24, 2011

A phrase that is frequently heard but never quite fully understood is "playing the race card." The phrase calls attention to the socially created phenomena known as race.

In America, society acts like only two significant races exist; they are the black race and the white race. This race game has been played in America since America's beginning. The phrase was created by the majority society (European Americans) and is used in a number of ways, but usually with reference to African Americans. The figurative language of the phrase reflects the actions relative to a card game or an argument where a trump card or point is used to control or get an advantage in the action. The reference to race indicates a reference to the historical significance to America's race experience and initiates an emotional response in a positive or negative way.

The race card can be used by any Politian regardless of party or gender. For example, if a political candidate makes the claim that his opponent is using the race card, the expectations of the candidate are either to gain support from people who believe his claim and support his assumption. One the other hand, the candidate knows that some people will see the claim as part of a strategy to discredit his opponent's argument. The risk in using the race card is that it can work both ways—for or against the user.

Many national figures have found ways to invoke the race card without making a direct reference to it. They have developed code words that serve the same purpose. For example, if a speaker wants to gain the support of people who are biased against African Americans, he can use words like Affirmative Action and civil rights as being negative social elements, and he knows that those who support those beliefs will line-up behind him. On the other hand, a speaker who wants to appeal to liberal minded people can use other coded words to the opposite effect, words like birthers, conservatives, and right wingers. So, regardless of the position desired by the speaker, words and phrases are available to affect the race card.

Generally speaking, when a claim of using the race card is made, it is usually made by someone in reference to African Americans and certainly not by African Americans because that would defeat the purpose.

For example, many Americans, not African Americans, say that Barack Obama was elected president because he is an African American. That statement would be an instance of using the race card. The argument is not a valid one, however, because if his ethnicity was the only criterion used to elect him, why weren't Jesse Jackson, Al Sharpton, Alan Keyes, or Shirley Chisholm elected president? So, the claim falls flat because it has no rational basis for support. However, in making the claim, many biased people will readily agree with the claim that, indeed, Obama was elected because of his ethnicity. The agreement comes because of the bias created by pitting one ethnic group against another.

Another example of using the race card occurred more frequently in the late '60s and continues today to some extent. With the passage of the '64 Civil Rights Act, employers were asked not to discriminate on the bases of color, gender, religion, and race (ethnicity). Also, some stipulations regarding diversity of workforce were required of employers depending on the number of employees they had. In refusing to consider some applicants for employment, some company representatives use the race card by saying that the applicant's chances for employment were not possible because of Affirmative Action, or because of a Government quota. The so-called Government quota required the company to hire a certain percentage of ethnic minorities, so that left them out of consideration.

Regardless of who uses the race card or when it is used, the primary issue involves whether African Americans are being discriminated against or being made to be the victim of an unjust and unfair society. What is generally missing from the use of the race card is the history that created the value for the phrase.

Too many Americans have forgotten and too many never learned the fact that ethnic bias, especially against African Americans, was a way of life for a few hundred years. Society would not have corrected the discrepancy on its own. After all, women did not get to vote until 1920. So, the government had to make the corrections. If looked at from another perspective, one might say that the majority ethnic group in America (primarily males) enjoyed liberties and privileges for three hundred years, not shared or enjoyed by other ethnic American citizens.

So, when the term "playing the race card" is used, one must take the time to see who is using it and for what purpose. The chances are that someone is trying to protect some special privilege or interest and wanting to keep it from being shared with others. In essence, the phrase is a "divide and conquer" tactic or strategy that is used to either gain an advantage in an argument or discredit one's opposition. The phrase should not be used at all, but if it is used, it should be changed to "playing the ethnic card," since race is no longer an accurate term.

The fact that the term race is used at all is an indication that the user still sees the different American ethnic groups as separate races. Instead of someone trying to identify the playing of the race card, he should realize that playing it at all is a foolish game that no one wins.

Race Language in America Needs Change

July 24, 2010

America needs to stop and take an accounting of itself in the wake of President Obama's election. What on the surface seemed like a country coming together as of lately seems like a country more divided than ever. The claims of progress in our democratic society seem to be unfounded in light of the barrage of negativisms hurled toward Obama.

Americans and Obama made history when they elected him as president. Something else happened as well, a calling up of ethnic hate and fear that had been laying semi dormant for a while. With Obama as the leader of the country, the fear and hate began to rise to the surface because people who did not want Obama and the country to succeed felt an urgency to stop him at all cost.

One of the primary changes America needs to make involves language. As human beings, we have the gift of language that helps us to identify and choose good from bad, right from wrong. When we use language for negative reasons, we should not be surprised to get negative results.

When Americans believed that people were identified as belonging to a race by the color of their skin, the word race seemed appropriate. The derivatives of race such as racial, racist, and racism were used to identify a specific aspect of race. Today, Americans know that the belief of race by skin color is not valid, so the obvious actions would be to discontinue the use of the word race and its associated words. Therein lies the problem. Race was used as the bases from bigotry, bias, discrimination, and prejudice.

Unfortunately, race is still the basis today for much of the fear and hatred surrounding politics on every level of government.

Let us be clear on the definition of the word racism; The American Heritage Dictionary defines it as "The notion that one's own ethnic stock is superior." In America, the ethnic group to hold and promote that notion has been the European Americans. The very nature of the words bigotry, bias, discrimination, and prejudice informs us that any and all humans can and usually do possess a degree of these feelings. But each of these terms is different from racism or racist because they represent a group of like-minded people.

So, when the word racist or racism is directed towards, for example, an African American or Asian American, no bases exist in America to validate the claim. What usually is meant in reference to calling non-European Americans racist is one of the other terms. The language of race or racism does not fit.

The negative language used by some members of the Right in America has created and promoted the feelings of fear and hate directed especially at Obama and his administration. In an effort to try and justify their notion of superiority, they focus their attention of Obama or African Americans as the enemy. Just what is the enemy doing? Absolutely nothing, but that is beside the point.

They use the fear and hateful language to stir-up the European Americans who are led to believe that they are losing or giving up something important to non-European Americans, but especially to African Americans. If these Obama critics find anyone even remotely associated with Obama and his administration that can be used as a symbol of racism, that person is exploited because he or she helps to make their case for being bias.

If we reflect on Obama's recent past, we have little difficulty remembering incidents that were used to paint a picture of him showing preference to some African American individual or group and using that as proof of his being bias against European Americans. The most recent victim of this type of negative action is Mrs. Shirley Sherrod. She gave a speech at an NAACP meeting that underscored her belief in helping poor people, regardless of their color. In explaining her epiphany, she used language that was later taken out of context to try and show her to be a bigot.

Because of the altered language being broadcast over the airways, her boss heard about the claims of racism via the broadcast, but not the circumstances surrounding it and rushed to judgment, not wanting to be seen as condoning biased behavior, and forced her to resign. Once the full story of her speech and activity was made known, she was completely exonerated and offered a new position. President Obama called her personally and apologized to her and offered her a new position, since she was forced to resign from the previous one.

What did not follow was an apology and explanation from the media that created the first mistake of labeling her a racist. In her speech, Mrs. Sherrod used the word black and white to describe African Americans and European Americans. The use of the first terms feed directly into the plans of biased Americans. The language matters where race is of concern.

Language in and of itself cannot and will not eliminate bigotry, prejudice, discrimination and the like, but it can help to correct a wrong and set a course in the right direction. Since race is still a major problem in America we can use language to help us resolve it.

For example, the word bastard has a denotation and a connotation. When the denotation is used the meaning is clear and effective; however, when the connotation is used, the intent is negative. So, regardless of the word preceding bastard, the connotation remains—nice bastard, good bastard, Christian bastard, etc. The word race acts the same way by suggesting that other human races exists. The words black and white are used with the intention of race following them. Rational human beings know when language is right or wrong, good or bad.

Once we begin to use the appropriate language regarding ethnicity, we will lose the issue that continues to keep the nation divided—race. Yes, by changing the language of race some Americans will lose their sense of privilege and superiority, but, hopefully, they will gain membership in a larger group of patriotic, God-fearing, freedom-loving, fair-minded Americans who want to see America realize its full positive potential.

Changing the language will not automatically change a person's perspective. Bigotry, biases, prejudice, and discrimination will continue to exit, but from individuals, not groups called racists. If we persist in maintaining the negative, fear and hate-creating syndrome, we will only prolong the time when reason can step forth and take its rightful place in the hearts and minds of those citizens who really love this great country. Reason will prevail eventually; it will just take more time to overcome the ignorance that continues to try and block it.

Beck's Actions Show Bigotry

June 5, 2010

Glenn Beck's bigotry shows ignorance and stupidity. According to an old saying, "it is better to be thought a fool than to speak and remove all doubt." This saying is appropriate for the conservative talk show host Glenn Beck.

Beck recently used a segment of his radio show to make fun of President Barack Obama's 11-year-old daughter, Malia. He poked fun at her by affecting a young person's flimsy voice and trying to imitate her in a dialogue with his radio co-host, Pat Gray. Both men displayed a total lack of character and decency by their actions. Beck, however, was the instigator of the ruse and so deserves the focus of attention. By his actions, Beck showed his ignorance, stupidity, and bigotry.

President Obama made the statement during a press conference that his daughter, Malia, greeted him with the question, "Did you plug the hole yet, Daddy?" In an effort to try and denigrate this young lady, Beck missed the opportunity to show that this 11-year-old was very astute. She recognized the responsibility her father, the president, had regarding this national concern by asking the question. She also showed concern for the people living on the gulf coast by asking the question. Finally, she showed concern for the environment by asking the question. Had Beck been of a mind to address the issue with class, he would not have tried to make fun of a serious situation. However, he does not stop here.

Pat Gray, in an effort to imitate the president, responded to Beck with "Honey, not yet...Not time yet, honey. Hasn't done enough damage." The implication is that the president is deliberately waiting for more damage to occur before taking corrective measures. Why would Beck and Gray want to cast aspersions against the office of the president and indeed, the president himself regarding such a critical situation? Also, what kind of person would give such a negative answer to an 11-year-old girl?

They evidently have little or no regard for either the office of the presidency, the president, or an 11-year-old girl, for that matter.

Do they not know that in the oath of office for the presidency, the first duty of the president is to protect and defend the country? Since that is the oath he swore to uphold, why would he want to do harm to the country via the oil spill on the gulf coast? In this regard, the action and language of both Beck and Gray reflect ignorance and stupidity.

The game continues for Beck as he again mimics Malia asking the question of her father concerning the oil spill. Beck then makes a comment regarding "the level of their education." The statement is incoherent except that Beck is trying to impugn the intellect of the president and his daughter. Ironically, his language and questioning a level of education seems to backfire on him. As stated earlier, the question from an 11-year-old girl shows more character and concern then the imbecilic action of two grown men with a national radio show. One wonders about their level of education.

Beck and Gray finally enter into an area that clearly shows their ignorance, stupidity, and bigotry—ethnicity. Beck once again talks in his idea of Malia's voice and ask "why do you hate black people so much?" The idea of this child asking such an absurd question is clearly unthinkable. The suggestions from the question is that the president has done or said something in the presence of his 11-year-old daughter that would lead her to believe her father hates someone. What would motivate Beck to place such a question in the voice of this child?

Our first answer might be stupidity. However, when we hear the response of Gray, we know the answer is bigotry.

Gray playing the role of President Obama, responses to the hate question saying "I'm part white, honey." That response shows the depth of ignorance, stupidity and bigotry expressed by Beck and Gray. The terms black and white are no longer correct or accurate. Neither term defines or depicts a person's ethnicity or culture.

We now live in the 21st Century and must make the necessary adjustments in an effort to educate ourselves. When we make those adjustments, we raise our level on consciousness to accommodate a more realistic perception of ourselves and others. Their use of the words black and white reflects a mindset that is held hostage in a world that places a value on people of various skin complexions with white being supreme. Beck and Gray see themselves as superior because they identify themselves as white (European American), they feel comfortable and at ease ridiculing people they view as inferior to themselves. They apparently still believe in races—black, white, red, brown etc.— none equal to their white race. Hence, we see the bigotry.

Beck issued an apology the next day because of complaints he received. However, being true to his biased perspective, his apology was not made to the president or Malia. His comment simply said that he was sorry only for breaking his own rule about not bringing children into politics. In other words, he feels that had no one complained, or he'd not gotten caught, all would be well.

When a person has no standards or values, he or she has nothing to stand on or for that matter is worthy of respect. People with biases and hatred against others can never rest or feel at peace for fear that they might miss an opportunity to express their negative feelings. Fear comes from ignorance. Ignorance can be corrected by acquiring information.

Stupidity and bigotry, like water, will exploit the point of least resistance. Silence is often used by the wise to hide short comings, but a loud voice will expose a fool every time. As the saying goes, "A word to the wise is sufficient."

Chicken Little and Obama Naysayers

July 3, 2010

Ever since the Obama election, some Americans, namely Republicans, tea partiers, conservatives and other Obama naysayers have been acting like the world is coming to an end. He has been characterized as a socialist, communist, fascist, antichrist, devil, alien, joker, Muslim, Hitler, tyrant, and a host of other equally complimentary terms. In addition, he is said to lack intelligence, courage, drive, common sense, integrity, Christian values, and male dominance qualities. He has been described as having a tragically flawed character.

As one might assume, all these features are negative because to them, his represents the voice of doom. The problem with this picture is that the representations are really reversed. The only loud and negative voices proclaiming doom and destruction of Americas are the naysayers. They are best characterized as belonging to the Chicken Little club.

If we recall they story, Chicken Little is hit on the head by a falling acorn which leads her to believe that the sky is falling. The Obama naysayers believe that his election as president signaled the sky falling or a loss of their privileges and control. What happens next is that fear and anxiety takes control of the club and they must spread the word that disaster and doom is imminent in America because Obama is now president. Every conceivable argument is employed to convince the people that the sky is calling or America has been taken from them by Obama. Since the story of Chicken Little has numerous endings, we will visit several to show how they fit the club.

One of the endings to the story suggests that when disaster strikes, one must face it head-on calling up as much courage as possible to meet the challenge. Unfortunately, the only courage the naysayers have conjured up is reflected in their fear and anxiety or their Obama name-calling and rejections.

Nothing created and/or promoted by Obama gives cause for believing the doom and destruction of America is imminent. After

all, America has three arms of government to make certain that
no one branch takes total control of society. What the action being
employed by the Chicken Little club shows is them simply being
chickens.

Another ending to the story involves both Chicken Little and
her listeners. As she makes her way to tell the king that the sky
is falling, she informs all the people she encounters. Rather than
question the validity of her information, they simply go along
with her.

Well, last weekend in Oklahoma City the epitome of the
Chicken Little story was being told by none other than Glen Beck
and Carl Rove (for a price). The title of their tale was not "The Sky
is Falling," but "Taking Back Our Country." The message is that
"real Americans" must stop and think about what has happened to
their country and once they realize that it is being held and changed
by Obama, they must fight to take it back. Unfortunately, many
of the story listeners and club members do not think, but simply
accept what is being said as valid and react on those bases. They
need to realize that "real Americans" do not believe everything
they are told; they check the facts first.

Another ending to the story involves the use of an outside
motivator who selects the bearer of the ill tidings in an effort to
convince the listeners. What happens is the outside motivator
wants a certain message presented to some people who will accept
it without question. So the outsider selects the dumbest person
available and convinces him or her that the sky is falling. That
person will proceed to go out and convince others that the message
is true. How does this happen? Most intelligent people will hear the
dumb person's message and assume it to be factual because they do
not believe the dumb person is not capable of manufacturing that
message on his or her own. Unfortunately, everyone in the story is
duped because they do not verify the information being presented.

The Chicken Little club and their activities fit easily into all
three of these scenarios because they are gullible and trusting. The
American public is at no loss to hear and see the talking heads on
radio and television warning them of the imminent disaster about

to befall America because Obama is the president. The reason for all this activity is fear that the world is coming to an end, as in the Chicken Little story.

But what is the cause of the fear?

Had Chicken Little stopped to examine the acorn that hit her on the head, she would have realized that only one acorn fell. Had the characters Chicken Little met on her way to the king asked her how she knew that the sky was falling, they would have discovered that she was over-reacting. Had the people who were convinced that Chicken Little's message was factual considered the source of the message, they would have reconsidered their response.

What is the fear of the Chicken Little club? Society, as they knew it is changing. One of the effects of that change is a loss of privilege and control over non-European American citizens based on color. Breaking old habits is difficult at best when few options are available for retaining the status quo. When change forces a departure from the old, comfortable, and convenient habits, the first reaction is defensive.

Change cannot occur in an undisturbed environment, so some adjustments must be expected. Common sense and reason will dictate to most Americans the actions that need to be taken if indeed the sky starts to fall or that we must take our country back from Obama and his Democrats before it is utterly destroyed. The power of fear is that it controls those who have fear, not the one creating said fear.

Chicken Little was just a dumb bird.

West's Remarks Reflect Negatively on Him, Not Obama

May 22, 2011

Recently a Princeton University professor, Cornel West, made some disparaging remarks about President Obama referring to him as a black puppet and a black mascot relative to his dealings with Wall Street and other entities. West's remarks are surprising in that they display more of him than of his characterization of the president. One generally expects the remarks of a noted professor to be informing, instructive, enlightening or even entertaining; that, however, was not the case this time.

West first characterized President Obama as a black puppet. All Americans have the right and privilege to speak freely, even about the president. West, however, showed a lack of respect for the office of the president by suggesting that he is an inanimate doll with strings attached to his limbs and head. The strings are controlled by others who manipulate the doll to resemble and suggest human movement. Certainly, one can disagree with the decisions the president makes, but to suggest that he is constantly being manipulated by others is an insult based on ignorance. The insult is not directed at Obama, but at West for making such an asinine remark.

If West believes that the president is being influenced by others and that influence negatively affects his decision making, then he should say so. Calling the president a puppet strikes at his character, not at his actions. If West came to the conclusion of Obama being a puppet based on his observations of Obama, then the problem is not with Obama, but with West's expectations of the president. In other words, because Obama is not doing what West expects or expected him to do then he must be a puppet, controlled by others.

West next characterized Obama as a black mascot. A mascot is defined as an animal, person, or thing adopted by a group as its representative symbol and it is supposed to bring good luck. Although most mascots are viewed favorably and with pride by the group they represent, West seems to suggest something nefarious with the use of this term and its association with Obama.

Again, the remarks attack the person and not his decisions. Obama is operating in new and challenging territories as president. He has and will make decisions that will not be well received by everyone. Making decisions that causes disagreements is part of the job of being president. West seems to be not in touch with reality when he criticizes Obama for being a mascot rather than for making decisions with which West does not agree. Maybe if we all knew Obama's thoughts prior to his making a decision we would be in a better position to assess it. Unfortunately, that is not the case.

What really casts a shadow on West and his remarks about Obama is the reference to black—black puppet and black mascot. One has to wonder about West's use of the term black in the context in which it appears. Is the reference to a black puppet a reference to a color or a cultural identity? If it is for a color than what is the significance of the color—bad, Evil? If the reference is to a cultural identity, then it is meaningless—black is neither a cultural identity nor an ethnic identity, African American is. So, what is the significance of the color preceding the noun?

The only sense it makes is to seemingly associate it with slavery and bigotry where the African slave was often forced to do his master's bidding. West seems to be stuck in the past with his reference to black puppet or he is deliberately trying to demean Obama by attacking his character. What comes to mind, however, is the character of West and his motives for making the remarks.

The reference to a black mascot occasions similar remarks as does the reference to the black puppet. The complexity of the president's responsibilities are not restricted to or evaluated by what is observable to the average citizen or even a well-informed citizen. So, for someone to assert that the president is not doing something or doing too much of something is pure conjecture because it is based on opinion.

West, apparently thinks that Obama should think like he thinks and act as he expects is foolhardy. West's reference to Obama as a black mascot seems to suggest that as in the days of slavery, African Americans were considered lacking in intelligence and incapable of making rational decisions. If that is the suggestion West is making, then he has no grasp of reality and Obama's record these past two years. Black is color, not an ideology or way of life. Obama knows that but, apparently, West does not.

Obama is not a black president serving black people. Although he received the majority of the African American vote in his bid of the presidency, he was not elected by black people. As president, Obama has to represent all Americans. West seems to think that Obama must address the concerns of African Americans specifically because of the biased treatment they encountered in the past and continue to experience today. West does not seem to understand that Obama as president cannot single out a group or groups of people for special privileges and treatment. If he was to do that, he would be accused of being biased, and rightly so. Just because he cannot address the problems of the poor and ethnic minorities individually does not mean that he is ignoring them. He simply must be allowed to do his work how and when he sees fit.

West is said to be a social activist as well as a professor. His concerns for the poor and unfortunate Americans are important to him. Whatever his efforts are in giving aid to these people, he cannot help their cause or his by making the kinds of remarks about President Obama referenced earlier.

West needs to understand that Obama is an African American who happens to be president of all the United States. Being African American is not synonymous with being what West calls black. To identify with the term black is to restrict one history to the American slavery experience and a total lack of self-worth and value except from a black perspective. Only those African Americans who want to hold on to the past and the bigotry it fostered accept the term black as an acceptable identity. Those who have moved on consider themselves African Americans.

Professor West might want to consider joining this latter group.

Eastwood's Antics a Matter of Subjective Interpretation

September 9, 2012

The classic song by Sly and the Family Stone "Everyday People" has a line that states "Different strokes for different folks," and this line came to mind when reading the various reactions to Clint Eastwood's appearance at the Republican National Convention. Those reactions revealed a world of differences among people who witnessed the same event but came away with different reactions. Regardless of the many reactions, Eastwood's performance showed ignorance, stupidity, and arrogance.

The reference to Eastwood's performance being ignorant is an assessment of him not knowing what was expected of him at that time. In effect, appearing before the audience during prime time carried a certain degree of importance to the organizers of the convention. Their expectations included a boost in support for their candidate by this famous movie personality.

Evidently, no one told Eastwood about the expectations, so he went on stage and improvised for twelve minutes with an empty chair. For the organizers of the convention, television time, especially prime time, was important for the party to get its message out to as many viewers as possible, so to have twelve minutes during prime time go for naught was not an effective use of time. According to some reports, Eastwood did not inform anyone as to what his plans were nor did anyone from the convention meet with him before his entrance on stage with the chair. So, the reference to ignorance points to a lack of information by Eastwood and the people responsible for the stage participants. Because no one knew what to expect from Eastwood, everyone was surprised by his performance.

Eastwood's performance as reported by the *Daily Beast* offered a sampling of remarks from a number of people. For example, Todd McCarthy, a critic for The Hollywood Reporter said, "It was very bizarre." He added, "To see this wackier thing happen is not in line with his super-cool personality that we're used to." Film critic Roger Ebert noted, "Clint, my hero, is coming across as sad and pathetic." Ben Affleck noted, "Even though I disagree with his politics, I've seen far more boring speeches in my day." Many other comments were given and they all represented a variety of reactions that reflected the uniqueness of the individuals.

To say that Eastwood's performance showed stupidity would be an understatement in light of the time and place he presented it. Since no one but Eastwood knew what was going to happen, no one was prepared for it. Since no one was prepared for it, time was wasted on the viewers trying to grasp just what was happening.

If Eastwood was to use his celebrity to enhance Romney's candidacy, he selected an ineffective avenue of approach to accomplish it. One must ask the question "what was the payoff in the performance?" Everyone witnessed the same spectacle of Eastwood on stage talking to an empty chair. Each individual had the opportunity to draw his or her conclusion about what was witnessed and its effectiveness. To many people, it was thought to be stupid and a waste of time.

Sometime after Eastwood's performance, we learned that he arrived at the convention about fifteen minutes before he was to go on stage. He had no prepared speech or notes with him. Just before he walked on stage he asked one of the stage workers to give him a chair. He walked on stage with the chair and proceeded to start a dialogue with an imaginary President Obama.

These actions reflect an arrogance that defies logic and just plain common sense, not to mention disrespect and absurdity. The show of arrogance comes from the willingness to assume to berate the President of the United States like a child being given a "time out," for whatever reason. Why would any person believe that placing any president in that position would garner respect from the performer?

The effort indicated a total disrespect for the office of the president and a lack of understanding of how both he and the imaginary president might be perceived.

In adding insult to injury, Eastwood impugned the integrity of the president by engaging in a dialogue that suggested the president used profanity in making a reference to Mitt Romney. This action was totally out of place and inappropriate for Eastwood. However, we must assume that he felt comfortable in doing it because of his celebrity that places him about regular folk and gives him license to do things regular folks cannot or would not do.

We still wonder about the purpose of the performance and the effect it was supposed to have on the viewers. We wonder if Eastwood was affecting a character from one of his many films or was he being himself. Either way, his lack of respect for the office of the president reflected poorly on him.

Some people might question the reasons for criticizing Eastwood and /or his performance since it only involved him having a conversation with a chair. His performance can be and was taken on a variety of levels and depending on the interpretation of the individuals and how they viewed the action and words, an assessment was made. The statement "Beauty is in the eyes of the beholder" provides an example of subjective interpretation, meaning that the criteria for making a judgment comes from the beholder. That being the case, we can understand how some people might have interpreted Eastwood's performance as a biased attempt to denigrate, disrespect, and dishonor President Obama, to "put him in his place" which meant an African American, regardless of his position, below and behind this European American celebrity.

Since subjective interpretation rests with the individual, we can simply go back to the words of the song to underscore the reality of "Different strokes for different folks. And so forth, and so on...."

Lowry Confuses Human Rights with Civil Rights

April 7, 2010

In a commentary, "Health Reform Fight Not Like Civil Rights," Rich Lowry (King Features Syndicate, 4-6.10) makes the claim that some Democrats and liberals are using the civil rights movement of the '60s as an example of that "era's expansion of freedoms." He adds that "when they denounce the bill's opponents, they compare them to segregationists."

He makes references to a number of African American congressmen who have recently encountered negative experiences by some of the opponents of the health care bill including John Lewis, and James Clyburn. In a comparison between the violence of the civil rights era and what is taking place today, he states that "It takes a clinical lack of proportion to draw a parallel between a mass beating of peaceful protester and some repulsive cretins shouting the N-word."

Lowry claims that when liberals place the negative behavior of health care opponents today with the behavior during the civil rights era that it is an abuse of history. Several references are made to Dr. Martin Luther King, Jr. and his philosophy and protest. Regarding the supporters of the health care bill, he states that they "invoke his (King's) movement now precisely because of their inability to persuade. Accusing the bill's critics of racism and comparing them to the segregationist mobs of the 1960s is about silencing and delegitimizing them." He adds that "It expropriates the unquestioned moral authority of the civil rights movement and then uses it as a political bludgeon. It substitutes rhetorical thuggery for argument."

Lowry obviously does not understand or appreciate just what society is experiencing since the election of President Obama and the civil rights movement. He talks about the civil rights movement of the 1960s as if there were not detractors or violence, hatred, and death. He fails to understand that the anger and violence of many of the opponents of the health care bill are based on fear and frustration.

Their fears and frustrations did not start with the health care bill; it started before the 1964 Civil Rights Bill. The election of Obama as president increased the level of fear and frustration to the panic level. What is the basis of this fear and frustration? They are afraid of losing their mythical place of privilege; their sense of being superior to all non-European Americans, but especially, African Americans.

What Lowry fails to see is that the health care bill is just veneer to cover the fear and frustration of losing their cherished identity of being "white," and the associated privileges of the past that it produced. The civil rights movement of the 1960s began the major process of eroding those precious rights, but many ways were used to prevent the total destruction. With the election of Obama, the truth has to be confronted.

Being "white" with all its privileges was just a game whose time has run out. Unfortunately, many so-called "whites" are not ready to give up their pseudo status, so they fight with any and everything they can to keep it. The truth be told, all the negative actions by Obama's opponents are against what Obama represents to them. Why make everything focus on Obama? Why is the health care bill called by opponent "Obamacare"? The worse possible experience so-called "whites" can have is to have a "non-white" be seen as their equal. Obama transcends the equal level as president, so the fear and frustration is traumatic.

Another point concerning Lowry's lack of perception is that what is being compared between the civil rights movement and the reactions of the opponents of the health care bill is attitude. Check all the Civil Rights legislation and you will not find a single reference to African Americans. Why? Because African Americans were intent on receiving the same rights enjoyed by the European American citizens. Civil Rights should belong to all Americans.

What the Obama opponents seemingly lack is a knowledge of and respect for human rights. Human rights are a matter of decency that no law can enforce. The general rule is to do unto others as you would have them do unto you.

When Lowry and the Obama opponents finally figure out that the world is not coming to an end, and that being on the same level with other human beings is an OK place to be, then maybe they can turn those fears and frustrations into something positive to help America become a better place for all. Taking pot shots at the president and his supporters might bring some temporary satisfaction, but lends to nothing positive to build on.

American Protest and Prejudice

May 8, 2010

When the pilgrims arrived in America, they brought with them the mindset that God had given them this country. They simply had to remove its present occupants and take control. We must remember that these were Christian people who saw themselves as the new Children of Israel, a concept known as topology. Their objective in coming to America was to first possess the land, and they believed that with God's help, they would possess it.

In addition, they were to practice religion the way they saw fit. This belief was based on their interpretation of the Bible, namely Deuteronomy 2:31-36, as well as other biblical references:

> *31 The LORD said to me, "See, I have begun to deliver Sihon and his country over to you. Now begin to conquer and possess his land."*
>
> *32 When Sihon and all his army came out to meet us in battle at Jahaz, 33 the LORD our God delivered him over to us and we struck him down, together with his sons and his whole army. 34 At that time we took all his towns and completely destroyed [a] them—men, women and children. We left no survivors. 35 But the livestock and the plunder from the towns we had captured we carried off for ourselves. 36 From Aroer on the rim of the Arnon Gorge, and from the town in the gorge, even as far as Gilead, not one town was too strong for us. The LORD our God gave us all of them (New International Version).*

This idea of God giving this land to these Europeans eventually turned into a policy known as Manifest Destiny. The belief was that America was a European American country, ordained by God. The fact that these Europeans thought themselves superior to the natives and non-European also informed their beliefs.

Incidentally, the Pilgrims and Puritans believed that a person should never try to rise about the social and economic status in which they were born. If God had wanted them in another social/economical group, He would have paced them there:

"Nevertheless, each one should retain the place in life that the Lord assigned to him and to which God has called him. This is the rule I lay down in all the churches" (1 Corinthians 7:17 New International Version).

Somewhere along the way a nation was formed with the guiding principles of democracy as its objective—the opportunity for life, liberty, and the pursuit of happiness for all. The idea was to not perpetrate on the new European inhabitants the same injustices that they had encountered from England. Over the years the experiment in government has been at work, striving towards it democratic objective with one primary exception—ownership of America. The idea of America being the land of European Americans has never been expunged from some of their minds in spite of the progress made in accepting the value of all human beings.

Today, much of the public dissent and protest comes from some people who identify themselves as Christian conservatives, Tea Party members, concerned citizens, American patriots and a host of other terms. The dissent and protest began in earnest when Obama was elected president. Following Obama's election was the appointment of a number of influential officials who just happen to be people of color.

The stated objection of the Congressional Republicans to any legislation offered by Obama became public knowledge. The fear that has come to surface in society today is based on the idea of a loss of country and special privilege by European Americans. Rather than embracing the idea of democracy, the protesters see themselves as victims of a process to deprive them of their country and their privileged citizenship. The reasons offered for protest, the economy, budget, immigration, health care and others are simply covers for the fear, hatred, and bigotry hiding behind the masks.

For proof of this fear one needs only to look at the various signs displayed at the public protest gatherings. Viewing some of these signs, one gets the impression that someone has taken the country away from Americans and they want it back; or that government is too big and needs to be brought under control; or that too much money is being spent by the government on things not needed or wanted. Even more signs present a likeness of President Obama in a negative way. Since no alternative suggestions are offered at these gatherings to correct the problems displayed in the signs, fear, hatred, and bigotry seem the only reasons for the protest.

At some point in America, reasonable minds might conclude that if we as a people and a nation are going to succeed at this democratic experience, we will have to come together. Coming together does not mean agreement on everything. The art of comprise is part of the political process if it is employed correctly.

Protest is also part of the rights and privileges of each and every citizen if it is directed at some reasonable objective. Protest for protest sake makes no sense at all. What many of the protesters must come to realize is that the fabric of their old belief in America as belonging to European Americans began to unravel once the Constitution became to law of the land. We are constantly reminded of our responsibilities as Americans every time we look at a coin that states "E Pluribus Unum."

America is a land of diverse ethnic and immigrant populations who came together to share and enjoy the blessings of life, liberty, and the pursuit of happiness. Part of our responsibility is to help protect these rights and privileges of and for each other. Biases, prejudices, and discrimination are all part of the human experience, but as Americans we can rise above these negative elements when we place concern for the betterment of our country above partisan, emotional, irrational and insensitive issues. Time limits on presidents and congressmen were established by the framers of the Constitution for the reason of addressing the people and the problems not to the liking of some citizens.

Regardless of the beliefs of some people, America never was a land given by God to European Americans nor is it a land that respects the rights of only some of its citizens. Too many Americans hold a restricted view of history and their implication in it. History is never static; it changes every time we learn something new about our past.

Please protest if that will bring attention to the problems or concerns at hand; that is a right and privilege. However, hiding hatred, fear, and bigotry behind reasons for protest will eventually manifest itself, and expose the fools behind the masks.

President Obama Signed a Bill Eliminating the Word Negro That Signals Change in Identities

August 15, 2016

When Africans were brought to this country and enslaved, one of the first things taken from them was their identity. Taking away their identity was important because it represented the history of who they were and that they were valued. Although each enslaved African would be given a slave name, they would all be commonly called black or Negro because of their skin color. The African identity was taken away from the enslaved, but the slave sellers and owners knew who they were, what they did (farmer, fisherman, craftsman, etc.) and where they were from because their selling price would be influenced by that information.

An example of the value of the African's identity was underscored in a 1764 poem by James Grainger, "The Sugar Cane." This poem was constructed using four parts called books; the fourth book, "On the Genius of Africa," shows the value of a slaver knowing the identity of the African captives:

> "Negroes when bought should be young and strong. The Congo-Negroes are fitter for the house and trades, than for the field. The Gold-Coast, but especially the Papaw-Negroes, make the best Field-Negroes: but even these, if advanced in years, should not be purchased."

This information focuses on males, for females the advice is when looking for a sound Negro:

> "Where the men do nothing but hunt, fish or fight, all the field drudgery is left to the women: these are to be preferred to their husbands."

The reference continues for males:

> "The Minnahs make good tradesmen, but addicted to suicide. The Mundingoes, in particular, subject to worms; and the Congas, to dropsical disorders."

(The Making of the Negro in Early American Literature, 2nd edition, Fountainhead Press, 2006, P. 38)

For enslaved Africans in America, their identity was taken away so their history and value would be tied to American slavery. If the only identity an enslaved person had was that of being American black or Negro (both terms mean the same), then they did not exist except in the system of slavery. The only personal identity they had linked them to their owner, as in the reference— John Smith's Negro, "Tom."

During the early 1700s, the term for slave went from Negro and black to simply "slave" due to the common coupling of the two phrase "black slave" or "Negro slave." However, many of the enslaved were still Europeans and American Indians, but the majority of the enslaved was African/ African American.

Once the government instituted the system of white supremacy and black inferiority, race by color became an important part of personal identity in American society. Americans were no longer able to identity with a particular ethnic or culture group. Kamala Kelkar, (PBS Newshour, 5/22/2016), noted that "In 1790, the U.S. Census counted people by lumping them into one of three categories—slaves, free white females and males, or all other free persons." The most important identity an American could have or want to have was white. The most damning identity one could have was that of either slave or Negro.

Immigration to America from around the world, but especially Eastern and Southern Europe, brought many changes to the invented concept of race. Although most European immigrants were not referred to as white, they all were willing to give-up their cultural identity to be called white.

For people of color, the term Negro was used regardless of their place of birth outside of the U.S. As recently as 2010, the census form still included the term Negro or black, but the list for other people of color had expanded. Kelkar explained that "The Department of Energy Act has for decades described "minorities" as, "Negro, Puerto Rican, American Indian, Eskimo, Oriental, or Aleut or as a Spanish-speaking individual of Spanish descent."

Because of the system of white supremacy and black inferiority, people of color were identified as "minorities."

For over two hundred years, the words race and ethnicity were generally undefined and used indiscriminately to the confusion of all, especially the U.S. Census. As recent as 2010, Americans in a number of categories were told on the census form to identify themselves as white, if they could not find an identity that suited them. This group included mixed-ethnic individuals such as Asian Americans, American Indians, and Hispanics.

In effect, the concept of race by color had reached a point of meaninglessness. The problem was that the term race was interpreted as pertaining to multiple biological groups of human beings or ethnic groups. The fact is that only one race of human beings exists—*Homo sapiens*. Ethnicity or ethnic groups pertains to the variety of cultural groups within the human race.

Every human being on the planet Earth has two identities—one ancestral or ethnic, one cultural. The ancestral or ethnic identity is represented by a person's biological parents; the cultural is the identity the individual selects. For example, an Asian American has Asian as an ancestral identity, and American as the cultural which he or she embraces. The terms Negro and black do not allow for either identity nor does the terms white and Caucasian. Fortunately, things are about to change.

President Barack Obama just recently signed H.R. 4238 "which amends two federal acts from the 70s that define "minorities" with terms that are now insensitive or outdated." In addition, the bill was sponsored by Rep. Grace Meng, D-NY, with 74 Democratic co-sponsors and two Republican ones;" it passed with 380 votes. The two words removed from the books are Negro and Oriental. According to Kelkar, "The new bill changes the language to, 'Asian American, Native Hawaiian, a Pacific Islander, African American, Hispanic, Puerto Rican, Native American or Alaska Native.'"

The changes in identity were inevitable because race by color was an invention based on false assumptions and beliefs. Black or Negro and white or Caucasian were never biological categories of the human race but were put in place because of the government's control. No one ever came to America with only the identity of black, Negro, or Caucasian or white; they always had an ancestral and cultural identity.

Once in America, however, the Europeans recognized the value of being identified as white and so they abandoned their ancestral and cultural identity for white. People of color coming to America realized the stigma associated with being called Negro or black and usually decided to retain their ancestral and cultural identity. Now the people of color who were previously called Negro can be specific in their ancestral and cultural identity—African American.

For whites and Caucasians, no official changes have been made although the term European Americans was used on occasion by the Supreme Court, but they always had the freedom to identify themselves using their ancestral identity such as Irish, Italian, Polish, German, etc. In any event, the fact is that identity-based on race by color is rapidly being deconstructed.

Real Changes in the Community
Must Come from the Top Down

September 9, 2014

When the Michael Brown tragedy occurred in Ferguson, Missouri, many people were dismayed that such a thing could happen. Sometimes, it takes a tragedy to bring to the surface other equally discomforting things as well.

We hear about people organizing to make things better for the community and especially for better police and community relations. Usually, the focus of attention is on the event that just occurred and what caused it. In Ferguson we learned that out of a total of fifty-three policemen, only three or four were African American, when the population percentage of African Americans is around 67 percent. The answer to resolving the police-community relations problem, according to some, is to hire more African Americans on the police force. Unfortunately, that would not solve the problem.

If we want to get to the heart of the problem that contributed to the death of Michael Brown, then hiring more police will not accomplish that objective. The real problem has to do with the treatment of African Americans with respect to fairness and justice. The problems of fairness and justice for African Americans will not be addressed or resolved by adding more African Americans to the police force if the perception, attitude, and behavior of the people in charge of the police do not change.

What incidents like the one in Ferguson shows is that the problem of community relations does not rest with the police force; the problem is systemic. The police behavior is simply one manifestation of the mind-set of the community leaders. The various elected officials from the mayor to the dog-catcher play a part in forming the attitude of the community relative to its citizens. Therefore, when searching for a cause of the problem relative to police behavior towards the African American community, one has to look at who controls the police.

One journalist looking into the community relations in areas near Ferguson discovered a pattern of unjust actions that places undue stress on the African American communities in the St. Louis area. For example, the greatest police-related instances taken from police reports occur in African American communities. The greatest percentage of traffic violations reported occurred in African American communities. The greatest percentage of arrest reported by the police occurred in African American communities. Why?

We cannot simply look at the police force for an answer.

Taken individually, the statistics seem to suggest African Americans are the worst drivers in the area, and they give the police more cause for arrest. However, when looked at collectively, we recognize that the majority of the African Americans stopped for traffic violations are poor, low-wage workers. When stopped by the police, whether they committed a violation or not, they do not usually complain. They do not complain because of the history of negative consequences associated with being African American and uncooperative with the police. The police not only know that African Americans understand this situation, but also depend on it working successfully in issuing tickets. The entire process is part of the system for general income for the community.

Many police departments depend on the poor, powerless communities of people of color to generate money to operate their local government. Usually, the poor do not have the extra money available to pay a large traffic fine. So, in some communities, if one cannot pay, they go to jail. If they go to jail, the family, friends, and often the employers of the jailed person will come up with the money. If not, the person jailed will usually lose his or her job, incur bills that cannot be paid, leave children to the mercy of available family or foster care, and in some instances lose their home and transportation. Why?

They get caught in the system because they are powerless and defenseless and therefore, easy prey. The cause of their problems is not the police force; they just follow the instructions of the administrators.

Part of the problem comes from ignorance and prejudice of European Americans towards the African American and people of color in the community. The ignorance and prejudice comes from perception. Sean McElwee, in an article for *Huffington*, "Five Signs We're Not a 'Post-Racial' Society" noted:

> "In the wake of the Ferguson shooting, a recent Pew poll finds that 47 percent of whites believe that "race is getting more attention than it deserves," with regards to the death of Michael Brown, while only 18 percent of African-Americans feel the same. Meanwhile, a similar Pew study found that whites are far less likely to see discrimination in the treatment blacks receive by the education system, the courts and hospitals. Such views are held by many Americans, who believe that "blacks are mostly responsible for their own condition." Police killings of unarmed blacks are certainly the most visible manifestation of systemic racism, but data show that racism still manifests itself frequently in everyday life."

The shooting of Michael Brown created an opportunity for all the citizens to see the actual conditions of the community and not rely on rumor and opinions. Armed with the facts of just how much African Americans are treated unjustly and unfairly, the citizens can begin to organize themselves into groups that will act to address many of these problems. When concerned people in the community realize the degree to which the poor and people of color are exploited, they should be moved to some level of action.

Change will come to the community, not just Ferguson, when the leaders from the top on down adjust their attitudes and become better informed relative to the people they serve, all the people they serve. Likewise, the poor, and people of color need to realize that they have power through the vote and public protest to make positive changes.

However, as McElwee stated: "In America, race determines not just where someone lives and what school he or she attends, it affects the very air we breathe. Although many whites wish to believe we live in a "post-racial" society, race appears not just in overt discrimination but in subtle structural factors.

So, the problems relative to the police and the African American communities are not simply police problems, but problems that involve the entire system of government that devalues and under represents many of its citizens of color. Problem solving, however, must begin at the top.

Effective Communications a Must in Replacing America's Ethnic Bigotry (Racism)

December 27, 2016

People from famous writers to Supreme Court Justices to presidents and even to everyday people have acknowledged the fact that America continues to be separated by color, and try as we may, little progress has been made to bridge that gap. Certainly, strides have been made to bring the two groups together, but nothing seems to work for very long.

The fact that ethnic bigotry was instituted at the very beginning of this American experience and continues today underscores its strength.

The social conditioning of Americans to respect the power and privilege of skin color manifests itself in everyday life in all of our society's institutions. Why cannot the gap that separates the two groups be filled? Actually, it can be filled; we just have to decide that we want to come together as one unified, un-bigoted nation.

When a group of European Americans was asked if it were possible would they like to live their lives as African Americans? They were asked to raise their hand if the answer was yes. Not a single European American raised his or her hand. Why?

Two reasons come to mind, one is that European Americans realize the privilege and power they experience because of their skin color and do not want to lose anything. Another reason is that European Americans know how American society treats African Americans and they do not want any part of that treatment. These two questions also represent the reason many European Americans do not like to talk about race. One question that these two reasons bring to mind relative to European Americans is since they know how they feel and know how African Americans are treated in society, why do they not speak out against it as unjust and unfair? One answer is a lack of effective communications between the European Americans and the African Americans.

One of the main points of contention involving effective communications between African Americans and European Americans is the fact that they have different perceptions of reality. The European American cannot tell the African American how to address his problems because he does not perceive the problem as does the African American.

For example, the problem involving a lack of good relations between the police force and the African American community is that the police still have the perception of bigotry and fear towards the African American. For them, the remedy for this problem is more troops and more training—for African Americans that is the wrong answer. The actual remedy would be an education that replaces the bigoted image of the European Americans towards the African American community to one that embraces all people as part of the human family. By doing so, the development of organizations that work together for the betterment of the communities can be constructed.

Unfortunately, many European Americans believe that their perception of reality is fair and just; they are mistaken. Society has conditioned them to see people of color as inferior and European Americans as normal and superior. No one has to teach them this bias; our society in all its institutions continues to reinforce this concept. When all the suggested solutions offered by European Americans continue to view two separate groups of people, then that is not a solution. The first order of business in resolving a problem is to recognize and understand the problem. If the problem is perception, then that is the first problem to resolve.

Blame and criticism for different perspectives should not enter the discussion, only the fact that they are different and must be made acceptable to both sides. Since society has conditioned European Americans to assume superiority as normal, not pretentious, they need to be shown that their view is biased. Achieving that particular accomplishment will be extremely challenging for as Dr. Robin DiAngelo noted in her study of white fragility that: "It became clear over time that white people have extremely low thresholds for enduring any discomfort associated with challenges to our racial worldview." She added:

"We [European Americans] can manage the first round of challenge by ending the discussion through platitudes— usually, something that starts with 'People just need to,' or 'Race doesn't really have any meaning to me,' or 'Everybody's racist.' Scratch any further on that surface, however, and we fall apart."

European Americans generally consider any effort to connect them to the system of ethnic supremacy as very unsettling and an "unfair moral offense. "None-the-less, the challenge must be made if any positive change is to be expected in replacing ethnic bigotry.

Another concern that bears consideration is the ethnic bias that is so deeply embedded in some European Americans that almost any challenge will prove ineffective. In an article entitled "The dark rigidity of fundamentalist rural America: a view from the inside," published in Forsetti's Justice, Alternet; 27 Nov. 2016) the writer noted that this group of people has their own way of viewing life in general, which differs from the way urban people see life:

"Another problem with rural, Christian, white Americans is they are racists. I'm not talking about white hood-wearing, cross-burning, lynching racists (though some are). I'm talking about people who deep down in their heart of hearts truly believe they are superior because they are white. Their white God made them in his image and everyone else is a less-than-perfect version, flawed and cursed."

The writer was writing from his experience as a resident of rural America.

From the nature of the above quote, and the deeply fixed notion of a racial identity, no amount of facts, evidence, proof or explanations will replace such a bigoted mindset. With all the changes taking place in our society and the world, the charade of races by color is not long for this world.

The sooner European Americans and people of color can begin to see each other as belonging to the same family of man the sooner all the confusion and myth-believing concerning race can be replaced. The changes will take place regardless of one's beliefs in a race, but being aware of the facts will help the transition occur smoothly rather than with great difficulty. The changes can only begin in earnest when the lines of communications that are free from ethnic bias are established.

American Democracy: Truth, Falsehood, Falsehoods as Truths, and Reality (Part One)

May 8, 2017

A young European American (white) man in his middle to late twenties was being interviewed on a television show; he was dressed in a suit and wore a tie. What he said during the course of the interview was in effect, that he was a white man, and he wanted to see America regain its rightful place as a white man's country. He was apparently upset because he believed that he was losing his power, influence, and privileges. From the expression on his face, it was apparent that the young man believed in what he was saying, and believed it to be the truth.

Some Americans might be surprised by what the young man said because they do not believe that he was speaking the truth. Well, what exactly is the truth as far as the young man was concerned? The problem of truth began with America's beginning.

Before we can begin a discussion about truth, we need first to have a working definition of truth. We might suggest that truth, in a statement, is represented by fact or reality. In another sense, we might suggest that truth is relative to the individual regardless of facts and reality. So, where does that leave us regarding truth? How can both suggestions be accurate? The key to the answer has to do with how we view facts and reality.

What we find in American society is evidence that truth is viewed as both relative to the individual and based on facts and reality. Here is how it works. Society first proclaimed certain truths, then proceeded to ignore them, inventing falsehoods in their place and convincing the people to accept the falsehoods as truth. Now that the falsehoods have been uncovered, the people do not want to accept the truth.

To demonstrate how this happened, we need to look at history. We begin with the words from the Declaration of Independence: "We hold these truths to be self-evident, that all men are created equal, that they are endowed by their Creator with certain unalienable Rights that among these are Life, Liberty, and the Pursuit of Happiness."

The first thing we note in this statement is the word "truths," which carries with it the semblance of facts and reality. We generally accept the sincerity and honesty of the word truth. The next phrase is equally important to our understanding of truth as being "self-evident" or clear and acceptable to all. We have no reason to suspect anything being amiss about what follows this first phrase: "that all men are created equal." Well, if we know anything about early American history and the founding fathers, we know that the author of those words, Thomas Jefferson, as well as other founding fathers, were slaveholders.

How can one believe in the equality of all men and be a slaveholder? Easy enough make slaves less than human. But what about other men and women who cannot enjoy the equal rights of the wealthy European American men? Simply write laws that control their freedoms.

In the phrase that follows, three words stand out: "endowed," "unalienable," and "rights," all invite interpretation. The first word, "endowed" can be interpreted as a gift or something provided to the individual. The next word, "unalienable" can be defined as not transferable to another or not capable of being taken away or denied. The term "rights" can be defined as freedoms, entitlements or justified claims.

Following this introduction of privileges that cannot be denied and are freedoms available to all, we learn what they are: Life, Liberty, and the Pursuit of Happiness. These rights and those contained in the Constitution are called civil rights. All American citizens are entitled to celebrate and enjoy them. We could examine each one of these rights to show that all Americans have never experienced them in reality because of two important things associated with American history: slavery and bigotry.

The institution of slavery made certain that the words of the preamble to the Constitution would never ring true: "We the people of the United States, in order to form a more perfect Union, establish justice...." The remainder of the preamble loses its value when we realize that "justice" was never established while a system of slavery was in existence. After slavery, laws were instituted to retain control of certain groups of American citizens.

The young European American man who considered himself a white man represents the reality of a falsehood being believed as truth. He is not being an extremist or extraordinary with his assertions, he is simply saying what American society has conditioned him to believe. The social conditioning, he has received all his life is at its core a system that fosters a belief in European American (white) supremacy. So, regardless of what the Declaration of Independence or the Constitution, or even the Pledge of Allegiance says about all men being equal with all their civil rights, including liberty and justice for all, reality provides those truths for European Americans only.

The system of European American (white) supremacy was invented and instituted by the founding fathers and woven into all America's social institutions. What was unknown to the young European American man was that the system in which he was nurtured and conditioned was based on a falsehood. The system of European American (white) supremacy was based on the false concept of reality consisting of two races, one black, and one white. The European American (white) race was presented as being the model for humanity as well as America's standard of beauty.

European Americans generally do not picture themselves as belonging to a race. People who do not look like them belong to a race. Another characteristic of being European American was that they were to consider themselves as the center of the universe, superior to all people of color, so their only equals were other European Americans.

To ensure that the concept of supremacy was received and perceived as ordinary and normal, the government instituted segregation, which meant that European Americans could live their entire lives without having to interact with a person of color. Discrimination was instituted to ensure that European Americans receive privileges above and beyond what was offered to people of color, especially in education, jobs, health care, salaries, housing, and the law. In all these areas, the African Americans were denied opportunities to participate as first-class citizens and denied their civil rights.

American Democracy: Truth, Falsehood, Falsehoods as Truths, and Reality (Part Two)

May 14, 2017

Often time, when we see someone with a missing limb, we think about the disadvantage that missing limb is for the person. However, what we often do not realize is that if the person was born with the limb missing, then it was never considered by that person to be a disadvantage because to him, the missing limb is normal.

The young European American man was born into a society that conditioned him to view society as a normal European American along with the social biases towards African Americans and other people of color. His perception was, to him, natural and normal.

With all the freedoms and privileges working in his favor, little wonder the young European American identifies himself as a white man. Despite the numerous civil rights protests of African Americans and other people of color, many European Americans failed to realize that the objectives of the protests were for the protesters, fellow Americans, to share in the same rights, liberties, and privileges enjoyed by the European American citizens. Each protest brought by African Americans was a deliberate effort to enlighten the European American citizens that something was wrong in American society and that American was not living up to its creed and mantra of freedom and justice for all.

The problem, as we can ascertain from the young European American, is that with each social gain by the African Americans and other people of color, he believes some of his privileges are being lost or taken away. For example, when the Supreme Court of the United States ruled that school segregation was unequal and that integration must be instituted in an effort to remedy the problems it caused, many European Americans believed that they were losing their right to segregate themselves. Although none of the civil rights acts and laws ever mentions African Americans specifically, the fact that they were the citizens being denied their rights, made them appear as the enemy to many European Americans. The facts concerning all the civil rights laws enacted under protest by African Americans underscored the rights of all citizens, not just those of people of color.

Nonetheless, the fact that the changes taking place in the world and especially in America became more noticeable to the young European American due to the advances in cyber technology. His idea of America being a white man's country was starting to be challenged by all the social changes taking place. The one change that served as a major indicator of change in America for the young European American was the election of Barack Obama as President of the United States. All his life he had been conditioned to view the African American as inferior and lacking social value. Now all of a sudden, an African American is president. For him, too much was being lost too fast.

The young European American has been conditioned all his life to believe the falsehood to be true. We know from the works of people like Edward O. Wilson and Elizabeth Minnick that people can be conditioned to accept falsehoods by way of having heard it over numerous times and/or by trusting in a leader of a group and believing through a blind trust. That is, people can be conditioned to giving serious thought to anything their leader says while continuing strong support to that leader.

For example, during the presidential campaign, Donald Trump made the statement that he could shoot someone in the middle of a public street and not lose a single vote. His thinking suggested that his followers did not give thought to what he said; their loyalty was to him, the individual. Unfortunately, that characteristic of the thoughtless American seems to fit many Americans who cannot or refuse to recognize the falsehoods masquerading as truths in American society.

To understand the difference between the European American's perspective of reality and that of the African American based on both their social conditioning is like they are walking down a street and both see a piece of glass in the grass. The European American sees the sun shining on the glass while the African American sees the sun's reflection from the glass. They both are looking at the same piece of glass, but each sees something different. If we were to ask them what they see, their answers would both be correct. The fact that they focus on different aspects of the same piece of glass represents the problem with their not being able to communicate constructively. If both cannot understand and acknowledge the fact of their two different perspectives, effective communication is impossible.

The reality for the young European American man consists of viewing America as only a European American society. That is when phrases such as "the American people," or "we the people," or any references to Americans are used, the mental picture the young man receives does not include people of color. People of color, especially African Americans are not considered real Americans to the young European American; they are simply allowed to live in America. That perception to him is real and true based on his beliefs and social conditioning.

With respect to the truths and falsehood of the young European American, no change is possible unless or until he is able to replace his falsehoods with facts and reality. The difficulty in the European American acknowledging reality is that the European American's beliefs are based on falsehoods, so everything he says and does reflect that falsehood at its base, however, he cannot accept his reality as being false. The reason for his inability to accept the falsehood goes to his experiences living in a biased America.

All his life, Americans institutions from segregated schools and churches, to preferential jobs and education, have underscored his sense of privilege. So, to deprive him of what he sees as rights for him, he sees as a form of abuse and punishment. To make matters worse, society tends to point to the African Americans as the source of his distress.

American Democracy: Truth, Falsehood, Falsehoods as Truths, and Reality (Part Three)
May 21, 2017

American history has always been taught with a spin that underscores the importance of the European, Anglo-Saxon male. Starting with the pilgrims and subsequently the Puritans who came from England to tame and develop a strange, wild, land given to them by God. The average American educational system also underscores the inalienable rights granted by the Constitution to European American men.

The European Americans know from living in American society, the power, privileges, and supremacy available to them, but not to people of color. In addition, the European Americans also know that the system of supremacy denies the rights they enjoy to the people of color.

Chief Justice Taney's opinions in the Dred Scott Case, 1854, noted the founding fathers, the framers of the Declaration of Independence and the Constitution that:

> "They perfectly understood the meaning of the language they used, and how it would be understood by others; and they knew that it would not in any part of the civilized world be supposed to embrace the negro race, which, by common consent, had been excluded from civilized Governments and the family of nations, and doomed to slavery."

No one offered a disclaimer to that statement until the 13th and 14th Amendment. The laws changed, but the mindset of many European Americans remains as Taney stated.

Nevertheless, many European Americans do not see themselves as the reason and cause of people of color not enjoying their rights. The failure of the people of color not enjoying their inalienable rights European Americans believe it is due to their inferiority, some additional personal faults, and/ or maybe it is still God's will.

In any event, the perception of the European Americans of themselves is based on the false premise of a race by color, and a hypocritical view of democracy as presented through American history and public education. In essence, their sense and view of reality are based on falsehoods, however, to them, it is based on truth and facts. Consequently, African Americans face discrimination daily from European Americans who do not realize their actions are biased.

Many social changes continue to occur in America since the founding fathers instituted their system of European American supremacy and African American inferiority. The more significant changes involve the actions of African Americans seeking access to their inalienable rights granted by the Constitution and denied by society. Fortunately, America is a society governed by laws, and it is through these laws that changes in the social structure are available. The laws were written without respect to color, but the enjoyment of those rights was based on the ability for those laws to be enforced.

African Americans did not enjoy the support of society in enforcing the laws that discriminated and disenfranchised them. For the African Americans, their reality has been the constant and continuous struggle to obtain and enjoy those inalienable rights. A problem for some European Americans, especially the young European American man in question, is that with each gain for rights made by African Americans, represents a loss to them.

A problem consistent in interviews that involve extreme concepts of ethnic bigotry such as the one in question is the fact that the interviewer never challenges the young European American's concept of race. In other words, questions like: what does white mean? How can whiteness be determined and who determines it? What is a race? How can a percentage of whiteness be determined? He is allowed to continue embracing his false concept of race and, in fact, becomes emboldened in his belief because it is not challenged or debunked.

As long as the interviewer accepts the concept of race from the young European American's perspective, the conversation will remain cyclical, and his bigotry will go unchallenged. In order for change to occur in the conversation, facts and reality associated with those facts must be introduced and considered. The presence and contributions made to America by African Americans are not fiction, but real and documented facts of significance. The recently opened building, The National Museum of African American History and Culture, as well as the statue of Dr. Martin Luther King, Jr., situated on the mall, gives proof and evidence to the contributions of Africans Americans to American history and society.

The introduction of DNA and its findings are real and important to our understanding of truth and scientific facts. When the DNA scientists reported that their finding indicated that all human beings were 99.9 percent alike, we have no reason to doubt them. They concluded that race cannot be discerned from our DNA. While Americans can disagree with the findings that debunk the concept of race by color, they cannot change them. However, if the concept on which the system of ethnic bigotry is based is not challenged, change is not possible.

The young European American who sees himself as white must be presented facts and evidence to replace the falsehoods he has been living with all his life. His acceptance of the facts and evidence relative to race represents the problem as well as the challenge. What rational and logical people view as falsehoods, the young European American views as truth.

Changes in American society are taking place on a more rapid basis than in the past because of the many advances in technology and other areas. Many of the changes we are able to witness on a daily basis. One of those changes is in the demographics of society. More and more American society is browning because of the mixture of its ethnic population and the union of representatives of different ethnic cultures. The concept of races by color or culture is quickly fading and the significance of race losing its social value. The problem of race has become so confusing that the U.S. Census Bureau simply allows people to identify themselves by providing a space labeled "other."

However, what is needed is a concerted effort to bring out the factual truth and separate it from the falsehoods. All the lies, myths, deceits, hypocrisy associated with race and American history and society must be confronted and debunked. By doing so, we will be able to see who we are and what we want to be and to start to engage in sound communications. The choice is ours to make; we can be either agent of change or its victims. Either way, change will continue to occur.

The young European American man who sees America as a white society must be given the opportunity to see the falsehood that has been guiding his life as truths. If he is able to recognize and accept those falsehoods for what they are, then a positive change in his perception is possible. If he is unable to discern the truth from the falsehoods, then his life will continue to be filled with the disappointments and the loss of his sense of value and self-importance as a European American (white) man in an ethnically diverse society and world.

The ideal objective of our future society is for all Americans, especially the young European American, to replace his whiteness with actual truths and facts and be able to state honestly and freely the ending of the Pledge of Allegiance that underscores "liberty and justice for all."

POPULAR CULTURE

*"Pop culture is a reflection of social change,
not a cause of social change."*

JOHN PODHORETZ

Race and the Media

January 15, 2010

Whenever the subject of race occurs in society by persons of note, the media seems to jump on it like a group of sharks during a feeding frenzy. Expert after expert is asked to discuss his or her take on the subject and the circumstance in which the subject happened. Networks create programs to discuss the subject and the persons implicated in the matter in an effort to gain a better understanding of race and why it came to the attention of the public.

This pattern has repeated itself for the past fifty or more years. Ironically, after all the network programs, televised town hall meetings, interviews, and investigative reports, nothing concrete happens to dispel the myth and illusion of race. Why? Could it be because of society's ignorance, or the appeal for public attention or fear that the truth will destroy the payoff received from those who wish to continue the game?

With all the current information available regarding the sameness of all human beings, one would think that ignorance of all people belonging to the same family of human would be next to impossible. One scientist made the comment that humans are more alike than penguins. Sure, superficial differences occur in and among humans. These differences exist even in families where children have the same parents. So why does the media ignore the fact that reasons, other than race, come into play go totally unnoticed by them? Reasons of bias, bigotry, prejudice, and discrimination can and should be addressed anytime the subject of race causes attention. Evidently, the media thinks that the important area of concern is race, therefore, the legitimate reasons go unmentioned or reduced to insignificant matter. Why have they not ventured beyond race?

If ignorance is not the cause of the media's refusal to look beyond race in their reports, then maybe the reason is that fact that like sex, race will bring in the viewers and listeners. The subject of race is like the golden egg laid by the goose. Because of its supposed value to the public, it cannot be ignored. The more the subject is aggrandized by the media, the more attention it draws. History shows us that any number of people have gained notoriety from a chance meeting with the media where their bias opinions were expressed and thereby promoted.

We know that the word race unites and separates simultaneously, so what better way to garner viewers and listeners than by calling attention to race? Does the media realize that because of their lack of forethought and acknowledgement of the myth and illusion of race, they are the primary supporters, and promoters of racism and social disunity? Have they not come to grips with the fact that race has no genetic basis; that it is a social creation?

One reason for the media's attraction to race might be the payoff received from the attention of the viewers and listeners and the decision to ignore the fact. By ignoring the facts of race the game of myth and illusion can continue. If rational thinking people were given the opportunity to move beyond the ignorance and stereotype of race, progress might be possible in bringing about some element of social unity and togetherness rather than separation, bias, bigotry, prejudice, and discrimination. The media has an obligation to keep the public informed, but it has failed miserably in helping society move beyond race because of its ignorance, fear, or arrogance.

Confronting Stereotypes in America

June 26, 2010

One of the tools used in some societies to control its ethnic population is to stereotype them in ways that makes them less than human. Once this happens, the disrespect and denigration comes easily. Many people grow up in a society never realizing that the images they have of ethnic groups are nothing but stereotypical characterizations. Unfortunately, too many of these people never realize that the images they have of ethnic groups were created with a negative purpose in mind. These images are invoked when the majority society wants to exert control over these groups to accomplish some partisan and usually biased purpose.

In America, words like, redneck, white trash, slant eyes, jungle bunny, bean eater, wetback, redskin, camel jockey, goat roper and a host of other similar words bring immediately to mind a specific ethnic group or portion of an ethnic group. None of these words are meant as compliments; they are used to divide and conquer. Along with these words come lists of characteristics that create a negative depiction of representatives of each group. For example, the word redneck is used to denigrate a European American who usually works a low-paying manual labor job outdoors. He generally lacks much formal education, speaks improper American English, listens to Country music, parties on the weekend or until his money runs out etc. All these characteristics usually will not apply to every person identified as redneck, but some people will have enough to be identified as one. Any European American who does not consider himself or herself a redneck will usually resent being characterized as one.

Stereotypes are created by taking data from a variety of sources and putting them together to make a composite image. The information gathered is not in itself negative. However, when the information is arranged in a certain way that creates a picture of people with some of these characteristics, then a stereotype is created. Take, for example, African Americans, who in the past have been identified as the personification of sexuality, lewdness, laziness, hostility, and dirtiness to name a few of the negative elements. For certain, one will find some of these elements in some individuals within the African American population. The stereotype, however, pictures all African Americans as having these character elements. The reason for these stereotypes has to do with discrimination and control. No one will usually identify himself as a stereotype unless he is entertaining or has little self-respect or pride, because the intent of the stereotype is to show disrespect and distance.

Again, in America, the European American set the standards for normalcy in society, so whenever someone other than a European American displays some of the so-called normal characteristics he or she is looked at as being different. In other words, being different means different from the stereotype of his ethnic groups. Take, for example, Barack Obama. If we were to list the stereotypical element used for African Americans, he does not display any of them. How can that be? Since he is African American he must be hiding some of these elements from the public so he can be considered different. Some uninformed people will say of his speech that "he's trying to talk white." Since he is educated and has a poised demeanor, he is accused of "acting white." In essence, whenever anyone identified as an ethnic American falls out of the stereotypical image, he or she is not acting normal relative to his or her ethnic group.

Unfortunately, stereotypes have ruled the day in America for many years. Too many Americans have no idea of what America looks like without the stereotypes and that is why some Americans find it difficult to accept someone like Obama as president.

Once, a few years ago, an African American male professor went into his department chairperson's office for a performance evaluation. The chairperson was a European American female. She complimented him on his work and contributions to the university and department, then proceeded to give him an average review ranking. When the professor questioned her about the average review ranking, she mentioned to him that she grew up in a part of the country where "Negroes" were not considered average. He asked further, what that had to do with his performance. She replied that she had never been able to separate herself from that perception of "Negroes," so average was the best he could receive from her. This incident shows how stereotypes can affect individuals in negative ways and can be harmful to both the perceived and the perceiver.

Fortunately, America is starting to change its perceptions of itself—no longer a society dominated by European American standards and values. Stereotypes have for too long been a veil over the eyes of too many citizens. That veil has been the cause of biases and discrimination against many American citizens. At times, the Government created stereotypical criteria used to set apart two ethnic groups, as in the case of the Japanese and Chinese during the time following Pearl Harbor. The objective was to present the Japanese as bad and evil, and the Chinese as loyal and good. This example is only one of many. If one cares to examine the history, examples of biases through stereotypes created against many ethnic Americans are readily available.

However, we as Americans need to be looking toward the future and seeking ways to eliminate the stereotypes. This elimination of stereotypes can be accomplished through education, observation, and experience. We have an excellent opportunity to set our sights in the right direction with the example of the Obama family in the White House. Our actions generally follow our thoughts, so if we look for the best in our citizenry instead of the negative stereotypes, chances are we will find it.

Ann Coulter Uses Language to Create Attention

November 6, 2011

Ann Coulter has for years used her spin on information as an attention getter. She has created a persona that some people accept as genuine and credible. The problem with accepting the Coulter persona is that it is not reliable or trustworthy. Whatever Coulter has to say will always shed light on her first, then the information. For example, she was recently on Fox News talking with Sean Hannity about how the liberals were attacking the African American Republican candidate for President, Herman Cain. Although no proof was offered for the accusations, she nevertheless made the claim with confidence. Coulter has shown herself to be a manipulator of information to call attention to her and elevate her position with all the people who think and believe as she does.

While talking with Hannity, Coulter made the statement: "Civil rights laws were designed to protect blacks from Democrats, from Democrat laws, from Democrat segregators, from Democrat governors and Democrats in the White House wouldn't protect them." To hear her speak these words one would assume she knew whereof she was speaking. However, to anyone with a general working knowledge of history, Coulter obviously mixes movements, parties, and time periods to create simultaneously two different interpretations.

First, for people who are knowledgeable of American history, they know that prior to the Civil War, the Republican Party, the party of Lincoln, supported the elimination of slavery. They also know that the Democrats were the party that embraced slavery, especially in the South. For a better picture of the party differences prior to 1964, any informed reading of the Reconstruction Period in America will fill in the gaps. Coulter spins the information to make it appear current, which we know is not the case.

Second, for the people who are unfamiliar with American history, and share Coulter's belief and perspective, her words will appear as truth. What becomes obvious to the reader it that the messenger appears more important than the message. The attention that falls on Coulter is exactly what she wants. Coulter knows very well that it was the Democrats, President John F. Kennedy, and Vice President Lyndon B. Johnson who were responsible for the 1964 Civil Rights Bill. If any American knows anything about the 1964, 1965, 1968, or any Civil Rights bill, they know that never is there a reference to any specific American citizens. Civil rights are to be experienced by all Americans. The civil rights legislation sought to include those citizens that had not been included previously. The party for bringing the changes in civil rights is the Democrats. Most African Americans know this, and continue to support the party that supports them.

Whether Coulter is a bigot or not, she knows how to use language to create concern that might suggest bias. She made a statement to Hannity that suggests a kind of paternal ethnic bias that goes back to the days of slavery. She knows that many African Americans, as well as many Americans generally, question the rationale of ethnic minority citizens joining a political party that does not recognize their value. What the party does recognize in these ethnic minority members is a change to use them as protection against charges of bigotry. In essence, if we have ethnic minorities in our party, then we cannot be accused of bigotry. So, in an effort to stroke the egos of the ethnic minorities in their party, especially the African Americans, Coulter says that: "our blacks are better than their blacks." Therefore, African Americans who belong to the Republican Party are better people than those African Americans that belong to the Democratic Party. The fact that she uses the pronoun "our" indicates ownership and suggests that these citizens are not free to make their own choices, but simply follow what the party suggests.

Although the statement might have been offered as a show of support for African Americans, like Herman Cain, who are members of the Republican Party, the statement can also be seen as a slam on the inability of African Americans to recognize an insult or a back-handed compliment. In any event, the language of the statement was meant to arouse attention, which it did. The attention, however, fell on Coulter more than on the message. She knows how to spin the language and present it in a way that some people will not question it. She has also developed a style of over-talking anyone who questions the veracity of what she says.

Coulter manages to keep herself in the public eye by writing books or making claims that call attention to her for making the claims. If Coulter was an expert in some area or had some credentials that provided reasons to accept what she says with more than a grain of salt, then her claims might be taken seriously. Unfortunately, she has her mouth and her determination to dominate any conversation in which she participates. That evidently, according to Fox News, seems to be enough because when she brings up the famous Clarence Thomas phrase "High-tech lynching," with a reference to how she suggests the liberal media treats Herman Cain, Hannity does not seem to understand just what Coulter has done. She knows there should have been a reaction to that term, but Hannity is so accustomed to agreeing with her, the significance of it does not register.

Coulter generally comes across to viewers and readers as a person in control of the information she dispenses. The problem with that is those people who are uninformed, believe her. For the other people, they know she caters to bigots who rely on ethnic stereotypes to give meaning to her words. Coulter is the epitome of the person with a little knowledge being a danger. She is skillful enough to play around the edge of the mud pit without falling into it, but she will provide enough information for some to wallow in it.

To read her books or listen to her talk, one has to wonder if she is pulling our leg or is she really that crazy. With all the attention she gets and the money she makes, one might easily say that she's crazy—crazy like a fox.

Miss America Pageant and Ethnic Pride Confused

June 12, 2010

A recent letter to the "Your Views" section of the *Oklahoman* (6/12/10) makes reference to an article announcing six African Americans being inducted into an African-American Hall of Fame. The letter states that "If we had a White Hall of Fame, we'd be called racist. The same is true if we had a United White College Fund, White History Month...Miss White America Pageant..." He ends his letter with the statement that "We are a nation divided, when we should be just plain old Americans." While his intentions are good, his knowledge and information are greatly lacking regarding this subject. Rather than trying to deal with all of his concerns that seem to divide us as a nation, let us examine one and hope the discussion will be sufficient. Let us look at the Miss America Beauty Pageant.

Many people complain today about the variety of ethnic beauty pageants and some make the claim that they are biased because they exclude European Americans. Well, as a matter of fact, the opposite is true. The pageants represent the true nature of diversity in America. The Miss America Beauty Pageant began in 1921. America at that time was deeply involved with promoting the idea of European Americans as the only normal Americans. Support for this propaganda was given by the release of the D.W. Griffith movie, "The Birth of a Nation" in 1915, and the growth of the Ku Klux Klan—the subject of the movie.

In addition, one of the nation's worst race riots occurred in Tulsa, Oklahoma in 1921. Also, 59 African Americans were lynched in the United States that year. In Oklahoma, as in some other states, Klan membership was represented from the governor's office to the local policeman and fireman as well as many doctors and clergymen. So the idea of America being a European America was dominant. Enter: The Miss America Beauty Pageant.

America is, and has always been, a multicultural society. However, before the support and protection of the civil rights

of all Americans came into prominence, the ethnic Americans,
European Americans who called themselves white, thought and
behaved like America belonged to them alone; other citizens were
living here due to the good graces of the whites. Therefore, one
would not be surprised to learn that according to its laws, only
whites could enter and compete for the title of Miss America. The
very title suggests that the winner of the pageant represented all
of America. Unfortunately, we know that was not true simply by
looking at who could enter. So, what were the other non-European
American ethnic groups to do? Since they were not included in the
Miss America Pageant, they started their own, but with a marked
difference.

Ethnic American beauty pageants are not biased or
undemocratic simply because they do not purport to represent all
of American society, just their ethnicity and culture. The Miss
America Beauty Pageant, however, did not identify itself as a
European American beauty pageant, which would have been
acceptable and fair; it represented itself as the only representative
of American beauty. The fact that European Americans do not see
themselves as an ethnic group makes it difficult for them to realize
that other American ethnic groups have as much right to promote
themselves as do the European Americans. Rule number seven
stated that "contestants must be of good health and of the white
race." The term white excluded and included, the same as the term
black; so today, neither term is appropriate for identifying an ethnic
American group.

By excluding non-European Americans from the contest, The
Miss America Beauty Pageant promoted ethnic bias. The bias was
re-enforced until at least 1940 when contestants were required
to complete a biological form tracing their ancestry. The fact
that no African American female competed in the contest until
1970 should lend some support to the justification of other ethnic
Americans creating their own pageants. Had they not created their
own pageants, they would not have had an outlet available to them
for showing their ethnic pride.

In addition to promoting ethnic bias, The Miss America
Beauty Pageant captured and controlled the standard of beauty

for American females. In essence, the only females of beauty were European Americans and people who tried to duplicate that standard. In America today, some ethnic females still try to approximate their idea of American beauty with cosmetic surgery, hair dye, and make-up. Their perception of beauty has been influenced by the standards promoted by The Miss America Beauty Pageant so much so that they no longer see themselves as naturally beautiful.

Over the years, The Miss America Beauty Pageant has changed considerably. With the influence of the Civil Rights Movement, many doors have been opened. However, confusion still remains in the mind of many people who think of The Miss American Beauty Pageant. Many people believe that the ethnic American cultures should now abandon their pageants since everyone can compete in The Miss America Pageant. What they fail to realize is that The Miss American Beauty Pageant represents all of America and the ethnic pageants represent their specific ethnic culture.

The confusion appears when the question is asked where white American females compete. Because white and European American were formerly seen as one, the difficulty now comes in trying to separate them. White does not mean American anymore then black means Africa or yellow means Asian or red means American Indian. If European Americans as an ethnic group want a beauty pageant specifically for European Americans, then they can create one. But do not confuse ethnic American beauty pageants as being representative of all America. In its early years, The Miss America Beauty Pageant, when it expressed bias, was viewed as representing all of America. No longer.

So, as stated earlier, expressing pride in ethnic American culture is part of America's strength, not a weakness. For each ethnic American entity mentioned in the above mentioned letter, a similar story of exclusion or lack of representation can be found. Unfortunately, the absence of those stories lead to confusion about the reasons for their existence.

America is not so much a divided nation as it is an uninformed and ethnically ignorant one. Today we still hold on to the terms

race, racist, black and white as if they have some validity or
reflect some accurate and current social value. When we as a
nation become better educated and informed, then we will be able
to accept and express the multicultural beauty that is ours as a
country, and maybe even come to see ourselves as "just plain old
Americans."

Here We Go Again, the U.S. Census Bureau and Race

April 3, 2011

Here we go again. The U.S. Census Bureau is the gift that keeps on giving in regards to collected ethnic data—the more they give, the less we know. An article from the *New York Times* entitled "Black and White Married in the Deep South: A Shifting Image," was sent to me by my longtime friend and former high school roommate. The article mentions the laws and social practices prohibiting the marriage of individuals from different so-called races; not all so-called races, just African Americans and European Americans. Interestingly enough, laws were never created to discourage their procreation or intimacy, just their marriage. The problems with this article are similar to the problems associated with all the data collected using so-called race terms— biracial, mixed-race, multi-race. These terms and others including race, or a derivative of it, are based on false premises. Therefore, the data cannot be accurate or valid.

This article underscores the Census Bureau's use and acceptance of the term race and its derivatives as being valid, accurate, and acceptable. The term biracial makes the assumption that two pure and biologically different races exist—the black race and the white race. One wonders how they arrive at the purity of each so-called race since the term biracial refers to two so-called races. Actually, the way these two races are perceived in America is based on stereotypes that provide symbolic elements that characterize each race. Generally, the characterizations are made from color and/or culture. The irony comes into play when one is asked what two races are represented in the biracial person— human and what else? Since there is only one human race, the other has to be non-human.

Another term used by the Census Bureau is mixed-race. What is a mixed-race person? Could a biracial person also be a mixed-race person or does this term have some unique qualifying aspect to it? The assumption in the use of this term is that more than two so-called races participated in the creation of mixed-race people.

Since the term is never defined, we simply do not know. We can, however, assume that the bureau or its representatives look at the cultural make-up of the parents of mixed-race people to make their determination. For example, if a bi-racial person procreated with a person of Asian and French culture, then their offspring would be labeled mixed-race. This example would be laughable if it were not part of our reality. One wonders how a so-called mixed-race person sees himself/herself.

A comment from the afore mentioned article shows just how cloudy and vague the concept of race is:

> "In the first comprehensive accounting of multiracial Americans since statistics were first collected about them in 2000, reporting from the 2010 census…shows that the nation's mixed-race population is growing far more quickly than many demographers had estimated…"

If someone can tell me the difference between a multi-racial and a mixed-race person as mentioned in the above statement, they will deserve my eternal thanks. Is a multi-race person different from a mixed-race person? The statement seems to suggest that there is. Just how does one discern them? What are the criteria necessary to be identified as multi-race and mixed race?

In the early days of slavery, Africans, American Indians, and Europeans who were slaves frequently created unions and produced children. When this happened, the slave owners paid little attention to these unions because the offspring simply increased his wealth. However, when Africans became the primary focus of the slave system, laws were created to discourage and penalize such unions, but only between so-called black and white slaves. In 1661, Maryland passed a law forbidding blacks and whites to marry regardless of their status—free or slave. The concept of race during that time was based on color rather than culture, so law was the controlling factor. How does the Census Bureau make its determination today?

Since the U.S. Census Bureau promotes the concepts of biracial, mixed-racial, and multi-racial groups of human beings, it should rightfully be the agency that seeks to correct its errors. To suggest that these groups of human beings exist is to do a disservice to America society, and especially America's children. The Census Bureau creates confusion and disagreement in educational information and instruction when society is forced to accept these racial terms as accurate, reliable, and correct. If the Census Bureau intends to continue to use these terms, the least expectation of society is for the terms to be defined. As matters now stand, no one knows the differences among a biracial person, mixed-racial person, and a multi-racial person. So, what value is the data collected from these so-called racial groups if the data is flawed?

The Census Bureau can easily start to remedy the problems created by these inaccurate and inappropriate terms by simply eliminating the use of the words "race" and "racial." The Bureau can make this move to a more specific body of ethnic-specific terms to collect the data it seeks. For example, instead of saying that the mix of black and white marriages has increased in the South since the last census, it could be more specific and say that African Americans and European Americans have increased their marriages in the South etc.

The difference between using black and white and African American and European American is that the data will not be confusing about who is included in or excluded out of the data collection. As a matter of fact, the Bureau, by using the specific ethnic cultural identities, will increase the accuracy and reliability of the collected data because it would not have to wonder if the so-called blacks are African Americans or of some other culture such as Haitian, Jamaican, or just a dark-complexioned person.

When terms are not defined in any program that focuses on collecting data from a variety of sources, the end result will not be reliable because of the many unrestricted variables. The phrase most scientists use is "garbage in, garbage out." If the Census Bureau knows specifically what it wants from the data, it should construct its collection program to produce the desired results. Clearly, the program, process, and so-called racial terms presently in place will not accomplish its objective. The time has come to make a change to help Americans with better self-identity now and in the future.

Supreme Court Looks at Affirmative Action in UT's Admission Policy

October 14, 2012

The issue of Affirmative Action has come up again for the Supreme Court to decide its merits as applied by the University of Texas and its admission policy. The outcome of the case could impact the role ethnicity has in college admission. An article entitled "Supreme Court studies UT's race admission policy," by Mark Sherman with the *Associated Press,* noted that "The court heard arguments in a challenge from a white Texan who contends she was discriminated against when the university did not offer her a spot in 2008." The title of the article should be "Supreme Court studies UT's admission policy that includes race." No one is being admitted to a race at UT.

Abigail Fisher, a 22-year-old student, claims she was rejected because race was used against her. The problem relative to this issue is the fact that race is only one of the considerations used by the university to admit students. According to the university, if it is to have any decision in creating an atmosphere of diversity, then it has to have the power to use whatever criteria necessary to achieve that objective. Its admission's program was deemed earlier by the Supreme Court to be effective in its objectives: "The University says the program is necessary to provide the kind of diverse educational experience the high court has previously endorsed." So why was a suit filed based on race? The suggestion seems to be that race has more value than the other considerations.

The university notes that along with race, it considers "community service, work experience, extracurricular activities, awards and other factors. The bulk of its slots go to students who are admitted based on their high school class rank, without regard to race." We are led to believe that Fisher felt her high grade point average should have been enough to get her admitted. The state of Texas realized some years ago that admission of GPA only would lead to charges of being unfair to students who, for social and economic reasons, could not compete with middle-class and above students. Texas discovered that relying only on grade point averages for admissions would create a problem of admitting students with little or no diversity or as in the case of the University of California at the Berkeley campus, the majority of students being Asian American. The problem actually turned out to be one that was not so much concerned about grade point average as much as who got admitted.

The problem seems to be that some European American students believe in entitlements when it comes to getting what they want. From statehood until 1948, the only school of higher education African Americans in Oklahoma could attend was Langston University, at the time, an African American only institution. Even in 1948, George McLaurin, the first African American to attend the University of Oklahoma Graduate School, had to endure Jim Crow arrangements, separated and isolated from the class in the same room.

America, it seems to some, belongs to European Americans and they should receive preference over any other ethnic American. Never mind the many years ethnic Americans, especially African Americans, were denied admission to colleges and universities.

The purpose of Affirmative Action was to try and close the gap between the number of European Americans and ethnic Americans who were qualified to attend academic, as well as professional, schools but were denied. The only reason for African Americans not being considered for admission was their ethnicity, so in order to increase their numbers in schools, their ethnicity had to be considered. The problem with schools considering ethnicity as part of admission was a claim of discrimination of European Americans. Ironically, the courts agreed that in some cases, European American students were being discriminated. Many schools realized that they would face charges of discrimination if they continued their policies that gave value to a student's ethnicity, so they, like the University of Texas, changed their admission program to make ethnicity (race) one of the elements included in admission.

For many people, Affirmative Action is a program that gives the ethnic Americans and women, an unfair advantage over European Americans. In light of the facts that many ethnic American students graduate from academically inferior schools compared to those of many European American students, what elements should be employed by colleges and universities to create diverse student bodies that would be fair to all? The element of ethnicity must be included if the challenge of diversity is to be addressed. Sherman noted that "Opponents of the [University of Texas] program say the university is practicing illegal discrimination by considering race at all, especially since the school achieves significant diversity through its race-blind admissions."

The university needs the tools they believe are necessary to effectively perform their responsibilities in creating a diverse educational experience for their students. If the court takes away Affirmative Action, then nothing will prevent a campus from becoming predominantly European American or as the case might be, Asian American or Hispanic American. In essence, who would be the most qualified students? Who would decide what students to select, and what criteria would be used in making the selection? At each stage of the process, individuals could file a charge of discrimination based on ethnic bias if the court fails to recognize the reason for the creation of Affirmative Action in the first place.

Common sense tells us that if we are riding in a car and it has a flat, the car must be stopped, the flat tire removed and fixed or replaced before the car can continue it travel. The point is that a problem cannot be addressed if the program is not interrupted. Change can only come when an interruption to the status quo occurs. For education in America to reflect ethnic diversity, change must be made— excluding ethnic American students from the experience is like the flat tire, Affirmation Action is the replaced or repaired tire. If we ask the question of what is in the best interest of the country regarding education for all, we must answer a diverse educational environment. After all, if our schools do not diversify, who cares?

Hank Williams, Jr. Apologizes for Obama Comparison to Hitler–Not

October 9, 2011

Hank Williams, Jr. the country singer whose song opens the Monday Night Football games, made a big mistake just recently during an interview. The mistake was not so much about what he said as it was about where he said it. He made a statement that compared President Obama to Adolf Hitler and referred to him and Vice President Biden as "the enemy." The problem is not so much what he said, as it is where he said it and why he said it.

Scratch the surface of a bigot, one will likely find a hypocrite. Scratch the surface of a hypocrite and one will likely find an irrational person. All three conditions usually go together because they complement each other. All three conditions can usually be found in people who make statements that call attention to themselves. Whether Hank Williams Jr. is one such person is not the question here. What is of concern here is his mindset and how that reflects the three conditions.

Most people know enough about history to not confuse Obama with Hitler, although it has been done numerous times. The idea behind the comparison is to picture Obama as a horribly despicable person. One would have to find some evidence to support the claim if it was to be believed, however, since Obama has not done anything so terrible to qualify him for that comparison, the only obvious reason for the claim is a gross dislike of Obama. One could easily say that William's statement indicates a dislike of Obama. The obvious question to follow is why does Williams dislike Obama so much? The reason could be politics—Obama is a Democrat. We might be able to accept that reason were it not for the fact that Williams has criticized Obama in the past.

One of Williams' mistakes was not realizing where he was during his interview with Fox News. One might assume that he thought he was in a comfortable, secure, and friendly setting where people thought like he thought. He probably based his thought on his knowledge of Fox News' reputation regarding its coverage of President Obama. Unfortunately, for Williams, he forgot the fact that he was closely associated with ESPN and Monday Night Football, and that viewers generally separate their football from their politics. When ESPN reacted to Williams' comments by pulling his television spot, he offered an apology.

Evidently, Williams saw nothing wrong with what he had said during the interview because he did not apologize for his comments. He does say that he is "very sorry if it (his comments) offended anyone." He never considered his comments were inappropriate, just a little extreme. Although he says he has respect for the office of the president, he must view the occupant of that office as somehow separated from it. In any event, one gets the message
that Williams does not like Obama.

No laws are broken when someone dislikes another person. Usually, when someone dislikes another person that dislike is based on something specific. Williams makes no mention of anything in particular he dislikes in Obama—just Obama. If someone is disliked enough to compare him with Adolf Hitler, but the comparison seems out of place, one reasonable assumption might be bigotry. Some Americans live in communities where ethnic diversity is not readily accepted. Some people believe that the color of a person's skin determines how they should be treated. American History shows that for many years African Americans were not given any value in society. As a matter of fact, an old saying actually measures the degree of value placed on the African Americans when it says "a N—– ain't worth s—."

Many people grow up hearing that sentiment, and others equally offensive, expressed on a frequent basis. Today, if the environment is considered safe, people who would not utter these sentiments in public would say them around friends who agreed with them. If any of these people are ever caught in the act of say disparaging remarks about an ethnic American, they will quickly apologize, not for what was said, but for being caught or "if" anyone was offended.

It goes without saying that former President Bush was compared to Hitler many times, and these comparisons were just as inappropriate as the ones relative to Obama. Fortunately, with President Bush, his comparisons were made regarding some action he had taken or not taken. With Obama, the comparison is made and we are left to draw our own conclusions. What can we make of Williams' comment that "My analogy was extreme—but it was to make a point?" What was the point? We are given nothing on which to base a reaction. His statement seems hypocritical because he does not say what he really means, whatever that may be.

In offering his apology Williams stated that "The thought of the leaders of both parties jukin'[sic] and high fiven'[sic] on a golf course, while so many families are struggling to get by, simply made me boil over and make a dumb statement, and I am very sorry if it offended anyone." The he adds, "I would like to thank all my supporters. This was not written by some publicist." Maybe he should have had a publicist write his apology because what he says makes no sense at all except if one takes each phrase at a time and try to associate it with something reasonable. One might assume he feels that the two leaders should be some place working to resolve the problems of the poor, and since they are not doing that, he gets upset and makes a "dumb statement." What he says later about the two men being total opposites adds to the confusion. We are left either to try and decipher what he means or simply to forget the entire matter and go on with our lives.

What teams are playing Monday night?

Comments about Gabby Douglas' Hair Are Out of Bounds

August 5, 2012

America watched in amazement as Gabby Douglas displayed her Olympic Gold talent and skills to win the title of the best female gymnast in the world. At the age of sixteen she has achieved something that is reserved for the most exceptional athletes on the planet—an Olympic Gold medal. All who watched her performances knew they were witnessing greatness. While most people were happy to see the young American female earn her medal, some individuals thought that Gabby's hair was more important than the accomplishment she had just experienced. Those individuals who tweeted comments about Gabby's hair were ignorant, insensitive, and asinine.

Athletes are dedicated and driven individuals who focus on perfecting their skills while developing their talents. Unless their physical appearance relative to fashion is a necessary aspect of their training, they concentrate on more important things. Depending on the sport or activity, the athletes' hair fashion is not of primary concern, unless it gets in the way of the performance. Otherwise, most of the athletes' concern is on perfecting their skills.

With respect to Gabby's hairstyle, we can assume that she wore it in a manner that allowed her to complete her programs with the least bit of distractions. Those people who made comments about Gabby's hair were ignorant of the fact that gymnasts like Gabby, as well as other athletes, come into contact with water and perspiration on a daily basis. Most women know what moisture on the hair does to it as far as fashion goes that why many prefer to keep it short and manageable. If those people writing comments about Gabby's hair knew what her training regimen was they probably would not have made those comments. But to some people, ignorance is bliss.

Regardless of the ignorance of some people regarding athletes and their hair, the comments were not in keeping with good taste or manners; in fact, they showed a gross insensitivity. The world had just witnessed a spectacular performance by a 16-year-old female gymnast and for some people, in praising her accomplishment they negate the praise by complaining about her hair style. We know that athletes are conditioned to manage their emotions so as not to interfere with their performance, but unnecessary and insensitive comments about a beautiful young lady's hair shows a total lack of class. What makes the hair comments even more insensitive is the lack of thought that could have a negative impact on a young female's self-image. If the hair comments were made to address the hair specifically, that is one concern that could be handled; however, if the hair comments were made with respect to Gabby's overall appearance, then they were totally despicable. Most young people at or around the age of sixteen are experiencing an identity change, and any little element of self-doubt can have a great impact on how they see themselves. Fortunately, Gabby knows that she is both beautiful and talented.

At a time when we Americans should be celebrating the accomplishment of Gabby Douglas for representing her country so well, we should also be mindful of the fact that negative comments about her should have no place in our hearts and mouths. We should be thankful for the devotion and sacrifice of this remarkable young lady in wanting to give America and the world her best efforts. So, for some people to praise her on one hand and criticize her hair on the other is just plain asinine.

A consequence experienced by people who make asinine comments is that the criticism they seek to place on others actually falls on them. They are seen as suffering from a character defect that prevents them from giving credit where it is due. One has to wonder what goes through the minds of people who cannot simply give credit and praise without including personal digs or what could be interpreted as insults. Gabby, as well as the other Olympic athletes, deserves our appreciation and support for their efforts in representing us and our country.

Chances are when we get a look at Gabby once the Olympic Games are over, and she is making the media rounds for her well-deserved honor, we will see a beautiful young lady whose personal appearance suits her environment. We are proud of Gabby for the challenges and triumphs she experienced in the face of many obstacles. Most of the people watching her perform probably paid little if any attention to her hair style, which is as it should have been. The only thing she should have heard from the people was "Go Gabby! You go girl!" And she did.

Slanted Cross-Cultural Homework Causes Parental Complaints

January 15, 2012

Recently in Atlanta, Georgia, the station, WSB-TV reported that some African American parents were very upset about their children's math homework that made references to slaves experiencing abuse and doing demeaning work. An example question asked "Each tree had 50 oranges. If eight slaves pick them equally, then how much would each slave have?" Another said, "If Fredrick [Douglass] got two beatings per day, how many beatings did he get in one week?" Other questions were along the same lines. When the school district was questioned about this problem, a spokeswoman stated that "teachers were trying to do a cross-cultural activity, combining math problems with social studies lessons." If the proper steps had been taken by the school and its educators, the concept of cross-cultural lesions could work very well. Unfortunately, the proper steps were not taken and the results were negative and unproductive. The proper steps should have involved preparation, execution, and expectations regarding the children, the educators and the parents.

Many times, educators with good intentions can create ill results by failing to prepare carefully and thoroughly the material to be taught. While the idea of using social history in a math class is generally a good idea, the selection of the material to be employed should be the top priority. What the educators in the above referenced incident did not do was prepare properly. They did not consider if the effect of the information presented was offensive in any way because it was taken from social history. But if we examine what was taken from the history, we discover that the information promotes and sustains the idea of African American inferiority and European American superiority.

What is generally taught in history about Frederick Douglass was his contribution to the civil rights of African Americans and women and his meetings with President Lincoln to convince him to allow African Americans to serve in the military during the Civil War. He was so successful that the Army created the 9th and 10th

Calvary—all African American soldiers. Because the questions all chose to picture Douglass as a slave, they did a disservice to his story.

With proper preparation, the educators could have selected aspects of the social history that presented a positive construction of Douglass. Since the question did not identify the ethnicity of the slaves, everyone would assume they were African. During the early years of slavery, American Indians as well as European Americans were slaves. The reference in the questions easily suggests they were African /African American. Proper preparation would dictate that all students receive positive reinforcement from the experience. The objectives of the questions should be on enhancing and learning the subject-matter, not picturing the historical vehicles employed in an unflattering context.

Once the homework questions are created, the execution of the exam should not cause undue stress on the students. The questions referenced above could have actually caused emotional problems for students, regardless of the ethnicity. For example, the questions about Douglass showed him as a victim, a slave, and therefore in an inferior condition. Since Douglass serves as a representative for African Americans chances are many of the African American students recognized inferiority underscored in Douglass.

On the other hand, the abuse and forced labor of Douglass and the slaves in general, came at the hands of European Americans and serve to represent superiority. Obviously, no one is suggesting that the questions were written deliberately with this in mind, but the results are the same regardless of the intent. What if a question stated "Benjamin Franklin fathered one and one-third, out-of-wedlock child per year? How many children would he have fathered in five years?" Where would the real emphasis lie in that question? Certainly not on the number of children but on Franklin because of his notoriety. That type of question would probably distract from the pedagogical objective and therefore be ineffective as an instrument of learning.

Generally speaking, most homework is given by the educators to measure the progress of the students' learning and control of the subject-matter. An expectation is established for each question as well as for the entire experience. One wonders just what the expectations were for the students doing the homework in question. The reported response of the spokeswoman that "This is simply a case of creating a bad question," shows a number of things lacking with the educator. For one, a lack of sensitivity for African American students who would have the concept of inferiority underscored. Another would be the lack of a considered expectation due to the nature of the question's objective—not just the number of beatings received, but the number that Douglass received. Still another concern is the lack of educational preparedness on the part of the educator relative to the sensitivity of the diverse students in the classroom and the effect that that disregard for feelings has on the non-African American students.

Most parents expect the school their children attend to reflect an atmosphere of safety and comfort from undue stress. In addition, they want to believe that the schools value each student's physical and mental well-being. When incidents like the one in question occurs, the parents are well within their rights to complain and demand to know what is at work. After all, had the parents not reacted the way they did, one doubts that the educator as well as the school would have ever realized that what they were doing was in fact counterproductive to a wholesome education. By calling attention to the problem, the educator as well as the students can benefit from the changes to come, and the parents can re-establish their expectations for their children's education, but always with watchful eyes.

Teens Hunt, Beat, and Kill an African American for Fun

August 14, 2011

A disturbing news story out of Jackson, Mississippi, carried on CNN this past week was about some European American teens who deliberately hunted down an African American man, beat and killed him. According to the story, the victim "James Craig Anderson, a 49-year-old auto plant worker, was standing in a parking lot, near his car. The teens allegedly beat Anderson repeatedly, yelled racial epithets, including 'White Power' according to witnesses." The real tragedy of this story is the fact that America does not find it appalling. This story does not represent one tragedy, the beating and murder of Anderson, but three tragedies when we add in the fate of the teens and the complicity of society.

How long will it take for an African American or any person of color to believe he or she can safely enjoy the freedoms and liberties guaranteed by the Declaration of Independence and the U.S. Constitution? Mr. Anderson evidently thought he had the right to be where he was, doing what he wanted, and observing the law in doing so. He committed no crime, caused no conflict or created no disturbance before he was attacked, beaten, and killed. America has laws that address the rights and privileges of its citizens as well as people to enforce the laws.

Unfortunately, some people believe they are above the laws or can ignore them when the objectives of their irrational beliefs can be hunted down and killed. A man has been deprived of his life, liberties, and freedom because of the fear his skin complexion caused in the minds of some European American teens.

Robert Shuler Smith, District Attorney for Hinds County, where the crime occurred, was "asked if there could be any doubt whether the intent was to actually hurt and kill a black person, Smith responded: 'No doubt about it. They were going out to look for a black victim to assault, and in this case, even kill.'" What a tragedy for Anderson.

Anderson was in fact not the cause or the reason for his tragic death; the cause was the fear, guilt, and anger the teens felt within them that needed an outlet. For them, that outlet was an African American person. The officials called the crime a "hate crime" since the specific target was an African American. The hate was inside the European American teens who seemingly felt a sense of loss of their power and privilege. The fact that they yelled "White Power" suggests a cry for help in that they were feeling a sense of loss and needed to fight to protect themselves from that loss. In essence, they evidently believed that African Americans represented the taking of their power of privilege and prestige, so they felt compelled to defend it.

Some European American teens, like their adult counterparts, have not accepted the precepts of democracy where in a diverse society each citizen has the same rights. They instead want to hold on to the false belief that America is a European American country exclusively, and any non-European American living here is a threat to their rightful ownership and rule. Their hurt comes from the fact that they are losing their 'white identity,' which is the only thing of value they have. If they lose their sense of superiority of having a white identity, then they would be just like all the other ethnic Americans in society, and that to them would be a tragedy. The real tragedy is that they still have not entered into the 21st Century as far as their thinking and perceptions are concerned. The cry of "White Power" for them is defining and confining; they are seemingly trapped in an outdated mindset that leads only to trouble for them, society, and the people they hold responsible for their hurt.

Society shares a great deal of responsibility for the acts and thinking of the teens regarding this crime. Why has there not been more vocal effort in dispelling the myths and fallacies of race by color? Too many Americans today believe that a so-called black race and white race exist. The fact is that neither exists. They were created by a bigoted society for social and economic reasons. Through the years many efforts have been made, along with laws passed, to address and to try to correct the problem of bigotry.

For teens today to yell "White Power" indicates that society has not done its job in educating its youth about the principles of democracy and life in a diverse society. What kind of society lets teens feel comfortable in going out to hunt for another human being to hurt, and subsequently kill, simply because of the color of his skin? Where do teens get the idea that they have the right and power to take another person's life just because of his skin color? Instead of society being so concerned about teens doing drugs and driving drunk, equal attention should be given to their sense of value and respect for other human beings, especially, non-European Americans.

Historically, in America the concept of a so-called white race has never been publically debunked for the obvious reasons of privilege and power. Scientifically, the concept of the existence of multiple races of human beings has been exposed as false for many years. Nonetheless, society continues to ignore science and continue the practice of calling some people black and others white—in essence, using color as a form of ethnic identity. The problem with that belief is it is inaccurate and confusing because a dark skin or a fair skin represents no hint of ethnic identity. In addition, skin complexion is no indicator of intelligence.

If America does not begin to address the problem of ethnic bigotry at the grassroots level and above, the occurrence of tragedies like the one in question will continue. Some might call this murder an isolated incident, but the lack of respect for other human beings, regardless of how they look, does not grow in an isolated environment, it is as dangerous as a deadly, contagious disease. If America does not make concerted efforts to correct this problem through education now, then when will it? Tomorrow never comes.

Cross Burning a Sign of Ignorance and Stupidity

July 24, 2011

If the incident that occurred in San Luis Obispo, California last month is any indication of how America has progressed relative to ethnic relations, then American has a long way to go. The newspaper account, The *Oklahoman* 7-23-11, states that "Four people have been arrested and charged with setting a cross on fire next to the home of a black family in a mostly white central California city." Strangely enough the answers come before the questions.

Throughout American history we are told about the burning cross as a symbol used by the Ku Klux Klan for a variety of reasons, but one in particular was to frighten and intimidate helpless African Americans, especially those living in the South. A lot of the stated symbolism for the cross burning makes no sense at all:

> "Many citizens thought it was a sacrilege to burn the cross, but the KKK defended themselves by claiming they burned the crosses as a symbol of their faith in what their belief system was. The KKK killed not only blacks, but whites and also a few politicians along the way." (answer.com)

And what they believed in was white supremacy. They believed that the color of their skin (white) made them superior to all non-European ethnic Americans. The incident cited above shows a degree of ignorance, fear, and insecurity on the part of the four people arrested for the act. First, they apparently used the burning cross as a form of intimidation against the African Americans. The cross is supposed to say to the African Americans that "you have no power; we control your life."

The fire added to the cross meant something else, it "was called 'cross burning or cross lighting' to let other KKK members know where to meet and to defend what they considered their territory and to terrorize blacks and whites alike that disagreed with their Aryan order." (answer.com)

The problem for the cross burners is not that others disagree
with their beliefs, it is because they know their belief is based on
a false premise, but cannot bring themselves to accept that truth.
Burning the cross actually indicated a fear on the part of the
burners that their belief would be exposed as false. The African
American family did not have to do anything to represent a threat
to the lack of common sense and decency imbedded in the minds
of the bigots. They evidently thought that their burning of a cross
would cause the African American family to leave or maybe just
disappear. Their illegal act was a form of defense of their belief and
proof to their fellow believers that they were willing to take a risk
for the cause.

Under the Declaration of Independence, they have a right to
think whatever they want, but they do not have the right to deprive
another of life, liberty, and the pursuit of happiness. Because of
their actions they were charged "with felony arson, cross burning,
terrorism and conspiracy. The charges come with hate crime
enhancements." Chances are these cross burners will have some
time to think about what they did and consider the wisdom of their
deed. The unfortunate part of this entire experience is the lack of
learning and understanding that is missed. Bigots are allowed to
be bigots in America, but not to the point of interfering in the lives
of other citizens. The only reason for someone to protest the rights
and privileges of another person because of his color is because of
ignorance.

To most people, the cross is a Christian symbol, but the
elements of Christianity are lost when the cross is set afire and
used as a protest against people simply because of their skin color.
The burning cross shows a contradiction in the so-called Christian
faith and belief of the bigots generally. However, if their faith and
belief in God tells them that they are superior to all people who
do not look like them, then they believe that their act is a form
of protecting and defending that belief. They also believe that
America belongs to them because God gave it to them, so they
have a right to say who lives where. Evidently these people either
have no knowledge of the Declaration of Independence and the
United States Constitution, or they totally ignore it. Maybe during

the time given to them by the state of California, they might become acquainted with those documents.

Cross burning is unfortunately not a rarity in America today. Once a common tactic of the Ku Klux Klan, it is now done by individuals who just seem to want to prove to themselves that they are special and privileged because of their skin color, which represents their identity. The fear of having an ethnic American look them in the eyes means they have lost their position of power and must fight to regain it. The fact that the U.S. Government has labeled certain illegal acts committed against citizens as hate crimes indicates the seriousness of the offense. When we examine such acts as cross burning, we find nothing that speaks to Christianity and democracy, but rather ignorance and stupidity.

When people base their identity on things that lack concrete support and proof and must be defended by irrational and false claims, they face a constant challenge to find value in themselves. Too often that value comes at the expense of their denigrating others, and if that denigration comes in the form of action against other citizens, then a crime has been committed. In this case, crime does not pay.

Michigan's Affirmative Action Problem

July 4, 2011

To many people, the case for civil rights for all people in America was fought in the 1960s and we as a nation have put that all behind us. Not true. The case for the merits of Affirmative Action is still being fought in the courts today. A July 1, 2011 *New York Times* article, "Court Overturns Michigan Affirmative Action Ban," made it apparently clear that the fight for civil rights is far from over. The article stated, "A federal appeals court on Friday struck down Michigan's 2006 ban on the consideration of race and gender in public-university admissions and government hiring in the latest round of the decade-long fight over the University's Affirmative Action policies."

What exactly does that mean?

Many of the good people of Michigan voted in 2006 to ban the use of race and gender, among others things, in admission and hiring in a number of situations. They felt that an unfair advantage was being given to the recipients of Affirmative Action. These people were not familiar with or chose to ignore American history that recorded the discrimination and unfair treatment of African Americans and women for almost three hundred years. They were under the impression that some people were being given preferential treatment simply because they were African American or female.

The 1964 Civil Rights Act recognized that long years of injustice could not be wiped away simply by passing a law. So, in order to try and make the playing field more accessible to those who had not been permitted on the field, affirmation action corrections were set in motion. If one were to venture a trip down memory lane to the early 1960s, one would not find females or African Americans employed in a number of jobs and professions that were generally reserved for European Americans. These jobs and professions had nothing to do with merit per se. So, to break the monotony of European Americans only, the courts decided it was time to give the African Americans and women a break.

Some people thought that nearly three hundred years of privilege by European Americans was just fine until the African Americans and women wanted to share in the benefits. Suddenly, many Americans felt that to try and bring about some semblance of justice for African Americans and women was taking something away from them, so they protested. They actually believed that nothing should be done to try and close the gap of injustice caused by three hundred years of being locked out of schools, jobs, and positions. In essence, they believed that all Americans woke-up one morning in 1964 and found that everyone was equal. Believe it or not, some courts agreed with them. In Michigan in 2006, the people said that to try and remedy the injustice was wrong if it meant making room for some Americans because of their ethnicity and gender; the courts agreed with them until just recently.

The *Times* article stated that "The 2-1 ruling by the United States Court of Appeals for the Sixth Circuit, in Cincinnati, said the voter-approved ban—unconstitutionally alters Michigan's political structure by impermissibly burdening racial minorities." For the African Americans and women who had been systematically prevented from school admissions and jobs simply because they lacked the education and/or training for positions they had been prevented from enjoying, and blaming them for these deficiencies, smacked of hypocrisy. Without Affirmative Action the diversity that America enjoys today would not exist. For certain, women and African Americans would not enjoy the many freedoms and liberties made possible through Affirmative Action.

One wonders why recipients and beneficiaries of Affirmative Action, like Supreme Court Justice Clarence Thomas and former University of California Regent Ward Connerly, both African Americans, would oppose it. What has changed in society that would make Affirmative Action no longer necessary? If anyone thought that the issue was resolved simply because of the court's decision, well guess what? "Michigan's attorney general, Bill Schuette, promised Friday that he would indeed appeal the decision overturning the ban known as the Michigan Civil Rights Initiative through a formal request for rehearing en banc [the full court] by all 16 judges of the court."

Will someone please explain how one goes about trying to right a wrong committed against a people because of their ethnicity and gender when neither of those conditions can be used in the attempt to correct the injustice? What the voters of Michigan voted on was known "as Proposal 2 and prohibited public institutions from giving preferential treatment to any individual or group on the basis of race, sex, color, ethnicity or national origin." In essence, the very criteria used to exclude them from participation in society justly could not be used to help them recover from the unjust treatment.

Basically, the opponents of Affirmative Action evidently believe that nothing should be done to try and bridge the gap created by segregation, discrimination, bigotry, and injustice against African Americans and women for three hundred years. Their sense of equality and fairness defies logic and common sense by their thinking that if no changes are made, everything will right itself. Their idea of justice and fairness is to leave everything the way it was before the Civil Rights Acts of 1964 and on course, Affirmative Action.

Many people will point to President Obama and say that because he is president and African American that Affirmative Action is no longer needed. What many people do not understand about Affirmative Action is that this program simply provides an opportunity for African Americans and women to access entrance into schools and jobs. Students who gain admission to schools through Affirmative Action must still experience the same curricula as the other students. Employees hired with the help of Affirmative Action must still perform their job the same as the other employees. The key component of Affirmative Action is access to opportunity. The end result is a better society for all Americans.

Jasper, Texas, a Study in Historical Bigotry and Social Control

July 1, 2012

If the name Jasper, Texas sounds familiar, it is probably from the news created in 1998 when an African American man named James Byrd was killed. Byrd was walking home at night when three European American men picked him up, took him to a secluded wood, tied his hands and feet, and then tied him to the back of the truck. He was then dragged for several miles until he was decapitated from that experience. An enormous amount of media attention was paid to the incident, which produced a variety of activities, some from the Ku Klux Klan as well as the Black Panthers. After the arrest, trial, and conviction of the perpetrators, the town seemed to undergo a dramatic change regarding ethnic relations—a positive change. Unfortunately, the change did not last very long.

In a recent article in the *Washington Post*, "Racial tension still an issue in Jasper, Texas" 6/15/12 by Lora Stahl, healing and reconciliation didn't really take place. Since the killing of Byrd, a number of things happened to indicate that the town was dealing with some of the bigotry that is part of its history. Over the past few years, four African Americans had been elected to the City Council and the town had recently hired an African American as Chief of Police. The participation of these African Americans in the town's affairs seemed too much for some of the European Americans to take. So, something had to be done.

The nature of the problem in Jasper as well as hundreds of other towns like it is the unwillingness of too many of the European Americans citizens to come to grips with the bigotry that has been part of their lives since birth. The stereotypical view of the African American by European Americans is one of inferiority accompanied by negative elements such as ignorance, laziness, dishonesty, violence and a host of other descriptive adjectives. The problem stems from the belief that if African Americans occupy positions of leadership, then the value and stature of the European Americans is diminished. Therefore, that situation

should never be allowed to exist. The power and prestige of the
European Americans would be in jeopardy of being lost if African
Americans were to gain positions of power. So, when the presence
of African Americans in the town's government came to notice,
something had to be done to protect the real [European American]
citizens.

One of the first orders of business was to remove the African
Americans from the City Council. That was done through a recall
process. Apparently, the powers-that-be did not like the power the
African Americans managed or simply working with them, so they
had them removed using their power and influence. That power
and influence was generated through creating fear and hatred of
European Americans losing the place of privilege.

The article noted that "On Monday, 16 months after he was
hired by a black majority on the City Council, Police Chief Rodney
Pearson was ousted during a tense council meeting. The council,
which now has a white majority, voted 4 to 1 to terminate Pearson."
The reasons for Pearson's firing are not clear, except for the
article stating that the Mayor, "Mike Lout grilled Pearson during
a long session before the firing was announced. Lout reportedly
questioned the chief about how many hours he worked and why he
was not present at two high-profile crime scenes."

Evidently, the Mayor had to lecture the chief (read boy) before
he told him of his firing. The lecture was a show of power the
mayor wanted to underscore not only to the chief, but also to all
the townspeople. In effect, the European Americans were back in
control—they took their town back.

To understand the way this change in power took place we
have to look at a number of things that do not seem connected, but
are. The chief, an African American, was married to a European
American. On the surface, they had not encountered any problems
in Jasper. However, we are told that "Pearson's wife [Sandy] was let
go about three weeks ago from her job managing a medical office
because of 'low morale' in the workplace." By the business letting
Sandy go, it was suggesting that she was the cause of the "low
morale."

With the firing of Pearson, the powers-that-be in the town have successfully cut off the Pearson's livelihood. They, in effect, have said that they have the power to destroy your way of life and make your time in Jasper difficult. What apparently started the power change, according to the article, was Pearson's concern over the recall process: "Earlier this year, Pearson hired lawyers to represent him in an Equal Employment Opportunity Commission claim. According to a report in the Beaumont Enterprise, the claim was not mentioned by the council during the meeting this week." The complaint was not mentioned for fear that the dots would be connected and the truth comes out. The article continued with, "The complaint was apparently filed after a local recall election last month resulted in several black council members losing their seats to whites."

We are told that some African Americans launched a recall petition to unseat Lout, but were not successful. We need not wonder why. The irony of it all is that just when people start to believe that society is beginning to realize that all people live on the same planet, breathe the same air, and meet whatever requirements necessary to life and livelihood, fear and hatred in the form of bigotry and prejudice comes forth to take center stage. Yes, the powers-that-be in Jasper have been successful in delaying social progress. However, they must realize that all their efforts did no more than delay progress.

Their efforts to "take back their town" supposedly from African Americans are based on their fear of losing their sense of superiority. Their hatred comes from the fact that they realize they are fighting a losing battle and they cannot stop the inevitable loss. So, they do what they can to hold on for as long as they can.

Arrest of African American Teens Waiting for the Bus Show Challenges for Law Enforcement

December 9, 2013

By now, many people have heard the story of the arrest of three African American high school basketball players in Rochester, N.Y. for refusing to move away from the sidewalk where they were standing, waiting to catch a school bus. Their coach had told them to wait at that location for a school bus, which would take them to a school where they would play a scrimmage game. The arrest reportedly occurred when a police officer ordered the teens to move away from their location. At least one of the teens tried to inform the office that they were only following the orders of their coach. The explanation was not accepted, if even heard, by the officer that proceeded to handcuff the teens. The basketball coach arrived on the scene to see his players handcuffed and in the custody of the officer. The coach's explanation as to why the teens were waiting for the bus in that location was also ignored by the officer. The officer even threatened the coach with arrest if he did not stay out of the incident.

The teens were taken to jail where their parents had to pay $200 for release of their sons on bail. Fortunately, after the District Attorney reviewed what had transpired, she dismissed "the charges in the interest of justice." The Rochester Police Chief said, however, that he believed "the arrest was justified." Evidently, the location where the arrest took place had been the scene of disturbances at some earlier time. Regardless of the reasons given for the arrest, the incident reveals a number of problems involving police and certain ethnic American citizens.

If anyone has difficulty understanding why the police and certain ethnic American populations have relationship challenges, this incident should serve to underscore what is at the core of the challenges. First, from the perspective of the African American teens, the police failed to recognize them as valuable human beings. Next, the police ignored what the teens had to say as irrelevant to his objective; finally, the police acted on the basis of stereotypes in going about making the arrests.

First, the one thing that all human beings expect from other human beings is validation. That is, when one person says hello to another person, a reply is expected as normal behavior. If a reply is not forthcoming, then some form of rationalization is provided to satisfy the lack of a reply. However, in most cases, a reply is usually forthcoming. The reply lets the first person know that he or she has been recognized and validated. For someone not to reply could signal a rebuff or a deliberate lack of validation. In most cases the greeting is followed by a reply. What the officer did, relative to the teens, in not allowing them to explain their presence was to not validate them; that is, to show them that what they had to say was of no value to him.

When the officer handcuffed and arrested the teens, he further communicated to them that he did not value them as human beings worthy of common decency and respect. If someone accidently steps on another person's foot, a quick comment of "excuse me" is generally offered to show respect for the person whose foot was stepped on and to acknowledge regret for the offense. Because the officer ignored what the teens said about their presence and the fact that they were handcuffed and arrested without any acknowledgement as to their humanity, we might assume that they felt helpless and certainly not valued.

In addition to what happened to the teens, they also witnessed the way the officer treated their coach and the lack of respect given him. Some people might excuse the officer for showing a lack of respect to the teens, but the coach was a responsible adult who deliberately spoke to the officer in a respectful manner. The officer not only ignored the explanations of the coach for the teens' presence at that location, but also even threatened to arrest him as well. The actions of the officer suggest that he was the only person with any rights and value that mattered. Had it not been for the presence of other people with cameras and access to the social media, the results of this incident might have very well meant a criminal record for the teens and legal expenses for their parents. From numerous past experiences we know whose words would be viewed as true in a court of law when the balance is between the officer and the accused.

Most national polls (Gallup, 7/13) reveal that two out of every eight African American and Hispanic American men have had some direct negative contact will law enforcement. So, there should be little doubt why African Americans and Hispanic Americans regard police officers as the enemy rather than friend or protector.

What does this incident say about the challenges of the law enforcement establishments regarding relationships with minority citizens especially African Americans and Hispanics? If the people that the police are to protect question the motives of the officers, little or no cooperation or respect will be forth coming from those people. Too often officers are ill equipped and uneducated to serve successfully in minority communities. In the above incident, the arrest and subsequent actions could have been avoided had the officer given the teens a little respect and valued them as human beings rather than following negative stereotypical perceptions.

One of the teens said in remembering the treatment received from the officer that "not all teens are bad;" in other words, why would the officer assume that these teens were bad since they had not done anything unlawful? The answer to that question comes from a lack of adequate instruction and education relative to how police are perceived by minority citizens and why they are perceived in such a negative way.

In far too many cases the police seem to forget their mantra "To Protect and To Serve" when it comes to certain minority citizens. Too often they forget that they represent the laws of the people they serve; they are not themselves the law. One approach to changing the negative perceptions of minorities toward police would be for the police to ask themselves how would they like themselves or any member of their family to be treated? Once they have answered that question, they should proceed to meet their objective.

Tonya Battle and Another Case of Ethnic Discrimination

February 17, 2013

Ethnic prejudice is still so engrained in the psyche of some Americans that they continue to do irrational, illogical, and stupid things. A case in point was reported by the *Huffington Post* 2/16/13 in an article, "Tonya Battle, African American Nurse, Sues Michigan Hospital for Race Discrimination." According to the article, the lawsuit states, "Tonya Battle was barred from treating an infant patient at Hurley Medical Center because she is African American." In addition, the article noted that in the complaint, "Battle claims that the newborn's father showed her supervisor 'a swastika of some kind' and asked that no black people be involved in his child's care."

Why would someone living in a diverse society like America, make such a request thinking it was a proper thing to do? The answer is that at one time, not very long ago, ethnic prejudice against African Americans was common practice. The laws against such practices began to change in 1954 and continued through the 1960s to today; however, the psyche of many Americans still remains entrenched in ethnic prejudice. If blame is to be placed on anyone in this case, it should be with the hospital and its representatives. Three things happened in succession that should not have taken place when the request was made: acknowledgement, acceptance, and activation.

The problem began when Battle's supervisor acknowledged the request as legitimate and reasonable. Anyone can make a request for anything, but to acknowledge the request as reasonable usually takes an understanding of what is being requested and if the request is appropriate. Evidently, the supervisor did not stop to consider her African American co-workers when she acknowledged the request. Instead of discounting the request as being absurd, inappropriate, and unreasonable, her actions made it seem legitimate and reasonable.

After the requested was acknowledged, the supervisor then took the next step and accepted it as legitimate. Her actions, in essence, indicated to the father that she agreed with the reasonableness of his request. Again, the fact that her acceptance of the request affected other people at the hospital seemingly did not cross her mind, or if it did, she quickly dismissed it. The supervisor, apparently, was not aware of, thinking about, or was ignorant of U.S. Equal Employment Opportunity Commission (EEOC) regulations that prohibit discrimination. In any case, she was not conducting herself appropriately in her position with respect to her co-workers. She must have thought that European Americans still have to power and privilege to discriminate when they desire to do so.

The next step taken by the supervisor, putting the request into action, is the most serious action of all because it not only ignored the well-being of the African American nurses but also put the hospital in jeopardy. The article noted that nurse Battle said that she "was shocked, offended, and in disbelief that she was so egregiously discriminated against based on her race and re-assigned." We are told in the article that "Battle, who was taken off the case, was allegedly later told by a supervisor that the patient's request was granted. The [law] suit also states that a note was appended to the patient's file that read 'No African American nurse to take care of baby.'"

Today, as American citizens, we look around and see examples of how society is starting to embrace its diversity in a positive way, and we often forget that just because laws were written and instituted to remove elements of discrimination in society that all is not well. We need look no further than our political system to verify that all is not well. Many Americans have yet to accept Barack Obama as president simply because he is African American.

We must acknowledge that the prejudice that was ingrained in the European American's psyche for several hundred years will take some time to be removed, if ever. In some cases, we will rely on Mother Nature for assistance, otherwise we must look to education and information for help.

The Battle lawsuit should serve as a reminder to all of us that much work remains to be done regarding eliminating ethnic prejudice. Some of that work should come in the form of education that debunks the false concept of multi-biological races. Science has proven beyond a doubt that all human beings are 99.9 percent alike—that skin color, eye color, and hair texture are all superficial elements. Human blood and organs are not assigned an ethnic designation regarding use, so why should we be so ignorant about physical appearance? The longer we accept and recognize the false concepts and assumption about race, the more we will see examples like Battle's.

The hospital where this incident took place should institute a program of ethnic education for all its employees in order to avoid a repeat of the Battle experience. The education should not focus on how different we are, but how much alike we are and the minor differences are just that—minor. The fact that the supervisor acknowledged, accepted and activated the biased request showed ignorance and a lack of regard and sensitivity toward all the African American employees, not just the nurses. The supervisor's decision led to a collapse of communication among professionals, and a reassessment of standards and values by everyone involved in the hospital environment. An apology will not be sufficient to remedy the harm that has been done to the African American employees because from the action of the supervisor, the problem is systemic, not arbitrary.

We as a society need to get to a point where anyone making a request that discriminates against any ethnic person or group would feel uneasy doing so because he or she knows that it will not be granted. Getting to that point, however, will require consistent attention and hard work.

Evidently, we still have a way to go.

The Media Fails Its Responsibility in the Trayvon Martin Case

April 1, 2012

Who is Joe Oliver? If you have been following the Trayvon Martin case, then you know that for a few days Oliver was on all the major news shows telling the audiences what a good friend he is to George Zimmerman, the killer of Martin. Why was Oliver on all the news shows? The answer is because the media did not do their jobs. They took the word of some unknown person and let him have an audience with the programs' viewers. The media is at fault for creating much of the confusion surrounding this case.

Without first checking his credibility before allowing him air time, the media did the public a disservice because what Oliver had to say contributed absolutely nothing to our understanding of this case. One reporter, however, Jonathan Capehart, a writer for the *Post*, realized that Oliver was seeking publicity and had nothing concrete to share because it was not based on facts. Oliver convinced the media that he was "a man who knew the man who shot Trayvon Martin on Feb. 26 in Sanford, Fla. A man who could vouch for Zimmerman's personal growth and character. A man who knew the gunman so well that he was certain that the voice screaming for help on one of the 911 calls was Zimmerman's." According to Capehart, while Oliver might have believed all this, the facts proved otherwise.

The game Oliver had been playing with the media came to a head on the MSNBC show The Last Word, with Lawrence O'Donnell. Capehart was also a guest on this show and took part in asking questions of Oliver. Any number of responses from Oliver to the questions put to him by O'Donnell could have proved Oliver's lack of credibility, but one response to a question sealed the deal. Oliver said, "I wouldn't put myself out here on the line like this if I didn't know in my heart that George Zimmerman was in a life-or-death struggle." All the guests realized simultaneously that they'd been had. What does knowing something in "your" heart have to do with hard facts? Nothing.

Finally, Joe Oliver was no longer invited to talk on any of the news shows simply because he had nothing to contribute. Why didn't the media know this beforehand? We might assume that part of the reason is the desire to be first in presenting what has been called "breaking news." The problem with this concept is that the line defining news has been blurred to the point that one questions what really is defined as news today. Reporters and journalists used to verify their information before offering it to the public. However, since the advent of "breaking news" it seems that speed is more important the accuracy. Oliver is not the only person seeking "air time" regarding this case and the media has, in a number of instances, accommodated them.

Another problem that the media seems to create in a subtle way involves the subject of race. When a question about race is raised by a reported or journalist, then race enters the story. From the introduction of race comes the question of racism. Once racism has been introduced, the charges of being or not being a racist become the center of attention. For some people, simply knowing someone of a different ethnicity is proof enough that the accused is not racists.

Unfortunately, once the bridge to race, racism, and racist has been crossed the water beneath the bridge becomes too tainted to be of use. Using race as a decoy has become a popular ploy to try and defuse an issue. With respect to the killing of Trayvon Martin, we do not know for certain that it played a part. We do know that Trayvon is dead. As a society we need to stop using the words race and racist as catch-all words. In reality, bigotry might have played a larger part in the activities surrounding Trayvon's death than did racism. A person can have prejudices and not be a racist.

One thing the media can help the public to understand is that racism and prejudice is not the same thing. If they want to be accurate in reporting, they should try and ascertain the difference before assuming that race was involved. By not making a clear distinction between racism and bigotry the media is complicit is promoting the confusion. If they do not know the difference, then they should avoid using the words because their use creates a definite impression with the public. After all is said and done, if the public is not made aware of the misuse of the words race, racism, and racist, chances are we will be back at the same place as before the news story of Trayvon broke—uninformed.

We have been led to believe that the media has a responsibility to the public, and part of that responsibility involves reporting facts. If we cannot depend on the media to provide us with the facts, then they have outlived their usefulness to us and the public good. Unfortunately, what passes for news today is little more than entertainment, and not good entertainment at that.

So, who is Joe Oliver and why do we want to hear what he has to say? Mr. Capehart was right when he said, "Don't trust Joe Oliver's 'gut feeling' about his 'friend' George Zimmerman." My response to that statement is: why did I have to listen to Joe Oliver in the first place?

The Martin and Zimmerman Case Underscored the Biases Present in American Society

July 21, 2013

Following the decision of the jury during the Trayvon Martin trial, the primary question asked about the trial was—was race involved? That question, unfortunately, was the wrong question to ask. Many Americans are great pretenders when the subjects are race and justice. They pretend that both race and justice exists for all Americans when they know for a fact that it does not.

First, the term race is inaccurate, misleading, and incorrect because it supports the divide that is inherent it the term's usage. Human beings belong to one race, so the appropriate terms should be ethnic groups or ethnicity when speaking of personal identity. Injustice in America, we know, is a fact. All one has to do is look at the number of women imprisoned in Oklahoma, or look at the gap in the jobs between African American and other American youths, or the arrest and imprisonment of African American males across America.

So, the question following the Trayvon Martin case should be: how much did ethnic bias influence the decision in the case?

Not having an ethnic bias in America is impossible for anyone who has been here for a week, because we recognize that different ethnic groups are stereotyped by society in general in everyday life. What that stereotyping meant for the Trayvon Martin case was that the decision against Martin was a forgone conclusion once the jury was selected. Americans like to think that our criminal justice system is fair and impartial when we know that the outcome of any trial commonly depends on the level and degree of representation one can acquire. We know that a person who can afford a top tier lawyer stands a better chance of receiving a favorable verdict than a person with a Public Defender. Yet, we simply place our hope in our belief that the system works. What we do not consider is the fact that ethnic bias is a fact of life for all Americans. In addition to the ethnic difference, we must recognize that social and economic differences also take a toll on the justice system.

When we look at the ethnic differences involved in the case, we must consider that everyone involved came to this experience with some long-standing ethnic assumptions. Zimmerman, for example, assumed that Trayvon was a suspicious-looking person. We do not know why Trayvon was assumed to be suspicious to Zimmerman, but common sense dictates that if it is raining and one has a hood, then one will use that hood to protect one's self from the rain. According to Zimmerman, the identity of past perpetrators were African American, so it stands to reason that he assumed Trayvon to be African American. Although Zimmerman's ethnicity is Hispanic, the jury considered him to be "white," like most of them. So, the division of ethnic bias was present in the perception of the jury regarding Martin, Zimmerman, and themselves. Since they identified with Zimmerman, and not Martin, they would offer a decision that was more in line with their perception. We must remember that Martin and Zimmerman are not viewed equally by the jury even thought they might say they are; ethnic stereotypes held by the jury were involved in the jury's decision.

Our justice system says that we are to be judged by a jury of our peers, but we know that happening is next to impossible. The decision against Martin was made by a jury that had no idea of what his life and social environment was like. Without the ethnic associated with Zimmerman, the jury had no knowledge of his life as well. The lives of the individuals on the jury have no resemblances to that of Martin—they would never meet in the same church, neighborhood store, park or school except by accident. Their social lives are completely different from that of Martin, so they form assumptions about his life as a young African American accompanied with all the negative stereotypes associated with those assumptions. They do the same with Zimmerman also, but from a totally perspective—he is considered "white."

For many years in America, certain ethnic groups were not permitted citizenship because they were not considered European American. Included in that group were Polish, Irish, Italians, Jewish, Hispanics, Asians, and numerous others. After World War

II, the government began to consider many of them as "white," and because of this change, many were able to benefit economically, socially, politically as opposed to the opportunities of African Americans. Many of these new "whites" became staunch defenders of their new group, actually fighting against some other ethnic groups attempting to acquire social fairness and justice; they became more "white" than the European Americans in wanting to preserve the rights, privileges and power of their new group.

Today, the U.S. Government and the Census Bureau allow any number of ethnic Americans to identify themselves as "white;" even Zimmerman could identify himself as a "white Hispanic." The term "white" is inaccurate and incorrect as well as misleading. A person either has an ethnic identity or is considered European American, not white. So, what does this have to do with the trail? Simply stated, the members of the jury could not relate to Martin from an economical perspective because they do not live in the same or similar environment based on their economic status. They have no occasion to interact or get to know Martin, his family or the millions of families like his. And, yes, ethnicity biases did play a major role in this equation.

As a society, we need to recognize the fact that America is separated on many levels because of economics, education, religion, politics, and other elements, and that all citizens are not and, for now, cannot receive fair and equal treatment through our justice system. The Martin case provides us with an opportunity to not only open a discussion about this problem, but also to create actions for addressing them. We are merely begging the question when we ask if race had anything to do with the Martin v. Zimmerman case because we know that ethnic bias is a part of the American social fabric.

What we must do as a society now is to create and implement plans that will bring us together as one society with diversity rather than a society separated because of our ethnic diversity. Too many Americans do not realize or recognize their bigotry because of their level of separation from parts of society, in many instances; their "level of separation" not only keeps others out, but imprisons them.

Fairness in the Criminal Justice System and Society is the Focus of the Protest

December 2, 2014

In the wake of the Ferguson, Missouri grand jury decision, one thing has become crystal clear—many European Americans have no clue as to why African Americans do not trust law enforcement in general, and the justice system in particular. Many European Americans do not take the time to get the facts relative to incidents involving European American police officers and African Americans; they simply side with the police. In addition, since the majority of law enforcement officers reflect the majority society, the relationship between these two groups is generally good. No so with respect to law enforcement agencies and African Americans and other people of color.

The element of distrust of the justice system regarding African Americans and people of color has proven to be correct in far too many cases. Whenever a conflict arises involving justice for an African American victim and a European American law officer, the officer is usually exonerated. When African Americans protest a decision and the lack of justice, as they see it, from the justice system, many European Americans take the side of the law establishment, regardless of the actual situation, evidence, and facts.

No amount to evidence, facts, and data will convince a bigot that American citizens, regardless of their ethnicity, have a Constitutional right to protest against the justice system as to what they perceive as an injustice. Rather than sticking to a specific issue or concern presented by the protesters, the bigots will try to bring in other issues to try and weaken the objective of the protest. For example, when protesters talk about the number of killings of unarmed African American males by European American law officers, the bigots want to bring into the discussion the number of "black on black" murders.

The problem with this inclusion is that it has nothing to do with the problem of unequal justice. The African Americans who commit murder against other African Americans are generally apprehended, tried, and if found guilty, sent to prison. History shows that most European American police officers who shoot and kill young African American males rarely go to trial, and if they do, are usually set free. Michael Brown's case is only one of the most recent examples.

One of the problems with the difference between how African Americans see the criminal justice system and the way European Americans see it is how some, usually bigoted, European Americans perceive African Americans in general. In many instances, European Americans see African Americans at extremes: either well-to-do, educated, and professional or poor, ignorant, prone to violence, dishonest, collect food stamps, and criminal. Little room is ever given to seeing African Americans as ordinary human beings as they, European Americans, see themselves.

Because of these perceptions and bigoted attitudes, fear and hate can be easily generated by people who want to polarize each side. For example, an article in the *Oklahoman* 11/29/14 by *Wall Street Journal* editorial writer Jason L. Riley entitled "A Discussion No One Wants," does just that, whether deliberate or not. Apparently, Riley does not realize his bigotry. Using language and information that casts a dark shadow on the character of Michael Brown, Riley tries to build an argument justifying Brown's death. He added,

> "Racial profiling and tensions between the police and poor, black communities are real problems, but these are effects rather than causes, and they can't be addressed without also addressing the extraordinarily high rates of black criminal behavior—yet such discussion remains taboo."

This reference is a good example of mixing several different concerns and trying to blend them into one—the black problem. First, racial profiling and tensions exists among African Americans and police regardless of the communities; the focus of the police is usually on the skin color. The "black on black crime" is a problem that is being addressed even by the president, so that concern should not be included in the discussion. African Americans want to have the discussion, however, they must have it with people willing to listen and act positively.

Riley offered some unsubstantiated information that serves to underscore his bigotry: "But so long as young black men are responsible for an outsize portion of violent crime, they will be viewed suspiciously by law enforcement and fellow citizens of all races." The statement suggests that all young black men are criminals and are responsible for committing a large portion of violent crimes. Where are the facts, stats, or evidence? By now Riley should know that human beings belong to one race, not many.

Riley wants his readers to think that the entire problem in Ferguson is simple to assess:

> "Pretending that police behavior is the root of the problem is not only a dodge but also foolish...Ferguson's problem isn't white cops or white prosecutors; it's the thug behavior exhibited by individuals like Michael Brown, which puts a target on the backs of other young black men. Romanticizing such behavior instead of condemning it only makes matters worse."

There we have it; all that needs to be done to solve the problem is to get rid of the young, black thugs.

What Riley does not understand in his bigoted perspective, is that Michael Brown and Ferguson are not what is being protested, per se, but the injustice of the American criminal justice system. Responsible Americans of all ethnicities are involved in protests all across America and some foreign countries in an effort to get America's attention regarding the years of injustice perpetrated against African Americans and people of color. These protestors are not causing violent disruptions, but civil unrest and civil disobedience. The American Psychological Association defined violence as "an extreme form of aggression, such as assault, rape or murder." Some extreme and small elements of some protest groups have destroyed property and burned buildings, cars, and businesses. These acts are reprehensible and have no places in the protests and are never condoned. With respect to violence, however, the violence in most cases is not committed by the protestors. When we look at the definition of the word violence, we certainly cannot describe the protestors as violent; they do not assault, abuse, or murder the police or law enforcers.

"*Spinning into Butter*," a Lesson in Bigotry

April 23, 2010

The movie "*Spinning into Butter*" (*2007*) is both simple and complicated depending on how one views it. The simple approach is to take the movie's story at face value and follow the development of the newly hired Dean of Students, Sarah Daniels, a European American, at the elite Belmont College. Daniels left an ethnically diverse college in favor of a predominately European American one because of the biases she developed at the former school. Unfortunately, she becomes challenged at her new place of employment when an African American student starts to receive hate messages. In essence, the simple story follows Daniels as she moves from one stage of prejudice to another.

The complicated view comes in a number of approaches. We can look at the entire story through its theme—bigotry. If we follow this approach, we will have to consider the five major areas of concern: the European Americans Dean of Students, the European American faculty and administration, the defiant African American student, the African American news reporter, and the student body with representatives from different ethnic groups. When we take this approach we discover that biases exist in all the groups. Each group has its own challenges of bigotry to confront.

Another complicated approach to understanding the story is to look at it as an expression of American society and its approach to dealing with the nature of bigotry. This approach seems to provide more food for thought. For example, the movie's title comes from the story of Little Black Sambo. Although this story was initially about a young African boy, a series of cartoons were created featuring an African American boy. The cartoons represented a negative stereotype of African Americans symbolized in the character of Sambo.

American society found the dehumanizing and belittling of African Americans quite entertaining. Why? Because seeing in full view the demeaning and negative qualities created in the cartoons and exhibited by a little stereotyped character gave the European Americans a sense of self pride and importance, even a feeling of superiority based simply on their skin color. The fact that America enjoyed the negative stereotype of African Americans underscores the lack of value placed on being African American. The movie captures European American attitudes and the variety of expression they take in society.

Bigotry, biases, prejudice, discrimination and ethnic hate are common practices by European Americans toward African Americans even though they were not always outward and obvious. All are included in the movie, with the exception of racism. Sure, the words race and racism are used, but they do not fit because most intelligent and rational people know that racism is an illusion created to divide and conquer ignorant people. The human race is composed of many ethnic and cultural groups, but only one race. Therefore, racism cannot exist in isolation; bigotry, biases, prejudice, discrimination and hate can be confined to individuals.

Bigotry knows not color, gender, religion, culture, because it belongs to the individual. In the movie, we observe the characters from the five areas aforementioned expressing and exposing their form of bigotry. Daniels does not understand that what she is experiencing and reacting to is not caused by the students, but by her own ignorance. We see this clearly when she tries to talk a Hispanic student into being identified as one group rather than the one he embraces in an effort to give him a scholarship. The scholarship will make the college look good, but at the student's loss of identity. He finally rejects the scholarship; his identity is too high a price for him to pay. The Dean never really understands this.

The militant African American student reacts to what he believes is a lack of acceptance, as a human being, by the school and the students, by posting the ethnically sensitive comments and creating the other acts that call attention to the bigotry he knows exists, but the school and students are hiding. He wants to bring out the bigotry in full view. He sees his challenge as a contest in which one wins or loses. He loses.

The African American news reporter is an opportunist. He understands the situation of bigotry at the college and wants to capitalize on it. He would have enjoyed the publicity he and the college would have received if the claims of bigotry had been forth coming. When his chances for national television, and a possible move up, are destroyed, he loses interest in the story and moves on.

The school's administration and faculty, as represented through several characters, show a total ineptness in not only recognizing the problems of bigotry, but also in knowing how to address it. Although they are supposed to represent the educational and intellectual elite, they are exposed for their arrogance and ignorance. The epitome of their ignorance and ineptness is shown when Daniels is told to come up with a ten-point plan to solve prejudice on campus. They are so ignorant that they fail to perceive their own ignorance.

Finally, the students expose their bigotry in an open forum, but otherwise hide behind the mask the militant student tried to expose. They are products and representatives of American society. In attending an educationally elite college, they are encouraged to feel more than special and privileged; they are elitists with feelings of passive bigotry. A quote at the beginning of the movie mentions that one never forgets how he or she is made to feel, that sentiment is underscored in the movie through a number of students.

Although the movie presents the many sides of bigotry, it never comes close to addressing avenues of approach to understanding it. What becomes apparent throughout the movie is an unwillingness of any of the symbolic characters to address their bigotry. Why? Because they are stuck in their cultural box of race and fail to see that the box is the major problem.

The college, via the administration, shows the least intelligence regarding ethnic bigotry by suggesting that it could be resolved with a number of rules and student interaction. As the intellectual leaders, they should be the ones addressing the problems for themselves. However, they never realize that they are ignorant of the problem and their superior attitudes will not allow them to listen to anyone they feel is beneath them.

"Spinning into Butter" is an excellent teaching tool for educators who operate outside of the "race box." The problem of bigotry cannot be honestly or accurately addressed using

the language of race, black and white or any stereotypical or generalized language. Seeing the problem of bigotry fully while in the "race box" is not possible, so the perspective must change in order to fully appreciate the opportunity to learn teach and learn.

At the movie's conclusion, Daniels is seen going back to Chicago and the ethnically diverse school she left for Belmont. The suggestion is that she now understands her bigotry and what it means to be an ethnic American of color. Unfortunately, she does not get it—bigotry is not addressed from the outside in, but from the inside out. The movie does not address or resolve anything relating to bigotry. Each major symbolic character stays in his/hers/their corner of the "race box"—they are so at a loss to try and get out because they all accept the status quo.

"All in the Family," a View of American Bigotry

December 16, 2012

An old saying that "hindsight is 20/20" makes reference to the possibility of people looking back on something in the past and getting a better, more clear picture and understanding than the first time they experienced or saw it. That might be the case for some people, but not for all. Sometimes the look backwards does not change at all; the change depends on who is doing the looking. A good example of this type of experience can be observed in the famous television show "All in the Family."

The show was centered on the Bunker family who lived in a house located in Queens, New York. Information about the show states:

> "Archie Bunker was the main character... He was television's most famous bigot, crass, downright rude. Yet he was loveable, with a soft side just beneath the surface. Edith Bunker was his somewhat dizzy wife whom he called 'Dingbat.' Archie and Edith had a daughter, Gloria, who had a husband named Mike, but was called 'Meathead' by Archie."

We are told that "The stories revolved around many controversial topics including, rape, sex, homosexuality, death and other topics that were relevant to the '70s, especially political strife and inflation." In addition, we are told that "Archie Bunker was probably the first character in a situation comedy to use racist remarks referring to blacks and other minorities."

What makes this show important is the fact that Archie complains constantly about the changes that are occurring in society. The audience sees him as a bigot, but he never sees himself as such, and rightly so, because his society conditioned him to hold the social perspective he possessed. If we look at some of the lyrics of the show's theme song, we get the full flavor or Archie's protest: "Boy, the way Glen Miller played. / Songs that made the Hit Parade. /Guys like us, we had it made. /Those were the days."

Archie remembers, according to the song, what to him were the "good old days," when European Americans (whites) were the people of privilege in society. The song also underscores his attitude about himself and other European Americans concerning the present state of affairs: "Didn't need no welfare state. / Everybody pulled his weight. /Gee, that old LaSalle (car) ran great. / In other words, he had a good job, a nice affordable house, an automobile, and he lived in a segregated neighborhood. Those were the days!

For Archie, conditions in society are changing in a way that allows other Americans to begin to share in many of the benefits of society. The problem for Archie is that he wants to retain the level of privilege he believes is his by virtue of his being European American. To be more specific, the government promoted European American privilege, segregation and discrimination. Richard Rothstein, in an article, "Government-Sponsored Segregation," published in The American Prospect, tells us how Archie was able to purchase the house in Queens. He states:

> "The government has an explicit policy of not insuring suburban mortgages for African Americans. In suburban Nassau County, just east of Queens, for example, Levittown was built in 1947; 17,500 mass-produced two-bedroom houses, requiring nothing down and monthly payments of only about $60."

This payment, we are told,

> "(was considerably less than the approximately $75 unsubsidized charged in Woodside Houses for apartments of comparable size.) At the FHA's insistence, developer William Levitt did not sell homes to blacks, and each deed included a prohibition of such resales in the future."

Archie's house in Queens more than likely had a housing restriction that prevented African Americans from living, owning or renting them. So, the attitude of privilege that Archie reflected, along with the bigotry, was not unusual for his generation. Those social elements were cultivated in him by his society.

Again, we are told that although the Supreme Court ruled in 1948 that racial restrictions were legally unenforceable, the FHA and VA continued to insure such mortgages. By 1950, the federal agencies were insuring half of all new mortgages nationwide. Many white families, who before the postwar housing boom lived in urban neighborhoods in proximity to African Americans, were relocated to more isolated white racial enclaves, created and promoted by government policy. (40)

To Archie, the privileges and special attention given to European Americans was normal and expected. What would have been seen as out of the ordinary would have been fair treatment to African Americans. Other forms of advantages given to European Americans came in the benefits of belonging to labor unions, a membership that denied African Americans. But housing was a major element in the make-up of American society because it was the foundation and center from which most social elements revolved. When we look back and see just how unfairly African Americans and other minorities were treated by our government, we can recognize how the gaps in economics and education were created. Much of the problem relative to accepting all Americans can be traced back to the government's role in sponsoring segregation and discrimination.

Rothstein makes the point that with public housing, federal and local governments increased the isolation of African Americans in urban ghettos, and with mortgages guarantees, the government subsidized whites to abandon urban areas for the suburbs. The combination was largely responsible for creating the segregated neighborhoods and schools we know today, with truly disadvantaged minority students isolated in poor, increasingly desperate communities where teachers struggle unsuccessfully to overcome their families' multiple needs. Without these public policies, the racial achievement gap that has been daunting to… educators would be a different and lesser challenge. (41)

So, now when we look back at Archie Bunker and the constant protest he made about the changing society in which he lived, we can understand why he complained. What we might not appreciate from him is his concern for people who do not pull themselves up by their bootstraps. What we now know that he never considered was that the African Americans and other poor minorities could not pull themselves up as easily as the European Americans; they had to work for their boots. The government literally gave Archie, and the generation he represented, the boots, the straps, and a little incentive just because they were European American. Now that things are changing, we no longer have to wonder why he lamented "Those were the Days."

We certainly thank Riley for his article because he gave us a picture of the problems American society faces regarding valuing all citizens and insuring that we all receive justice and fairness regardless of what we look like or where we live.

TV's "Good Times" Was an Example of Government Sponsored Segregation and Discrimination

December 9, 2012

When most people think of history, they think of it as being static; however, to do so would be a mistake because it is dynamic. Whenever additional information is added to an historical event, that information changes the way the event is interpreted. An example is the television hit show of the middle to late '70s, "Good Times." We were told that the show:

> "follows the challenges and joys of the close-knit Evans family—patriarch James, mother Florida, eldest son and accomplished amateur painter J.J. (James Evens, Jr), brainy and beautiful daughter Thelma, and youngest son Michael, a political and social activist—who live together in a high-rise housing project on the South side of Chicago."

While the show was presented as humorous, the truth of the matter is that the show was about a representative African American family living in the projects, struggling to survive in an environment of government sanctioned segregation and discrimination. The government and society created at least three boundaries restricting the freedoms and advancement of many African Americans.

For many Americans living in large cities during the so-called New Deal, the only reasonable and affordable place to live was in public housing. For African Americans, however, the living conditions were quite different from those of European Americans living in public housing. For example, the housing for African Americans was generally located in an existing low social, economic, and predominantly African American community.

For European Americans, the public housing was generally placed in economically established European American neighborhoods. For anyone with a passing knowledge of "Good Times," we know that the Evans family lived in the projects.

What we did not question about that fact was the projects was like a prison with its boundaries, inhabitants, and restrictions. The government required the inhabitants of some projects to be African Americans, which meant they were segregated.

Living in the projects is like living in a unique and isolated world where every aspect of one's life is of concern. For the African Americans, living in the projects meant being totally inconvenienced from goods, services, employment, school, and security. Because of the location of the projects in the less attractive and economically secure area of the cities, the problems associated with crime, drugs, unemployment, transportation and a host of other concerns were part of everyday life. These concerns were not the same for the European Americans living in public housing. Their locations placed them in or near the conveniences needed to carry on a "normal" life for the brief time they would live there. Many of the problems faced by the Evans family were from their immediate living environment.

The next challenge faced by the Evans family came from the location in which the projects were built. Since the community was low social and economically, the chances for employment in the community were slim to none. Since unemployment was also a feature of the area, we know that crime would be a close companion along with the drug culture. Any child living in such an environment had to be concerned with his or her security because of the presence of gangs and their activities.

Fortunately, the Evans children were not associated with gangs because of the strong and constant influence of their parents. Children living in the real world are not always so fortunate. Like the conditions inside the projects, the local community was segregated and reflected signs of discrimination and neglect, especially in the schools.

We were told that the Evans family lived in public housing located in Chicago's South side—reportedly the "baddest part of town." What that meant was the government did not pay close if any attention to what happened in this area primarily because its inhabitants were poor African Americans. Although the Evans children had talents, the avenues available to them for further development were extremely limited.

The two primary institutions available to the children for creative expression were the church and the school, both segregated and in the African American community. Segregation is a form of discrimination that places, for African Americans, a challenge to participate in whatever they are being denied. What we see of the Evans family in "Good Times" is a daily struggle to survive in a society that has stacked the deck against them.

In an article by Richard Rothstein in The American Prospect 11/12, entitled "Government-Sponsored Segregation," he comments on public housing in New York, but could easily include other cities like Chicago, Philadelphia: "Whereas in the mid-1950s most New York public-housing tenants were white, [European American], today they are only 5 percent white, as the decampment of middle-class families to segregated suburbs has been completed." He adds that "The public and media stereotype of project residents has become one of entrenched poverty and social dysfunction. By 1973, President Richard Nixon could describe such projects as 'monstrous, depressing places—rundown, overcrowded, crime-ridden.'" So, living under such conditions, how was the Evans family to progress?

When we consider "Good Times" as a form of entertainment—humor, we suspend reality because the Evans fight back with the only weapon at their disposal—laughter. When we assess this show seriously, we must see it as an absurd creation. The only relief they experience in their daily struggle for survival is through laughter. The words to the "Good Times" theme song underscores their short-lived joys in life that mirrors the show's name: "Any time you meet a payment. Good Times." This experience suggests that trying to meet payments is a constant struggle. The point hits home in these lines "Any time you're out from under. / Not getting hassled, not getting hustled. / Keeping' your head above water, / Making a wave when you can."

The conditions described indicated—above all—not good times, but desperate times. If one has to try and keep his head above water, we do not have to guess where the rest of his body is located. None of these situations are a laughing matter.

"Good Times" ended its television run in 1979; Rothstein noted that "Although housing authorities nationwide had ceased purposefully segregated projects in the last quarter of the 20th Century, they never took action to reverse the effect of previous policies." What is even more disheartening, is how society characterizes many African Americans who live in public housing as lazy, uneducated, drug-taking, free-loaders with little or no initiative simply because of where they live. Rothstein informs us, "In 1984, The Dallas Morning News sent reporters to federally funded projects in 47 cities. They found that the nation's nearly ten million public-housing residents were still almost always segregated by race [ethnicity]." What he says next underscores the claim of discrimination against African Americans: "The few remaining predominantly white projects had superior facilities, amenities, services and maintenance in comparison to predominantly black [African American] projects."

A gap in the social, economic, educational, and political conditions of African Americans and Europeans was created by government sponsored segregation and discrimination, and to this day has not come near being closed. The irony of this gap is that the African American is seen as a villain when he tries to close the gap. History, we know to be the record of past events, but we also know that the more information we obtain about those events, the better able we are to speak to their significance.

The Movie "*12 Years A Slave*" Provides 12 Valuable Lessons for America

March 23, 2014

The movie, "*12 Years a Slave*," won an Oscar award as this year's Best Picture, and well it should have because of the picture of slavery it presents. Many viewers based their evaluations of the movie on how the system of slavery dehumanized and denigrated the slave, showing the harshness of the punishment and pain endured by the slaves. In those cases, once the movie is over, the memories of the viewers rests with the experiences of the slaves. However, the movie's most valuable and significant element rests in its intrinsic objective—to provide a gift to America as a valuable teaching tool.

The movie, followed by mature and informed discussions, should be a requirement for all Jr. High and High School students, because of the way the movie presents the concept of slavery, and how it reflects American life. By doing so, we all can gain unique lessons from it. Let us take a look at twelve of the most obvious lessons we learn from slavery. These lessons are not arranged in an order of priority and most of them overlap, but relate to slavery as viewed from the movie.

First, the movie shows how the enslavers become dehumanized when they treated the slaves as animals. Watching a human being degraded through inhumane punishment and pain reflects on the ones inflicting the actions and the reasons for doing so. The power to whip a human being to death does not make one a human being for using that power, but more a brute for dropping to that level of behavior.

Second, the movie shows how the actions of the enslavers to dehumanize the slaves represent a form of insanity. Although the slaves were human beings, they were viewed and made to view themselves as animals; most people treat their animals with a degree of respect for the service they render. So, when the action of an enslaver goes against common sense, and what is considered normal thoughts, the result is a form of insanity.

Third, the movie shows that all African Americans were not slaves; many were free, educated, business and property owners. For example, Paul Cuffee owned several sailing ships, made and sold sails. In Louisiana, Cyprian Ricard owned almost a hundred slaves—yes, even some African Americans owned slaves, but not all African slaves; a cabinetmaker from North Carolina, Thomas Day, employed a number of European Americans; and in New York City in 1924, seven African Free Schools were supported by the public. The schools were called African Free Schools, not Negro or black or colored because those terms lacked specificity. So, Solomon, being a free man, was not an isolated case; not all African Americans were slaves.

Fourth, the movie shows how all European Americans were not supporters of slavery. Had it not been for the characters played by Brad Pitt and Mr. Parker, both European Americans, Solomon would not have regained his freedom. We also note the behavior of Solomon's first young master how Solomon was treated with a small degree of respect for his knowledge and skills. All enslavers did not treat their slaves the same.

Fifth, the movie shows how slavery created guilt—feelings in some of the European Americans who knew that slavery was a false concept and that the Africans and African Americans were human beings, just like themselves. The guilt came from the fact that they knew slavery was wrong, and in contradiction to the Declaration of Independence and the Bible. Yet, the suspension of truth and reality was substituted for the make-believe concept of viewing human beings as animals and property. The fact that any form of formal education was denied to the slaves to promote the idea that they could not learn. This action was a deliberate effort to hide the truth and protect their guilt.

Sixth, the movie shows how laws regarding the ownership of property were generally respected. The laws of property rights reflect the world of finance and business. These laws seemingly took precedent over laws regarding human concerns. A man's worth was indicated not only in his money, but also in his property—including land and slaves. The laws were created and enforced by the wealthy property owners.

Seventh, the movie shows how the insanity of slavery helps us to understand many of the attitudes and actions of some people today, especially the concepts of ethnic bigotry based on skin complexion. European Americans firmly believed that the color of their skin was a biological fact of superiority. The reference to their color as a sign of power was used constantly, especially the European Americans who were hired hands.

Eighth, the movie shows how the belief in slavery promoted a false sense of power, privilege, arrogance, and prestige. For all intent and purpose, the movie shows how some slave masters viewed themselves as gods, controlling the total lives of their slaves. In addition, other European Americans believed that they were created to be masters over other ethnic Americans, so they behaved as though it was a fact.

Ninth, the movie shows how slavery used Christianity in a hypocritical way, for generating fear, intimidation, and discipline. In essence, if the slaves did not practice being good slaves, then God would punish them through the slave masters. Church service for the slaves was a mockery of Christianity since the preachers always quoted scripture that encouraged the slaves to obey the masters and be good slaves.

Tenth, the movie shows how some European Americans believed that the Declaration of Independence was for all people, and some European Americans believed it applied only to them. The European American property owners believed they were entitled to more power, privilege, and prestige than the average European Americans. The country, in essence, belonged to them.

Eleventh, the movie shows how the secular and Christian standards and values did not apply to the enslavers. If a master wanted to procreate with his female slaves, he did so without impunity. His neighbors and fellow citizens gave little thought to what he did to his slaves regarding morals and values.

Twelfth, the movie shows that wedding vows were simply a matter of convenience, not law, with regards to who the master slept or with whom he fathered children. The wives of slave masters knew their place generally, but none-the-less, witnessed daily the handiwork of their husbands in and around the plantation.

The movie, as an invaluable gift, should be used because it tells us who we were, how we got to where we are, and what we need to do to move forward.

"Shopping While Black" is Profiling Ignorance That Can Be Fixed

November 4, 2013

Although the phrase "shopping while black" has been used recently, the practice has been in effect since African Americans first started shopping. To those readers who are not familiar with this practice, an explanation is in order. Recently, the *Associated Press* reported a story 10-30-13 that focused on the problem of "shopping while black." The article related how a young African American teenager walked into a Manhattan luxury store and purchased a $350 belt. Shortly after he left the store he was arrested. Evidently, someone in the store thought that he could not afford the belt, so something had to be amiss with the purchase.

What would cause the store personnel to question the sale to this buyer?

Americans are conditioned by society to base some actions on what we see and how we translate what we see. The image of the African American by many in society consists of negative stereotypes that reflect a variety of socially unacceptable characteristics such as a lack of sophistication, due to a lack of education and experiences generally reserved for the wealthy; a lack of finance, due to the lack of quality and high-paying jobs; and a propensity for crafty deceitfulness, stealing, and lying. In addition, majority society tends to picture African Americans, especially young males, as violent and dangerous, so one should avoid contact with them whenever possible.

The irony of the negative concept held by many European Americans towards African Americans and other ethnic Americas is that the African American generations, beginning with the '80s, are not aware of how they are viewed, so they act as if they can enjoy the same freedoms and privileges experienced by the European Americans. What they are discovering today is that the stigma of negative stereotypes still exists. The concept is not restricted to the U.S. since we learned that Oprah Winfrey was denied access to a $38,000 handbag because the Swiss sales clerk decided Winfrey could not possibly afford it. Being denied the opportunity to examine the merchandise is one problem; the greater problem comes after the African American customer has left the store.

The article tells of the experience Trayon Christian encountered after he left Barney's New York; "it was what happened afterwards. In a lawsuit filed last week, the 19-year-old said that he bought a Ferragamo belt at the Manhattan store, and when he left he was accosted by undercover city police officers." What we further discover relative to the negative concepts held by the sales clerks, is that the police also hold the same or similar views of African Americans as the article showed: "According to the lawsuit, police said Christian 'could not afford to make such an expensive purchase.' He was arrested and detained, though he showed police the receipt, the debit card he used and identification..." Obviously, African Americans shopping at high-dollar stores are being profiled and will continue to be until some changes in the image of African Americans are made.

One of the contributing factors to the profiling of African Americans shopping in high-dollar stores has to do with who is involved in the experience. In the article, we were told that "Skewed views can affect who gets arrested for retail theft, said Jerome Williams, a business professor at Rutgers University who has studied marketplace discrimination." He stated, "Many people justify racial profiling by saying that black customers are more likely to steal. But one study has shown that white women in their 40s engage in more shoplifting than other demographic groups..."

Part of the problem of profiling comes from the fact that women of color are not seen in high-dollar stores as frequently as are European American women. When the sales clerks and police see the European American women, nothing seems out of the ordinary, because the European American women look like the clerks and the police.

Filing lawsuits against high-dollar stores for discriminating and profiling is one way to get their attention; another way would be to indoctrinate people in management and service at these large (and small) stores urging them to treat all people the same. Of course we know that neither of these suggestions will eliminate the problem of profiling, but they could raise the awareness of the people involved. We as a society continue to delude ourselves into thinking that much progress has been made regarding how we treat one another. Yet, when we read about ways African Americans are treated on a daily basis whether driving, walking, or shopping we have to question: when will it stop?

Many European Americans, when they learn of ethnic profiling, try to down-play it because they have never encountered it. They try to convince themselves and others that the occurrences of profiling are few and far between and usually isolated cases. The fact is just the opposite of the belief. The article referenced a young lady, Natasha Eubanks, who stated, "It's one thing if you don't understand. But don't ever tell me it doesn't happen to me." Eubanks who shops frequently in high-end stores in New York City stated, "You can't assume it doesn't happen just because it doesn't happen to you."

On the positive side, the ignorance generally associated with profiling can be fixed. Yes, we can learn that ethnic minorities are in many ways like European Americans in that they represent a wide variety of incomes, education, and finance. To lump them all in the same basket of negative stereotypes does a disservice to all concerned. The insult that accompanies the injury of being profiled is the arrest which can create a multitude of problems involving police, lawyers, and incarceration. In some instances, the profiling has led to personal injury and death.

The social conditioning of many European Americans causes them to view African Americans, as well as other ethnic Americans, with suspicion because of ignorance and a lack of exposure to a variety of non-European Americans representing a stratum of society that encompasses the working class to the wealthy. If the victims of shopping while black continue to file lawsuits against the stores, chances are the ignorance will start to disappear. Ben Franklin once said something to the effect that experience is a hard taskmaster, but some will learn in no other school.

Oprah Winfrey Experiences Discrimination in Switzerland Boutique

August 11, 2013

Oprah Winfrey recently reported that she experienced discrimination while shopping for a purse in Switzerland. The event occurred, according to Winfrey, when "a clerk at Trois Pommes, a pricey Zurich boutique, refused to show her a $38,000 handbag, telling one of the world's richest women that she wouldn't be able to afford it." Apparently, the clerk did not recognize Winfrey or she would not have refused to show her the purse. The more important question relative to this experience is why was Winfrey's request to see the purse rejected. Winfrey called the incident an act of racism, but there is more to this incident than meets the eye.

In the aftermath of the incident, we are told that "Swiss tourism officials and the boutique owner were quick to offer apologies Friday. 'We are very sorry for what happened to her, of course, because we think all of our guests and clients should be treated respectfully, in a professional way.'" The boutique owner, Trudie Goetz, tried to make excuses for the clerk by claiming that because the clerk is mainly an Italian speaker she lacked the proper communication skills and "I believe she [the clerk] rather said something like 'we have some less expensive—we also have some less expensive bags' and not 'it's too expensive for you.'"

Of course, Goetz's offering in defense of her clerk makes little sense because how would the clerk know what is and what is not in a customer's price range? Also, why would she assume that Winfrey could not afford the purse simply by looking at her? The fact is that she could not know whether Winfrey could afford the purse, but assumed simply by looking at her that she could not afford it. Why? Stereotypes. African Americans as well as other people of color are generally the recipients of negative stereotypes. Why? The negative stereotypes are the product of American and Western propaganda that presents and portrays African Americans as not worthy of significant social value or respect.

For many years the images of the African American sent out of America showed him to be poor, ignorant, literate, simple, lazy, dishonest, a liar, a thief, a clown, and generally lacking morals or decency—along with a host of other negative stereotypes. Few, if any, of the pictures of African Americans were complimentary. So naturally, people of color from other countries did not want to be viewed in that negative light; therefore, in spite of all the positive contributions African Americans have made to America and the world, being an American of color was not viewed positively.

Today, when people of color come to America, they deliberately retain their cultural and geographical identity for fear of being mistaken as an African American because of the stereotypes. If Winfrey had gotten someone to announce her arrival at the boutique, she would have received VIP treatment because wealthy African Americans who travel outside the U.S.A. are generally well-received if their presence is made known. The average African American, however, falls into the category composed of negative stereotypes.

To be sure, the image of the European American is equally composed of stereotypes, but they are generally the opposite from those of the African Americans. The images in question come from movies, news stories, magazines and books. For years, many people in foreign countries thought that European Americans did not work, but simply went shopping, golfing, or to the beach every day, always having fun and enjoying life. When images of African Americans were presented, the context was usually in a second-class role or some other negative stereotype, usually involving protest or violence crimes. Rarely was an African American pictured as wealthy, educated, and non-threatening.

So, once we understand the history of the African American experience relative to the negative stereotyped images of them outside of America, we can begin to understand that the discrimination Winfrey experienced was not necessarily based on her personally, but on the image held by the clerk relative to people of color or African Americans in general. We know for certain that Winfrey experienced discrimination, but we cannot say that it was based on ethnicity or race. People can be discriminated against for a plethora of reasons, so race does not have to be the primary or only reason. Many people in America are profiled and discriminated against every day, not simply because of their skin color, but also because they are assumed to be in a particular socio-economic class.

Whether in America or some other country, stereotypes for people exists and those stereotypes serve as the bases for discrimination. Winfrey's experience should serve as a lesson for business owners that serve the public—never judge a book by its cover, or a customer on how he or she looks. What was the worst thing that could have happened had the clerk showed Winfrey the purse? No sale. The best thing would have been a large commission for a sale.

No individual is guilty of racism because racism is a group identity; bigotry is the choice of the individual. To say the clerk was guilty of racism would indicate a so-called race of people of which he or she is only a representative; however, to refer to him or her as a bigot places the responsibility for discrimination squarely on his or her shoulders. That being said, it does not excuse or forgive what Winfrey experienced.

For certain, Switzerland's tourism officials and the boutique owner offered apologies for Winfrey's treatment, but Winfrey, on the other hand, might be correct is her assessment of her experience as racist, because the first paragraph of the *Associate Press* story 8-10-13 provides this food for thought: "Switzerland is a glamorous playground of the rich and famous, filled with glitterati from princes to movie stars. It's a land with a sometimes uneasy relationship with foreigners—especially when they aren't white." For people of color, knowing that piece of information before making the trip could be helpful. After all, for one to be fore-warned also means to be fore-armed.

Black Friday, not African American Friday

December 5, 2010

Although it might seem needless, now is as good a time as any to fully understand why it is important to change the usage of words black and African American. Black Friday was not an African American holiday. Sure, it might sound humorous to some people, but confusing the economic term black with the social usage of the word black can be problematic for those who do not know the difference.

America has gotten comfortable with using the term black and African American interchangeably, thinking that either one is sufficient for identifying African Americans. The fact of the matter is that the words are not interchangeable—they do not mean the same thing. However, when society adds to the confusion by using the economic term "in the black," the problem becomes more complex. The term Black Friday has a number of meanings in itself. September 24, 1869, a Friday, was the day after the market crashed because of an unsuccessful attempt by some money managers to control the gold market; it led to a depression and the term 'Black Friday.' In this context, the term has a negative connotation.

Recently, the day following Thanksgiving has been called "Black Friday" because retailers hope to make enough money to put their businesses back on the plus side of the financial ledger, or "in the black ink." The use of the term in this sense is a positive one because it is a financial term that speaks to the positive effect of money in a business or a financial market.

The term black has many symbolic uses, some positive, some negative; however, when the word is used to identify African Americans, no clear connotation or denotation is apparent. Why? Simply because the word black is basically a color that is being used symbolically to represent things too big for it to contain, namely, African Americans, their social history, and American presence. For example, when someone makes the statement that "Blacks today are better informed politically than blacks were in the early '60s," a problem is created. The question might seem legitimate on the surface, but exactly who is the question addressing–African Americans or all people with a black skin complexion? Since America is a country of multi-cultures and multi-ethnic groups with a large range of skin complexions, to who is the question directed? The assumption is that the statement addresses African Americans, but that is not what it says; it says blacks.

Historically, African Americans have been referred to as Negroes, blacks, colored, cuffs, spooks, and a host of other names—none of them appropriate or accurate. Since the terms were assigned to African Americans, they did not reflect the positive elements that are necessary in identifying and defining an ethnic group. If each of the terms were examined for their denotative value, they would all come up lacking in specificity. For example, the term Negro is from the old Latin language meaning black. So in essence, by referring to African Americans today as black, no progress has been made since slavery in creating and defining them as a unique ethnic group. As stated earlier, the term black identifies a color, not a language, a culture, a history or a people. So, for society to continue using the term black as a reference to African Americans shows either ignorance, disrespect or both.

No one is advocating changing Black Friday to some other name, because in the context in which it is used, it is appropriate. The change should come in discontinuing using the term black to identify African Americans. Any person familiar with the term black as a reference to African Americans and not familiar with the historical significance of the term might easily confuse Black Friday as having some connection to African Americans or blacks in general. As a matter of fact, Craigslist closed down a site that was written by a bigot trying to imitate an uneducated African American crook with the following text:

> "Damms Eyes ates at the mission got a freeze turkey that eyes stold. Blacks Friday is our nigger day, mees and leroy will be waiting on use at the malls."

The writer of the above text shows his/her ignorance in language, syntax, grammar, spelling, and logic. Whatever the text was attempting to represent failed because it fell flat on its face. No doubt that the day, Black Friday, was the stimulus for the text and the bigotry felt provided the fuel to create the message. This example of ignorance and/confusion proves my point that the term black should no longer be used as interchangeable with African American.

Friday has been called the unluckiest day of the week and many superstitions have accumulated around it. When the color black is added to it, all the additional negative symbolic references of black create a more powerful set of superstitions. The problem revolves around the lack of reason many Americans have which creates a stumbling block to their understanding of even simple things in life. They prefer to rely on someone else to tell them what to believe and defend. Lyrics from a still popular song by the Doobie Brothers state to reality of the problem clearly:

> "What a fool believes, he sees/ No wise man has the power to reason away/ What seems to be is always better than nothing."

Black History Month Must Change

February 6, 2011

Time has come to make the change from Black History month to African American History month. For too long, African Americans have been content to keep the black reference as an identity instead of moving ahead and claiming the term African American as the up-to-date reference. Why is it taking so long for African Americans to see that the term black aids and supports the false concept of multiple biological races rather than a single human race? Let's look at why we need to make this change.

When Africans were brought to this country—some came on their own—the powers that be, mainly slave traders, removed all vestiges of the Africans' identity and replaced it with the term black, negro, and slave. Later, a variety of other terms were added. The primary purpose of the name change was to deny the Africans any positive value other than in the slave market. All Africans were called Negroes or blacks regardless of their social status. Since Africans had no power to change or challenge the practice of being referred to as negroes or blacks, they had to go along with the program. Some African Americans in the late 1800s and early 1900s did try to change the name to Afro-American, but their success was short lived.

In 1915, a young African American named Carter Godwin Woodson, a PhD from Harvard (1912), was so concerned about the lack of information about African Americans being disseminated to the public generally, and the African American community specifically, that he created the Association for the Study of Negro Life and History (ASNLH). The purpose of this organization was to "promote, research, preserve, interpret, and disseminate information" about the life, history, and culture of the negro people.

Carter, whose parents were slaves, was born into a bigoted society that referred to all African Americans as negro or black. He did not seek to change or challenge the use of those terms. He was not alone in this regard. Many other influential African Americans accepted the status quo. Carter's concerns and efforts to educate African Americans and the general public did result in the establishment of Negro History Week (1926)—a week that focused on disseminating the accomplishments, contributions, and research of African Americans.

After the Brown v. Topeka Broad of Education decision in 1954, civil rights activity began to gain momentum and, by the early 1960s, had given birth to a full-fledged civil right movement. Another movement that accompanied the civil rights movement was the Black Power movement.

Many young people like Jesse Jackson, Julian Bond, Stokely Carmichael, H. Rap Brown, Eldridge Cleaver, and a host of others began to focus on the aspect of African American blackness. The intent of the focus on blackness was to change it from a negative concept that denigrated the African American's self-image into a positive one that up-lifted the self-image. Many creative artists and scholars joined in the movement that resulted in popularizing phrases such "I'm black and I'm proud," "Black is beautiful," and "Black Power."

While the movement was successful in changing black from a negative to a positive concept, the changes only affected the African American community. The bigots in society who referred to African Americans as negroes, blacks, and the n-word were not affected at all. The problem was that the terms forced on the Africans and subsequently, the African Americans persisted in denying them a positive self-image in addition to an ancestry and culture.

In 1972, the ASNLH went through an internal fight that concluded with the association's name being changed to the Association for the Study of Afro-American Life and History. This change was very important because it indicated a change in the self-perception of African Americans. Dropping the term negro from the association's name was a positive move, one that indicated the growth of a positive self-awareness that was not defined by slavery's legacy.

Fortunately, in 1976, the celebration of Negro History week was changed to a month of celebration, but unfortunately it was changed to Black History Month. The only difference between negro and black is the spelling; both words mean the same thing, and both words were the gifts of the American slave masters. So, this name change was a step backwards. Why would anyone want to preserve either of these slave master-given terms? An old saying speaks to the fact that when one knows betters then one will do better. If we do not know better, it is time we learn because the consequences can be devastating to young people.

If we look around us today, we discover that America has many African American-looking people who are not African American. If we try to identify them as blacks or African American, they will inform us of their cultural identity. For example, if we were to look at a few professional basket players like Tony Parker, Thabo Sefolosha, and Serge Ibaka, we might mistake them for blacks; they will tell us that they are not. But why is that important? Their names and cultural identity will tell us something about their history. If we ask an African American his cultural identity and he answers that he is black, we know several things about him immediately—he does not know his history and culture except from a non-descript black perspective. Black is a color that has no social significance except in parts of the world where people who are called blacks are not valued. Black does not indicate a country, ancestry, or culture.

When we continue to hold on to terms like negro and black, we are simply re-enforcing the confidence of American bigots who see society as a variety of races with the so-called blacks at the bottom of the social latter and so-called whites at the top. Changing the word from black to African American will not eliminate bigotry, but it will take away the re-enforcement of separateness of race.

The time has come to make the change. Back in the '60s, Curtis Mayfield and the Impressions recorded a song that aided in the civil rights movement. The song was "People Get Ready, There's a Train a coming." As we learn more about ourselves, we learn that growth involves movement. The train of change is in the station. Now is the time to move from black to African American, and like the words to Mayfield's song say, "You don't need no ticket, and you just get on board."

Riley Cooper Fined for Using an Ethnic Slur Avoids the Real Problem

August 4, 2013

Many Americans like to play a game called "Let's Pretend," where they know something to be real, but pretend that it does not exist or they have no knowledge of it. Such is the case with comments surrounding Philadelphia Eagles' wide receiver, Riley Cooper. The team fined Cooper for saying that "he would fight every 'n——' at a Kenny Chesney concert in Philadelphia." The pretending comes into play when many people react to the news like they did not know that many Americans still use the n-word. We know that this ethnic slur is used on a regular basis by many Americans, so what is the problem?

The problem with Cooper using the n-word is that he used it in a place he thought was safe to use it, but he got caught. He evidently forgot that being a high-profile person in a large city meant someone had a camera on him at all times. The owner of the Eagles, Jeffrey Lurie, remarked that "We are shocked and appalled by Riley Cooper's words," and continued by stating, "This sort of behavior or attitude from anyone has no role in a civil society. He has accepted responsibility for his words and his actions. He has been fined for this incident." (Upi.com/Sports) For Cooper, the fine is a reminder to make sure the area is safe before any word is used that could result in another fine. As far as behavior and attitude regarding non-European ethnic American players are concerned, Lurie should address his concerns with the entire organization.

With respect to Cooper and his use of the n-word, chances are he grew up in an environment where the word was used by people as part of their everyday speech. We Americans like to pretend that all bigotry and prejudice has been eliminated from society because we are now all civil. The reality is that many Americans did not get the memo about ethnic slurs being unacceptable in a civil society or if they did get the memo just ignored it. Many European Americans grew up in communities where the use of the n-word was a regular part of everyday conversations.

For anyone growing up in such a community, considering the n-word as something unacceptable was unthinkable. No one comes into this word creating his or her own values and standards, but simply learn and accept without question what is already in place. In many instances, some people do not learn until later in life that certain words are considered ethnic slurs. My statements are not meant to dismiss the use and power of ethnic slurs regardless of how they were acquired. My concern is that when a problem such as Cooper's occurs, simply fining him is not the answer to the problem. The problem is not that he used the n-word, but why.

Society has done a disservice to many Americans by not clearing the air concerning the myth of race. America is a diverse society, but also one that embraced bigotry and prejudice. When American slavery created the two races—black and white—it also created the element of color to be used to keep these races separate. When one so-called race is made to think it superior to other so-called races, then bigotry and prejudice comes into play. America has yet to debunk the myth, so many people still hold on to the belief that multiple races of human beings exist and are inferior to the so-called white race. We are led to believe that all is well in society because all people possess the same rights and privileges. While we know that bigotry and prejudice still exist, we pretend that they all in the past.

The fine assessed against Cooper does nothing to inform him relative to why the fine was given. The message that action sent to the other players was not to get caught using ethnic slurs. That is the wrong message to send because it does nothing to inform Cooper and others why the use of ethnic slurs is not socially acceptable. What Lurie should do is institute a program where his entire organization can learn about American diversity and how we are all human beings with the same social value regardless of our skin color. An explanation of why using ethnic slurs would be more beneficial than just a fine. To some people who see nothing wrong with using ethnic slurs as long as one is not detected, they lack the knowledge and understanding of their perception of themselves and others.

America gets its strength through its diversity, so when Americans are educated about diversity it should not focus on the things that make ethnic groups different from one another, but what makes them alike. The differences among ethnic groups are derived through human efforts—economical, educational, geographical, and cultural; these differences have nothing to do with biology. So, the idea of ethnic superiority has nothing to do with color. If programs spend time teaching the differences among ethnic groups, then these programs are counter-productive. The concern in teaching about diversity is to show just how much alike human beings really are, not what makes them different.

Cooper understands that what he did was not socially acceptable, he said, "I shouldn't have. I'm disgusted. And I'm sorry. That's not the type of person I am. I wasn't raised that way." We, unfortunately, do not know what he meant by "that way." He continued by stating, "I have a great mom and dad at home. And they're extremely, extremely disappointed in me. They are disgusted with my actions." What we see in Cooper's comments is a lack of understanding of why he made the comment; he knows that he should not have made it, we just see how embarrassed he was about the negative press he received and how it affected his parents.

In order to try and prevent a repeat performance, Cooper should be made aware of why he made the comment in the first place. He needs to know that he is not alone in this situation, that many of his colleagues are as ignorant as is he regarding the myth of race, diversity, and ethnicity; they just do a better job hiding their ignorance.

The Defense of the N-word by Charles Barkley Cause for Concern

November 18, 2013

Charles Barkley recently expressed his thoughts relative to the n-word and, in so doing, exposed some gross defects in his thoughts. Barkley confused his freedom of speech with his personal freedoms, not fully realizing the responsibilities of each freedom. In his comments on TNT, he stated, "What I do with my black friends is not up to White America to dictate to me what's appropriate and inappropriate." He is absolutely correct in underscoring his freedom to associate with whomever he chooses. The problems come from his willingness to promote the idea of races based on color, and thereby underscoring the concept of ethnic biases. His thoughts on the use of the n-word also helps to promote ethnic division in America.

As far as Barkley using the n-word is concerned, he is correct in exercising his freedom of speech. He is incorrect to think that his use of the n-word is excusable. Barkley is free to eat a gallon of ice cream in one sitting; however, his common sense should tell him that to do so would incur some negative repercussions: stomach discomfort, digestive discomfort, and dietary discomfort. So, although he has the right to eat the ice cream, he understands the negative effects of doing so. What Barkley, apparently, does not realize is the negative effects of using the n-word in any context.

What Barkley seemingly disregards is the historical significance of the n-word and how that significance does not change regardless of who utters the word. True, the emotional impact experienced when the word is used by someone historically associated with its negative context cannot be denied, but it is precisely the negative emotional experience related to the historical significance that creates the difference.

Barkley supposedly assumes that people who identify with the n-word are immune from its negative effects when the word is used by people like them. That assumption is false because regardless of the word's intent, its historical connotations remain intact. He

seems to resent the thought of a so-called white America dictating
to him what to say and what not to say. One wonders if Barkley
realizes that the n-word was first used by European Americans
to identify Africans and African Americans in a grossly negative
concept. The continued used of that term regardless of the user
simply extends its historically negative concept.

One of the underlining concepts to come from Barkley's
comments is the false belief in multiple races based on color. That
concept always serves to separate and divide human beings, one
from another, for false and illogical reasons. One of the results
of America's creation of two races, one black, one white, is the
prejudice and bigotry based on the assumed superiority of the so-
called white race over the so-called black. Whenever either word
black or white is used, the image of two different so-called races
comes to mind. A similar experience is possible whenever the
n-word is used. America is changing with respect to ethnic identity
and the use of the terms black and white will eventually come into
disuse. Society will come to rely more on ethnic identities that are
more accurate and precise.

For someone to stand on their rights of free speech with respect
to a socially unacceptable word make little sense. The user of
the n-word presents two pictures of himself or herself to society
simultaneously: one, a picture of someone who is ignorant of the
word's historical significance, and two, a picture of someone who
is selfish and intent on doing emotional harm to another. If, for
example, an African American believes using the n-word around
other African Americans is OK, then a false assumption is being
made.

Not all African Americans accept the use of the n-word with
respect to themselves as well as with respect to others. They
understand the negative implications of using the n-word. Some
African Americans believe that while their use of the n-word is
permissible, that is not the case for people who are not African
American. Why? If the thinking is that the word was associated
in slavery and afterwards with African Americans so it should
be reserved for their use only, then that thinking is faulty. No one
person or group has a monopoly on the use of a word. The fact that

one group sees the word as special to them only means that the word still retains some of its power to do harm.

The late great comic genius, Richard Pryor, used the n-word for years as a staple in his comedy routine. He even produced an album with the n-word in the title. He recalled receiving an epiphany on day during a visit to Africa. He was sitting in a hotel in Kenya and began to look around the hotel lobby; he described what he saw as "gorgeous black people, like everyplace else we'd [the people traveling with him] been. The only people you saw were black. At the hotel, on television, in stores, on the street, in the newspapers, at restaurants, running the government, on advertisements. Everywhere." Pryor realized something for the first time; he turned to his companion and said, "Jennifer. You know what? There are no niggers here…The people here, they still have their self-respect, their pride."

Pryor realized that the n-word was given to enslave Africans in America when their personal identity was taken away. Once he understood the historical significance of the n-word, he said that he regretted ever having uttered the word on stage. He went further in describing it as a wretched word and added that "To this day I wish I'd never said the word. I felt its lameness. It was misunderstood by people. They didn't get what I was talking about. Neither did I … So, I vowed never to say it again."

The historical significance of the n-word should discourage anyone from using it or even promoting its use. Regardless of what anyone thinks, changing the context of the word or the setting in which it is used does not change its negative, stereotypical connotations. No one wants to deny Barkley his freedom of speech regarding his use of the n-word, but he needs to be aware of its historical significance and the fact that freedom is not free.

Both Bill Maher and Sen. Ben Sasse Complicit is Reference to the N-word

June 7, 2017

What does one usually think of when the following pronouns are used: we, us, our, and my? Depending on the context in which they are used, Americans generally think they are included in those pronouns. For example, when we read or say the phrase "We the people of the United States," or "Our forefathers," and "My country tis of thee," we usually assume that we are personally included in the pronoun.

The fact is that people of color, including Hispanics and Asians, as well as many Eastern and Southern Europeans, were not included for many years prior to the 1900s. Those pronouns referred only to American Anglo-Saxon males for the most part until the early 1920s. Basically, when European Americans are asked to close their eyes and picture a group of a dozen Americans, the likelihood of the presence of people of color in that mental picture is not very great, unless the European Americans had frequent and close involvement with culturally diverse people.

Before school desegregation was instituted, many European Americans had little to no contact with people of color because the schools, churches, and communities were segregated. That segregation helped to condition the mental landscape of many European Americans to exclude African Americans as part of society. European Americans were conditioned to give little or no social value to African Americans which meant not viewing them as social equals. With the arrival of the 1964 Civil Rights Act, an awareness of African Americans as citizens with rights and privileges equal to those of European Americans, the mental picture of Americans began to change, a little.

One of the things that the Civil Rights Act did was to underscore the separateness of the various ethnic groups. This feat was accomplished through the use of language; the terms minorities and race underscore the existence of both entities. If so-called races did not exist, they could not be discriminated against.

Right? They can only be discriminated against and deprived of rights only if they exist. So, when the act outlawed discrimination based on race, color, religion, sex, or national origin, by naming the elements in the law, it underscored their presence in society.

The Civil Rights Act presented a series of new problems for European Americans because now they have to be mindful of other people in society besides themselves. The European Americans had to not only give social value to African Americans but also recognize the fact that they shared social rights and privileges with them. This law was a new and great departure from what was considered the norm for European Americans. The challenge to conform to the law still represents a challenge to many European Americans today.

Often, when European Americans are in the company of African Americans or know that an audience of African Americans will hear what they say, they will be consciously on guard to avoid any word or statement that might suggest ethnic bias of anything that might sound pejorative towards African Americans. However, if the European Americans are in the company of other European Americans, they will not be on guard relative to their ethnic biases unless the person or persons in whose company they are in are sensitive to ethnic slurs. Otherwise, the European Americans will voice their biases freely without concern for repercussions. Remember, these ethnic biases are not something extraneous to European Americans, but part of their normal mindset, part of the system of European American superiority and African American inferiority.

A recent incident captured on television involving Bill Maher and Senator Ben Sasse of Nebraska during an interview, demonstrates the challenges of replacing the system of ethnic bias. During the interview, Sasse talked about his new book and also about people who dressed up for Halloween. Sasse said that the practice was frowned upon in Nebraska. Maher then said that he has to get to Nebraska more. Sasse then said, "You're welcome. We'd love to have you work in the fields with us." Maher narrowing his eyebrows stated, "Work in the fields? Senator, I'm a house (n-word)." For the readers unfamiliar with the term "house n-word," the reference is to the duties given to African/African American slaves who were generally off-springs of the master or a male from his family. Their duties did not include the harsh and brutal work in the fields, but work in and around the master's house. In addition, the status of the slaves was reflected in the duties he or she performed.

Once Maher made the statement, the audience noted the offense to which Maher stated, "It's a joke." Neither man stopped to comment on the reference, but continued the interview. The point here is that nothing was said at the moment, with the exception of Maher's reference to it being a joke, to correct the disparaging remark and its reference to enslaved people. One possible reason for the lack of attention paid to the seriousness of the remark is the fact that the two men forgot where they were, and being relaxed and familiar with one another simply let their guards down. Had the audience not reacted to the reference, chances are that both men would have continued the interview never realizing that something amiss had happened. Both men are guilty of failing to acknowledge the effect of the reference and to apologize immediately. That did not happen because the reference to the n-word has been a part of their normal social language that it did not represent a departure from the normal until the audience noted it.

Many changes are taking place in our society, as well as in the world, that affect us daily. One of the changes has to do with the changing demographics and the growing cultural diversity that has become a part of our everyday life. For many European Americans these changes bring great challenges because they slowly deconstruct what was considered normal to them. What at one time was considered normal and acceptable to European Americans in American society is no longer acceptable and continued use can result in serious repercussions. That is no joke.

Use of the N-Word Never Acceptable in Society Even by Entertainers

June 17, 2012

All words generally have connotations and denotations regardless of their context. If a word's existence is based on its historical denotation, then that history becomes part of that word regardless of the context. For example, the word 'history' retains its basic denotation regardless of the context or connotations. However, if we look at the word 'bitch' and examine its denotation, we discover that it means a female dog.

When the term is used in other contexts it could mean the act of whining excessively; a person who rides specifically in the middle of a front-seating only car meant for two passengers; a woman considered to be spiteful or overbearing; a lewd woman; a man considered to be weak or compatible and a host of other meanings. In the other uses or connotations of the word 'bitch,' the denotation does not usually influence its use because the connotations generally attack or describe the character of a person. The denotation simply defines the word without making a social judgment.

The n-word, like the word 'history,' retains its basic denotation regardless of the context in which it is found. Recently, a discussion regarding the use of the n-word has again come to the fore, so we thought we would provide some comments regarding its usage. If we look at the history of the n-word we discover that its creation was usage was meant to denigrate people of African and African American heritage. The intended use of the n-word was to create a derogatory and socially unacceptable association to the people forced to accept it as an identity. The social value of anyone described as an 'N' was below that of excrement; hence, the common statement: "a 'N' ain't worth shit." Any use of the n-word carries with it that history regardless of the so-called context.

Any number of entertainers have used the n-word in their work and tried to rationalize its use as part of their First Amendment right to free speech. If one considers the right to free speech as permission to say whatever one wishes to say regardless of the implications, then the entertainers are correct. However, if the use of the word carries with it the denigration or insults to people forced to accept that term as an identity, then the use is certainly unacceptable as well as reprehensive.

For someone to use the n-word as part of entertainment suggests a lack of historical knowledge or a disregard for the negative implications it carries. The word cannot be recreated simply because it is used in a different context—the elements of character associated with the n-word persist regardless of the context. For one to try and argue to the contrary underscores a lack of sound judgment in the face of plain logic. Spelling the n-word differently does not change its history—the negative implications remain.

Some people maintain the belief that because the n-word was/ is used to identify them that they have the right to pass judgment on the use of the word. How stupid is that? What they fail to realize is that the word was forced on them in the first place, so whatever they try to do to the word is meaningless historically because they did not create or apply it initially. The fact that the n-word has been applied to African Americans and used by many African Americans within the African American community does not mean that the word has been accepted and approved by African Americans. As a matter of fact, the African American community disapproves of the n-word's use, and rejected its association to their identity. So, why would anyone want to use the word today and even make excuses for its use? The answer lies in the payoff. Who profits from the use of the n-word?

Since the African American community has rejected the use of the n-word for all the negative concerns it creates, why would some African Americans continue to use the word if not for profit? One might consider the use for shock value or just plain ignorance of history and no sense of self-worth. When did the African American community give their power to entertainers to decide who can use the n-word or not? If the word is reprehensive and pejorative to the African American community, why would it not be so, in general, to everyone? Also, why would anyone want to promote bigotry by using the n-word even as entertainment?

The fact of the matter is that the word is unacceptable for use in society under any circumstances. Those who use the n-word know that it is unacceptable in its usual form, so they change its appearance through spelling or some other construction. Regardless of its appearance, its history is still present.

Many of the arguments offered by proponents of African Americans using the n-word, lack solid evidence of it losing its sting. Some have said that the word is part of the culture and that it is OK to use it among those in the community. How can that be true when the community has rejected it? Certainly, the use of the n-word was common within the African American community from slavery up to, and including, some segments today. The early use came primarily from being forced to accept the word as a form of identity—it was a part of the slave culture. African and African Americans knew the word was derogatory, but were powerless to change it. Another use of the word came from ignorance experienced through slavery. However, even the African Americans who used the word before it was rejected by the national community realized the pejorative nature of the word, so they reserved it for people they wanted to insult.

So, the n-word is not acceptable under any circumstances with the exception of how it was used in literature of the past. The use of the n-word in literature marked a clear indication of the mindset of the individual and his or her society in the work. The use of it today marks a clear indication of bigotry, stupidity or arrogance. Those who persist in saying that the n-word is part of free speech and they have to right to say it, must remember one cannot have it both ways—either the word is unacceptable or it is not. Society has said that it is not.

If someone calls you a dawg, what does that say about your mother, brother, sister or you?

The University of Oklahoma's SAE Video Offers a Chance for Change

March 11, 2015

A recent video of students riding a bus enjoying themselves, laughing, and singing a song was broadcast via social and regular media. The young men singing the song were members of the University of Oklahoma's Sigma Alpha Epsilon fraternity.

The picture and the entire atmosphere on the bus seemed a fun-filled and joyous occasion, and it was—until the words of the song were revealed. The words of the song stated that "There will never be a n-word in SAE," and included, "You can hang them from a tree." This song was sung by these young people because they felt safe, secure, and comfortable on a bus that included no African Americans. Why did they believe that singing this song was acceptable? The answer is they were taught this by their parents, schools, and society.

America is, and has always been, a diverse society, not of races, but of people from different cultures and geographical locations. Generally, American parents teach or tell their children that America is a democratic society that respects the liberties, rights, and freedoms of all people. However, the actions of the parents contradict the words.

Whether conscious or not, children are made to see differences among themselves and others and the focus on group identity begins. As children grow, they learn to recognize the benefit of group identity, an identity usually reflected in the family relationships, with other people in school, church, neighbor, and community. So, the young people on the bus reflect a sense of community of like people.

In our schools, children are forced to identify with a variety of groups that include social-economical, cultural, and ethnic. Rather than focusing on the similarities of the students, emphasis is usually placed on differences which are few and minor. Students learn through social activities as well as curriculum to place social value on individuals. Although they are taught that all people should be treated fairly, the language and social practices underscore the idea of separateness.

The concept of many biological races has been debunked for years; yet, teachers continue to use terms such as black and white as if they were legitimate. American history underscores the lack of value places on the lives, value, and contributions made by African Americans as well as other people of color. Teachers and professors cannot teach what they do not know or accept.

Society tells our young people that bigotry is fine as long as they can keep it hidden; just do not put themselves on the spot by blatantly saying or doing anything in public that can be interpreted as biased. The young people of the frat bus thought they were in a protected environment, so they felt as ease in singing their song. In various aspects of society young people are shown that it is fine to discriminate against people of color; they see it in our criminal justice system, our educational and political systems. They are reminded time and again that African Americans have little social value, so denigrating them is perfectly okay as long as one is not exposed. Fortunately, the use of social media has provided an opportunity for all of society to see some of the things that have been happening in private for many years.

The behavior of the young people on that bus can be attributed to their parents, schools, and society. Their actions displayed an ignorance of a democratic sense of humanity and history; a belief in the value of each human being regardless of color, ethnicity, gender, social or economic status. Their actions showed an attitude of arrogance, supremacy, and tribal characteristics such "us versus them." The first two lines of the song underscore the idea of group or tribal separateness with the understanding that the reason for there not ever being a n-word in SAE is because of color and social value.

Their actions displayed stupidity. Why would anyone, especially young university students, want to sing a song about lynching? Along with an ignorance of history, and an arrogance of privilege and power, these young people forgot about the power of social media. Sometimes the speed of the social media is faster than a speeding bullet as many people have learned to their regret.

Placing the entire blame on the students for their actions would be to excuse the parents, schools, and society for their failures in preparing the young people for life in a diverse, democratic society. We can begin to correct many of these failures by starting with the truth—bigotry was part of the American fabric from its beginning. As a society we have allowed bigotry to continue and grow through systemic creations enforced by laws and lies.

The concept for multiple biological races is false; only one race of human beings exists. Intelligence, character, physical and mental attributes are not based on skin color. The history and struggles of African Americans, Asian Americans, American Indians, and Hispanic Americans to gain their civil rights have been glossed over and not made relevant todays' students, just as they were not valued by their parents. So, we arrive at ambiguity and ignorance in many young people; unfortunately, the only regret for some of these young people is the fact that their bigotry was exposed.

The concept of racism is irrelevant in today's society since only one race actually exists. To call someone a racist is to give approval to their false concept of races. An individual cannot be a racist in isolation because the term refers to a group. To ascribe responsibility to an individual accused of ethnic bias, the term is bigot.

Young people, as well as society in general, need to learn and accept the meaning and nature of living in America. Because the changes in society have become more apparent in recent years, the challenge of change makes life difficult for those who prefer the status quo. When any American is discriminated against or denigrated because of some superficial difference, all Americans are impacted because that thinking goes against what we say we believe in and stand for as citizens— life, liberty, freedom, and justice for all.

www.ingramcontent.com/pod-product-compliance
Lightning Source LLC
Chambersburg PA
CBHW030417290526
45786CB00001B/15